The Middle East Explained

The Middle East Explained

Answering the Critical Questions On America's Middle East Challenge

Richard Parker Robison

1663 LIBERTY DRIVE, SUITE 200
BLOOMINGTON, INDIANA 47403
(800) 839-8640
WWW.AUTHORHOUSE.COM

This book is a work of non-fiction. Unless otherwise noted, the author and the publisher make no explicit guarantees as to the accuracy of the information contained in this book and in some cases, names of people and places have been altered to protect their privacy.

© 2005 Richard Parker Robison. All Rights Reserved.

No part of this book may be reproduced, stored in a retrieval system, or transmitted by any means without the written permission of the author.

First published by AuthorHouse 10/13/05

ISBN: 1-4208-6199-9 (sc)

Library of Congress Control Number: 2005905385

Printed in the United States of America
Bloomington, Indiana

This book is printed on acid-free paper.

Cover design by Jabra Ghneim

To our skilled and dedicated military men and women, especially those "unseen," thank you for your sacrifice—a sacrifice tragically misunderstood and misrepresented by so many today. In the end, history, and a generation yet unborn, will vindicate your sacrifice and honor your service.

Contents

QUESTION 1   3

- WHY DID THE UNITED STATES INVADE SADDAM'S IRAQ?

QUESTION 2   23

- HOW CAN THE IRAQ WAR SECURE THE UNITED STATES AND BRING PEACE AND STABILITY TO THE MID-EAST AND THE WORLD?

QUESTION 3   33

- MUST MIDDLE EAST DICTATORS, SUCH AS SADDAM HUSSEIN OR OSAMA BIN LADEN, BE ELIMINATED TO ENSURE GLOBAL PEACE AND STABILITY?

QUESTION 4   51

- HOW AND WHEN DID THIS CHALLENGE FROM RADICAL ISLAM BEGIN? WHAT ARE ITS ROOTS, ITS CAUSES?

QUESTION 5   59

- WHAT SPECIFIC THREATS ARE THE MUSLIM FANATICS MAKING AGAINST AMERICA? WHY ISN'T THE MEDIA ACCURATELY REPORTING THESE THREATS?

QUESTION 6   71

- WHAT DO THE RADICALS, THE TERRORISTS, TRULY WANT? WHAT IS THEIR HIDDEN AGENDA?

QUESTION 7   79

- WHAT IS AMERICA'S MOST CRITICAL QUEST IN ACCURATELY UNDERSTANDING THE MIDDLE EAST?

QUESTION 8 — 91

- WHAT ARE THE PRINCIPAL FACTORS DRIVING UNITED STATES' MIDDLE EAST POLICY?

QUESTION 9 — 101

- WHY IS THE ISLAMIC REPUBLIC OF IRAN AT THE TOP OF THE PRESIDENT'S EXCLUSIVE "AXIS OF EVIL" HIT-LIST?

QUESTION 10 — 119

- TAQIYA—"WHEN A LIE IS NOT A LIE"—WAS A CRITICAL CHAPTER IN YOUR PREVIOUS BOOK. WILL YOU REVISIT IT HERE?

QUESTION 11 — 131

- BY TOPPLING SADDAM HUSSEIN HAVE WE MADE THE REGION SAFE FOR THEOCRACY, RATHER THAN DEMOCRACY?

QUESTION 12 — 147

- WHAT ARE SOME ESSENTIAL, YET LITTLE KNOWN, MIDDLE EAST CULTURAL INSIGHTS WE MUST UNDERSTAND?

QUESTION 13 — 163

- WHAT CAN KNOWLEDGEABLE ARAB SOURCES TEACH US ABOUT ARAB CULTURE, ABOUT MIDDLE EAST WAYS?

QUESTION 14 — 175

- WHY DO MIDDLE EASTERN SOCIETIES TREAT WOMEN AS THE PERSONAL PROPERTY OF MEN?

QUESTION 15 — 185

- WHY DOES ISLAMIC CULTURE OFTEN TEACH THAT MEN MUST CHOOSE BETWEEN THE TEMPTATION OF WOMEN AND THE RIGHTEOUSNESS OF GOD?

QUESTION 16   191
- WHY ARE MIDDLE EASTERN WOMEN AND GIRLS KILLED FOR THE HONOR OF THEIR MEN?

QUESTION 17   197
- WHY IS THIS WAR AGAINST TERRORISM ALSO A "WAR FOR AMERICAN VALUES," FOR DEMOCRACY, FOR FREE AND OPEN MARKETS?

QUESTION 18   205
- WILL SUCH MEN AS OSAMA BIN LADEN ALWAYS PLAGUE US, THREATENING GLOBAL PEACE AND FREEDOM?

QUESTION 19   211
- WHAT ARE SOME IMPORTANT TRENDS TO WATCH IN THE WAR ON TERROR, TRENDS NOT GENERALLY IDENTIFIED?

QUESTION 20   219
- WHAT ARE THE IMPORTANT, LITTLE-KNOWN LESSONS WE HAVE LEARNED THE HARD WAY?

QUESTION 21   229
- IN THE WAKE OF THE IRAQ WAR, WHY ARE BRUCE WILLIS AND PAULA ABDUL HANGING OUT ON MUHAMMAD STREET?

QUESTION 22   243
- WHAT IS THE END GAME? HOW DO WE FINISH TERRORISM ONCE AND FOR ALL?

QUESTION 23   259
- DOES AMERICA HAVE A MORAL OBLIGATION, EVEN DUTY, TO LEAD THE WORLD?

QUESTION 24   269

- WHAT QUESTION HAVE WE FAILED TO ASK THAT PERHAPS WE SHOULD?

ACKNOWLEDGMENTS   281

BIBLIOGRAPHY   283

END NOTES   289

INDEX   297

PREFACE

The 24 Key Questions
...and Answers

Some Americans are still unaware of the level of long-term responsibility we have shouldered in the Middle East. More importantly, our leaders have hesitated to explain the incredible equities cementing America to the region. Confused, many seek answers to questions raised by the attacks of 9/11, the war on terror, and the U.S. invasions of Afghanistan and Iraq. Each of these challenges appears exclusive. They are not.

I know of no way of judging the future but by the past, paraphrasing the American patriot, Patrick Henry. And we must understand the past if we are to understand America's quest for freedom in the Middle East. This has not come cheap, a quest of sacrifice, in blood, in the lives of our free citizens willing to give all they have, in the sacrifice of patriots, both past and present. Understanding and appreciating America's incredible history is vital to our quest. From that perspective, that foundation, and from well-placed modern sources, what follows are the 24 KEY QUESTIONS Americans should be asking on our role and purpose in the Middle East. Each of the book's 24 chapters stands on its own; each enjoyed without required input from any other.

Why did we invade Saddam's Iraq in 2003? Does the war against terror have to be a generation-long struggle? When will our military forces leave the Persian Gulf region? Why do France, Germany, and Russia so strongly oppose our ongoing Mideast presence? Why is China nervous about our "monitoring" of the world's most strategic energy storehouse? Why do Middle Easterners seem to hate us so, yet continually look to us to solve their monumental problems, to buy their oil and send our aid, even shed our blood to protect them from a world of enemies?

These and other vital questions are fully explored in the following pages, insights offered by a Middle East specialist of uncommon training and experience on the ground in the region.

What are the Six Principal Reasons the United States invaded Iraq? Chapter One leaps at that question with both feet. *How will the Iraq War secure the United States and bring peace and prosperity to the world?* That one dispatched by Chapter Two. Then, take your pick: *Must Middle East dictators be eliminated to bring peace and stability to the world? Who is responsible for past pathetic Mideast leadership? What are the Seven Shrouded Truths driving America's policy there? Why is it impossible to understand the strategic importance of the region without considering the "China Card"? Why is the Islamic Republic of Iran at the top of the President's exclusive "Axis of Evil" hit list?*

Since it is not possible to understand America's Middle East challenge without a touch of Islamic and Arab cultural history, several chapters illuminate key questions, such as: *Why is the ancient Mideast principle of* Taqiya *a potent weapon used against us by Islamic radicals, a weapon not yet generally recognized or understood in the United States? How did* Taqiya *cause us to be more vulnerable to attack on 9/11? What is the Islamic institution of the "Temporary Wife" or "Wife of Pleasure" and why is this important to America today? Why do Mideast societies treat women as the personal property of men? Why does Islam teach that men must choose between the "temptation of women" and the "righteousness of God (Allah)"? What important lessons have we learned the hard way?* And finally: *What is the endgame? How do we finish terrorism once and for all?*

We stand at a critical juncture, accelerated by the rise of Islamic-born terrorism and the powerful military move of the United States into the Persian Gulf and Iraq. America's collective will, its vision, and those actions we take over the coming decade, will determine the world's security and prosperity through this century and beyond.

The devastating attack America suffered on September 11, 2001 was partly the result of the United States' penetration into the House of Islam and our military occupation of Arabia and the Persian Gulf following the 1991 gulf war. Osama bin Laden, among other Muslim radicals, has pounded on this theme in multiple speeches at least since 1992. Sadly it was not until we were treacherously violated on 9/11 that we began to pay attention.

Since then, moving with determination, the United States has successfully strengthened its hold on the world's most strategically vital sandbox. Willingly we sacrificed many American lives and invested billions of dollars in what we hope will be a future of peace, stability, and security for America and the world. This is a critical age, the most important and far-reaching in Middle East history since Muhammad's camel soldiers burst from Arabia to spread the word of Allah nearly 1,400 years ago. What unfolds in the coming decade will impact us for generations, changing us forever as a nation, society, and culture.

We should, however, be optimistic. The future offers hope for America and the world, though dictatorial regimes from China to the Middle East are working to counter America's freedom-quest. What the enemies of truth fail to understand is that the tide of history—the tide of freedom—is with us; it is our ally, shining from the eyes of half-a-billion young Muslims from Marrakech to Bangladesh.

The following insights are not for the weak of heart; nor for the pessimist, the man or woman who says: *"The Middle East is a quagmire! What are we doing there? It's never been done that way before! Democracy? How can it possibly work with Arabs?!"* Such people scare me. In today's techno-driven, nanosecond world, such naysayers are passé, more so, they are dangerous. And they are wasting our time. If that's your best shot, get out of the way. The greatest miracles of history are about to sweep us. We cannot, we must not, shrink.

History is watching...

The Middle East Explained

Answering the Critical Questions on America's Middle East Challenge

QUESTION 1

- WHY DID THE UNITED STATES INVADE SADDAM'S IRAQ?

WINDOW TO THE SOUL

Enchantingly beautiful, the Middle East is like a mysteriously veiled woman, yet fortunately for us her raven eyes are visible, a window to the soul of a most foreign land and people. *Umm idduniya*, the "Mother of the World," the Middle East is at the center of each of us, whether we recognize it or not.

Yet, for political reasons I suspect, our national leaders appear to believe the average American is unwilling or incapable of understanding the true extent of America's role there. The U.S. Administration, it seems, refuses to utter the "O" word. Any discussion of oil or oil politics is absolutely forbidden. In the process, we are being told precious little of America's true Mideast equities, perhaps because our leaders fear we are not yet ready for the truth. I resent the premise and believe it is one of the very few mistakes being made by the U.S. Administration regarding its Middle East policy.

FIRST, LET'S LOOK AT WHAT WE ARE *NOT* FIGHTING FOR:

(1) OIL

"No blood for oil!" The anti-war crowd shouts to the skies, linking arms with their brothers and sisters in Hollywood, in France, and around the world in opposition to this war of liberation in Iraq, this "war for oil." Such incredible sophistry; such blatant foolishness. Quoting Patrick Henry in 1775, who was facing his own challenge from the trembling "peace at any price" crowd of his day: *"Our brethren are already in the field,"* he shouted to the hesitant assembly, *"why stand we here idle?!"*

We live in a global economy. Let's not fool ourselves; oil is critical to everyone. But if we were in the Middle East only to take their oil, we would have long since deposed the weak so-called "Gulfies" of Kuwait, Bahrain, Qatar, the United Arab Emirates, and especially Saudi Arabia, brutally annexing these oil-rich Gulf States. Militarily, such a move would take mere hours to accomplish. Who would stand in our way?

But stealing Muslim oil is *not* why we are there. The Gulf Arabs, *requesting* the military protection of the United States, have created for themselves one of the highest standards of living on earth with every citizen—royal or otherwise—benefiting from the incredible prosperity. We do not need to own their oil, or steal their profits, in order to accomplish our strategic, long-range goals. In fact, annexing these oil-rich lands and pirating the profits would be the last thing we would do. Such a blatant, even Neanderthal, grab for the "black gold" would be resisted from Beijing to Paris, from Tehran to Tripoli, as rightfully it should. Persian Gulf oil profits the peoples of the region. This has always been our objective. Only indirectly will America benefit and not so much by financial gain, but by our ultimately controlling the *strategic power* of this global energy storehouse. (More on this critical reality in a moment, a reality nearly everyone seems to be missing.)

(2) EMPIRE

The United States of America is the world's only superpower. We could, if we wanted, become a modern Roman Empire. Who would stop us? But look at history; when have we ever struck out into the world to pillage, rape, and plunder? I challenge you to show me the historical example. The dictatorships or totalitarian regimes we've defeated in war we've gone on to rebuild as prosperous democracies, and at *our* expense, nations free to pursue their own path in the world. Some of the wealthiest nations on earth today were once our virulent enemies, enemies we conquered on the battlefield.

For example, following our overwhelming defeat of the Empire of Japan, instead of occupying and plundering, we spent billions rebuilding and retooling that island nation, creating one of the world's most successful democracies. Add to that Germany. Utterly defeated and destroyed in World War II, we then invested billions of dollars we did not have, helping the German people to rise from the ashes.

Today Germany is a leading nation in the European Union, a large and prosperous democracy essentially restored and rebuilt by the hard-earned dollars and sacrifices of the American people. We have never had the desire to occupy and exploit German or Japanese lands, nor to reduce to servitude these great peoples. What conquering nation in history can claim such benevolence? What nation forgives its enemies so completely, even carrying them on our shoulders? I see no equal to the level of American generosity in the history of mankind, and our willingness to freely mentor other nations, expecting little in return.

In the Muslim world the United States faces a wall of mistrust where many want to believe that the U.S. *always* sides with non-Muslims to defeat and humiliate Muslims. History proves otherwise. In 1991, the U.S. led a mostly NATO force to liberate a Muslim nation (Kuwait); in 1995, again risking American lives the U.S. defended Muslims being massacred in Bosnia. Then in 1999, America helped liberate Muslim Kosovo, siding with Muslims over Serbian Christians. Currently America is helping Iraq establish a democracy in the heart of the despotic Middle East. Though the radicals shout that America does this for its own gain, do the math, run the numbers. The sacrifice in American blood, and treasure, proves time and again that this premise is false.

In reality, nothing points to anything beyond our sincere desire to create a free, secure, and prosperous Middle East. Ask the people of Iraq, privately, one-on-one, away from vengeful terrorists like Abu-Musab al-Zarqawi, or away from Saddam's brutal former security men, the dreaded *Mukhabarat*, or Saddam's Ba'ath Party loyalists, sympathizers, and renegades. Ask most any Iraqi. Terrorism scares them more than it does Americans. They live with it every day. Most welcome the arrival of America as liberators from one of the world's most murderous dictators. Ask the Shi'ites; ask the Kurds and Turkmen; ask Iraqi Christians. Taken together they constitute the vast majority of the people of Iraq.

In the end Iraq will be free and America will go home. That's the way it's always been.

O.K., THEN WHAT ARE WE DOING IN THE MIDDLE EAST?

1) FIGHTING ISLAMIC-BORN TERRORISM WITH AN IRON FIST

> *I don't think we have in the Middle East a "process of peace." We have in the Middle East a "war for peace."*
>
> —***Shimon Perez,***
> ***Former Israeli Prime Minister***

Iraq is the example. Any nation that harbors, trains, or funds terrorism is at risk from the United States. Iran, Syria, the Sudan, even Saudi Arabia, and a host of Muslim terrorist factions within Mideast and Southwest and Southeast Asian countries all get the message, and they tremble. We wield an awfully big stick. In Iraq and in Afghanistan we fought with both hands tied behind our back trying to spare innocent lives. The world witnessed the surgical destruction America rained on the enemy. The stick was raised against the tyrant; we do not apologize.

We cannot shrink nor capitulate when force is necessary to secure America and to liberate the captive. Have we so soon forgotten the treachery of 9/11? Have we forgotten our national vulnerability? Short of our strong, swift response in Iraq and elsewhere it will happen again on a grander scale. Next time the death toll in American lives could be tens of thousands.

I was once on the inside. I saw Saddam's connection to terror first-hand.[1] Saddam's Iraq propped-up and harbored some of the world's most bloody terrorists—brutal worldwide operators, hit-men, warlords, extortionists, blackmailers, and murderers. This is an incontrovertible fact. Though poorly covered in the media (for reasons that still baffle me), Saddam provided support, training and safe haven (or at least left them alone) to the Abu Abbas Terrorist Organization, to Abu Nidal, to Ansar al-Islam, a proven al-Qaeda ally, and others we know about. He sent hundreds of thousands of dollars to the families of Islamic suicide terrorists in Israel. I've seen these connections, personally, on the ground. Our leaders have reported these connections on several occasions. Why does our media tend to ignore the facts, or downplay them? But Middle Easterners, including their leaders (many of them allies) do not. What is ironic is that the dictators and terrorists in the region seem to understand the necessity of a swift, overwhelming U.S. response far better than most Americans. Why? Because you cannot negotiate with murderers and fanatics, nor can you build consensus or in the process try to cajole France, or Russia, or China—the Mercenary States—into agreeing with us. Each has its own self-serving agenda which is *not* in the best interest of the United States, Iraq, or the world.[2]

It is not possible to separate the war on terror and the elimination of the Saddam Hussein regime. Saddam was a cancer, clandestinely spreading his death and hatred throughout the Middle East and the world. With Saddam still in power, there could *never* be peace in the Middle East. Terrorists would continue to have a determined and capable mentor, backer, and most importantly, safe haven.

2) SECURING AND PROTECTING THE CRITICAL OIL RESERVES OF THE PERSIAN GULF REGION

> **"Oil is no longer a simple commodity, bought and sold like cattle futures, grain, or timber. Oil, the 'ultimate commodity,' fires economies, swells national treasuries, and projects military power into far off lands. Control of oil resources defines national security, including global prestige and political influence. Oil is pure *power*. And when the tap goes dry, you are left to the mercies of those with their hands on the spigot."**
>
> **--Richard P. Robison**
> **Seminar, "Why We Fought Iraq,"**
> **Lexington, Kentucky, May 21, 2003**

Remember, it is not about the price of oil, nor about the profits, even when those profits are outrageously obscene. It's the *strategic power* of oil that rules. Although America needs and buys some Persian Gulf oil, fortunately we have other sources, including Alaska, Venezuela, the Gulf of Mexico, Mexico, Canada, and West Africa. However, Persian Gulf oil, including vast reserves discovered in Iran and Iraq, is *the* critical energy storehouse for Asia, with Europe likewise growing increasingly dependent.

As strategically essential as the Persian Gulf region is today, its importance will grow exponentially over the coming 10 to 20 years. One in three of the world's barrels of oil are located under the sands of just two nations: Saudi Arabia (275-plus billion barrels) and Iraq (110-plus billion). Many experts suspect that those figures are too conservative, that future exploration will reveal that Iraq, particularly, holds perhaps two to three times that amount of recoverable oil. Several nations have lusted over Iraq's oil resources, particularly over the past decade, as fields in Asia and the North Sea have begun drying up.

The fastest growing customer of Mideast oil has been *China*. What Asian nation has more long-term potential, and in so many vital ways and areas? China is the world's wildcard.[3] No one, not even the finest China specialists in the CIA, knows where the Chinese are headed or the threat this nation will pose over the coming decade. The so-called "China Card" is just too great an unknown, an "onion": peel back one layer and what do you find? Exactly, another layer. But one thing is certain. China is, and will be, a major importer of Persian Gulf oil for the foreseeable future. Increasingly, China is industrializing and modernizing on the back of imported oil, the source of which they neither control nor influence.[4]

According to a recent study by the Rand Corporation commissioned for the U.S. Air Force, "Chinese interest in maintaining the flow of oil has led Beijing to cultivate relations with Tehran (Iran).... China's dependence on imported oil has grown steadily since 1994, and is likely to continue...thus (China) seeks allies in key oil-producing regions, such as the Persian Gulf. Chinese analysts believe that maintaining good relations with leading oil-exporting nations such as Iran is important to China's future energy security. The United States, however, has attempted to convince Beijing that

Iranian-backed instability (i.e.-the sale of modern weapons systems, including missiles and weapons of mass destruction) threatens the free flow of oil from the (Persian) Gulf, which could drive up the price of oil and jeopardize China's economic growth. U.S. officials claim that China's promises at the October 1997 summit to cut (their) nuclear cooperation with Iran occurred in large part because China recognized this danger."[5]

In other words, China has been put on notice. The above is diplomatic language for: *Your (China's) prime source of imported oil is being endangered by your irresponsible relationship with Iran (and Iraq, at the time). Either cut off these blatant sales of dangerous weapons to Iran and Iraq or risk your primary source of imported oil.*[6]

It is doubtful that China has gotten the message. Well-placed sources claim China has merely become more careful, more clandestine, in its Iranian weapons' sales. The weapons continue to flow to Iran, often through highly cloaked middlemen and in round about methods. The game continues.[7] Recently the U.S. government has renewed trade sanctions on eight Chinese companies discovered shipping restricted materials to Iran, materials which help the Iranians to extend the range and accuracy of their missiles. Such materials include missile components and high performance metals.[8]

Oil is vital to global stability and economic well-being. Every $10. per barrel increase in the price shaves a half a percentage point off America's GDP (gross domestic product). The evidence shows that a higher oil cost affects China's and Europe's profitability at least as much, perhaps more.

Persian Gulf oil must remain market accessible and free of strategic manipulation by any strongman or terrorist-supporting nation. Ultimately, it is up to America to ensure the global security of this irreplaceable treasure trove, *two-thirds* of the world's oil, and the best and cheapest reserves available anywhere. Following World War II, the United States determined to protect these strategic resources and ensure the free flow of oil to the world. Democrat or Republican administrations (it does not matter) have stood by this policy. Even the well-known pacifist President Jimmy Carter issued, on January 23, 1980, what is known as "The Carter Doctrine" stating,

"Let our position be absolutely clear: An attempt by any outside force to gain control of the Persian Gulf region will be regarded as an assault on the vital interests of the United States of America, and such an assault will be repelled by any means necessary, including military force."[9]

We cannot, we will not, leave it to others to secure this strategic resource. Protection *and* control of Gulf oil is the bulwark of worldwide global security, prosperity, and especially peace.

In March of 1992, then U.S. Defense Secretary Richard (Dick) Cheney stated in a speech to the insurance industry that "We're going to be involved there for a long time to come.... The U.S. must look out for its long-term interests and understand that the region is not such that will let us disengage in a week, or a month, or even a year. We will be there throughout my lifetime; and for the next century." He went on to say, "I don't see any prospect that the Persian Gulf region isn't going to be an area of vital strategic interest to the United States and our friends around the world."[10]

U.S. military penetration of the Persian Gulf, as well as access to vast tracks of Southwest Asia and the Caspian basin, is key to global security and stability in this new international order following the Cold War. These nations, dripping in sweet crude, are absolutely critical energy storehouses, and principal present and future suppliers for China and others.[11]

Both U.S. and Chinese intelligence experts maintain that America and China are headed for a possible, some say inevitable, conflict in the years to come, principally over strategic control of the Pacific Rim region. Several possible flashpoints exist: the Taiwan issue, North Korean nuclear proliferation, Chinese weapons sales to terrorist nations, the Chinese military expansion in Asia, and so on. With time, other flashpoints will emerge. Yet, by *our* design, China is growing more and more dependent on Persian Gulf crude.[12]

During the 1990s, the United States encouraged the Gulf Arab Nations to become the principal suppliers of Chinese imported oil and gas. Slowly, methodically, Gulf oil has become their energy jugular, a very real crutch and their addicting Achilles heel, with the determined Americans systematically, skillfully, and ultimately controlling these key storehouses.

In recent years, primarily since the mid-to-late 1990s, China has come to understand her growing vulnerability and it frightens her. According to a late 2002 report in the *Chinese People's Daily* newspaper, 56.2% of the year 2001's imports of oil into China came from Middle East countries. The report reads, in part: "The source and route of China's oil imports are...(coming) under others' control...(and) China's oil security is waiting to be tested in war."[13]

According to excellent research provided in the Wall Street Journal, China's principal point of energy exposure, even danger, lies in the Middle East. There China's energy lifeline is increasingly subject to control and, ironically protection, by the United States military which patrols and controls Gulf shipping lanes.[14]

Another source states: "Asia, led by its four largest economies—Japan, China, South Korea and India—imports 60 percent of its oil. The International Energy Agency in Paris expects this figure to rise to almost 90 percent by 2020, with a corresponding increase in Asian vulnerability to any oil supply interruption.... Dwindling reserves of crude oil in Asia, the resurgence of economic growth in the region... and *the Middle East's dominance of proven and probable supplies of cheap oil will make the 90-percent dependence level a reality much earlier than 2020.* (Italics added.) Virtually all Asian oil imports will come from producers in the Persian Gulf."[15]

The source continues: "While the U.S. economy is fed primarily by oil from the Gulf of Mexico (and other relatively nearby sources), Asia is being forced to forge new relationships with key Gulf suppliers... China Offshore Oil Company says it plans new ventures in the Middle East, especially (in) Iran, as well as in Central Asia (Caspian Basin region)."[16]

According to many experts, the future is Asia's, particularly the Peoples' Republic of China. The Chinese are unstoppable, *if* they are able and willing to take full advantage of the power shift rushing their way. Culture and history are often damning to a nation, which has been the case in China in the past. But today the world center of gravity is shifting their way, and towards India, at an accelerating rate. China was successful in attracting more than $50 billion dollars in foreign investment in 2002. 2003 was much higher. Such massive influx of capital usually has a transforming effect. How will the Chinese respond? Will they moderate, or will they militarize and expand aggressively on the back of a tidal wave of foreign investment and break-neck domestic growth? How will the United States respond if they do? These are the questions of our time. These are the questions we should be asking. For some reason we are not.

China, Russia, and Europe look at the United States with suspicion, (some would say jealousy), and fear, due to our superior technology, military prowess, and most of all freedom and prosperity. In China's eyes, such a system is a threat. Ultimately, in spite of market reforms, China is totalitarian. This is what they know best. And if possessed of the same power and force America commands today, Russia, China, and many in Europe would wield the sword of power much more aggressively. The fact that Americans have yet to use their power in a hostile fashion towards Chinese interests does not allay China's fears. Dictators always view the world through their own cynical eyes, measured by their own self-serving values and brutal agenda. China is the perfect example.

According to a recent report by the Brookings Institute in Washington, D.C.: "Chinese officials strongly disapprove of the foreign (American) military forces in the (Persian) Gulf. They characterize U.S. military involvement there as interference. Furthermore, they suspect that the United States seeks to dominate the region in order to exercise control over the Gulf's energy resources. Having only limited options in terms of power projection to the area, *Beijing views its arms sales to Iran as a critical element of its regional policy.* On the one hand, these arms sales, including…*nuclear and other "dual use" technology,* give China an opportunity *to gain a foothold in the region and build up a long-term strategic link to secure its growing energy interests.* On the other hand, commercially, the arms sales give China an opportunity to substantially decrease the cost of importing energy from the Middle East. This will be especially valuable to China in the future, *given the expected growth of the volume of Chinese energy imports* along with an increase in the market price of oil."[17] (Italics added.)

Such genuine vulnerability has forced the Chinese towards the Russians, recently signing treaties, commercial and military agreements that will steadily enhance the military capability of the Chinese and in the process provide the Russians with badly needed cash. On his first official trip abroad, the new Chinese Premier Hu Jintao stopped first in Russia, where he signed wide-ranging agreements in military and energy fields. In 2002, China purchased approximately *55 percent* of Russia's total weapons and military exports. China understands that unless they can rise to some level of parity, or military competence and projection ability, the Americans will continue to hamstring them on every front, frustrating their goal of becoming the next superpower. Russia can provide China with a better military and, at the same time, *may* provide some of the needed oil and gas which is currently China's principal point of vulnerability. Russia has considerable oil and gas reserves, though their ability to develop and deliver the oil is badly dilapidated and hardly dependable. Russia will require considerable capital investment in worn-out and obsolete oil "lifting," development, and transport infrastructure, money neither Russia nor China currently have. The endemically unstable, eternally corrupt Russian political and economic climate is another downside. For various reasons the Russians keep shooting themselves in the collective foot.

Regardless, China cannot accept world domination by a single superpower, especially one as potentially dangerous to them as the United States. Worried the U.S. will not stop with Iraq, both China and Russia appear to be planning a coordinated strategy to accelerate the formation of a "multi-polar world order," neither controlled nor dominated by the United States.

The U.S. Department of Energy reported recently that over the next fifteen years the U.S. will import approximately 35% more foreign oil than at present. Such increases will be vastly exceeded by the Europeans, and certainly the Asians. In essence, only one place on earth currently has the proven energy capacity to meet such expansive global demand into the future: the Persian Gulf.

Should a clash between China and the U.S. erupt, the United States can shut down the Peoples' Republic, or strangle it off, by cutting her external sources of oil, both at the source in the Middle East, as well as blockading the Straits of Malacca in Southeast Asia. Just the *threat* of such a move by the United States will likely be enough to rein in the always pragmatic and cautious Chinese, with U.S. government "arm-twisting" done behind the scenes and out of the public eye. The Chinese are incredibly vulnerable and growing more so every day as they become "junkies" for imported Middle East crude. American leaders have masterfully redefined the "catbird seat."[18]

China's growing dependence on Persian Gulf and Caspian Basin oil,[19] its source and access ultimately controlled by the United States' military, will help contain the world's last, and potentially most dangerous empire. (This point is critical. See *The Middle East War Process: The Truth Behind America's Middle East Challenge* [March 2003] by the author at: www.authorhouse.com.) Strategic oil management has a moderating and stabilizing effect globally and the United States and its allies do this very well. Yet, regarding oil and gas *profits*, Kuwaitis, Bahrainis, Qataris, and soon even Iraqis will fully benefit from the sale of their own oil. Saddam is no longer in charge of his massive army and potentially deadly weapons' program, bought and built by robbing his people of their oil inheritance.

3) MAINTAINING THE GLOBAL SECURITY AND STABILITY OF THE U.S. DOLLAR

Another critical element in the oil-control issue is maintaining and buttressing the primacy of the U.S. dollar at home and abroad. Few factors are more important globally than the financial stability of the United States and the U.S. dollar; yet during the past decade the U.S. has become the most indebted nation in history. Estimates show the U.S. owes the rest of the world around *$3 trillion* dollars in borrowed debt. To finance this unprecedented burden, some experts claim America requires an in-flow of perhaps $2 billion *per day* from investors outside the United States.

In 2002, foreigners owned 12.5 percent of U.S. government agency securities, 31.7 percent of U.S. Treasury securities, 20.7 percent of U.S. corporate bonds, and 11.4 percent of U.S. stocks. Foreign investors are currently looking at Europe because U.S. interest rates are so low by comparison to *euro* accounts. Foreign investors are also troubled by the ballooning federal budget and trade deficits. Beginning in 2004, European banks held about 70 percent of their reserves in dollar-denominated assets. Amazingly European purchases of U.S. securities had financed approximately 80 percent of the U.S. account deficit, according to the French Press Agency, quoting a European Central Bank report.[20] The report also said that European banks are moving reserves away from the U.S. towards Europe, which may make it harder for President Bush to finance the record U.S. account deficit.

To counter these concerns, in mid-2003 the Treasury announced plans to sell a record $60 billion in new Treasury notes to help finance the deficit.[21] Some U.S. Senators have proposed selling some federal lands close to major cities, estimating that these sales may be sufficient to eliminate much of the shortfall.

Massive U.S. trade deficits have forced the dollar to depreciate by around 15 percent since 2002 against major foreign currencies. Though a weaker dollar usually helps to increase American exports, which become cheaper in other countries, there are dangers. The steady declining value of the U.S. dollar can drag down the American stock and bond markets. When the dollar drops, foreign investors see their investments in U.S. stocks and bonds lose value. If this continues too long, many will yank their U.S. investments and find a more stable or profitable alternative, such as the European *euro* or the Japanese yen. That could lead to a collapse in the U.S. stock and bond markets.

That said, due to the incredible economic juggernaut that is the United States, the dollar remains the world's financial 800 lb. gorilla. Playing such a powerful, stabilizing role in the world, the U.S. attracts about two-thirds of global surplus investment. This is an amazing statistic. In its bulwark role, the dollar is *the* central international reserve currency. Most foreign exchange transactions are denominated in U.S. dollars. The dollar is estimated to make up approximately two-thirds of all externally held currency reserves, amounts totaling in the *trillions* of dollars.

However, the emergence of the *euro* by the European Union is becoming a potential and viable rival or competitor to the U.S. dollar in international markets. "We believe the dollar's structural descent will continue, and expect the euro to be one of the biggest beneficiaries," stated Morgan Stanley in a 2003 report on the slide of the dollar against the euro. "At this juncture, the investment strategies of the two major groups of currency players: (1) the Asian central banks, and (2) the owners of petrodollars, are likely to remain positive for euros...for some time, despite the inferior cyclical fundamentals in euroland."[22]

With the precipitous drop of the U.S. stock market in 2000, the dollar has come under global siege, falling about 25% against the euro over the past two years. This has led some OPEC (Organization of Petroleum Exporting Countries) producers to consider shifting the denomination of international oil contracts from dollars to euros. In 2000, Iraq made the switch in some contracts, in spite of Washington's protests. Iran has seriously discussed it as well. One point of leverage key OPEC oil producers have considered using on the Americans is the threat of "adopting euro pricing and payments for oil contracts" at some future date.

In many respects, world trade is a game in which the U.S. produces dollars and the rest of the world produces things which dollars buy. Many nations and investors abroad would like to shift the focus off the U.S. dollar for a variety of reasons. In the view of many, such a shift from dollars to euros in the international oil markets would be a rejection of U.S. political policy and a very real financial attack on the United States. Such a broad-based move would require major oil importers and exporters to shift oil transaction funds from dollars to euros, or other currencies, precipitating the liquidation of U.S. stocks, bonds, and other holdings—where surplus dollars are often held—in order to cover these currency transfers.

Almost certainly such a move would cause a sharp decline in the value of the U.S. dollar abroad, panicking foreign and domestic investors into liquidating dollar holdings in U.S. securities. At that point, the previously mentioned huge U.S. debt position would become an even greater albatross around America's neck in the eyes of world investors. An accelerating global and domestic nervousness could gut U.S. dollar-denominated holdings, leaving pennies on the dollar in value to those foolish enough to hold on.

Since 1991, Saddam's Iraq on occasion shifted to the euro to denominate oil payments, in spite of considerable financial losses resulting from this "cut off your nose to spite your face" action.

Iran as well continues to threaten such a move. Recently, Malaysian Prime Minister Mahathir Mohammad, a particularly bitter opponent of the U.S. war in Iraq, advocated dumping the dollar in favor of the euro.

Suddenly the *strategic power* of oil, denominated in petrodollars, raises its ugly head impacting not only the ability of nations to ignite industry and commerce, as well as back and field armies, but more importantly impacting our national financial security. A sudden, panicked flight by international investors from the dollar would be a potent "weapon of mass destruction" the United States can never accept. Such a financial strike on the U.S. would not necessarily be affected by either the *price* of global oil or U.S. *access* to it. However, if the United States remains in ultimate *control* of Iraqi, as well as Arabian Gulf oil, the U.S. will be better positioned to limit such OPEC shenanigans. The most effective means, our government seems to believe, would be through a pro-U.S. Iraqi government and U.S. military "protection" of the Gulf region. U.S. successes in Iraq will probably ensure the continuation of the status quo regarding the U.S. dollar.

Ultimately, however, pressure will come from Asia, principally China, as this increasingly powerful region decides the United States holds too much power over Asia's primary source of imported oil. Fumio Hoshi, from the Japan Bank for International Cooperation, stated in a mid-June 2003 oil and gas conference in Kuala Lumpur, that Asia's oil imports are projected to nearly triple over the next 25-30 years to 34 million barrels per day. With high dependence on Middle East oil, Asia must do three things immediately, he says: 1) Reinforce its international bargaining power on oil contracts through regional cooperation; 2) Strengthen "energy security"; and 3) Boost efficiency technology to better utilize available energy.

U.S. financial and strategic leverage on the oil market is key to impacting and managing both points one and two.

"They've got to sell the stuff (oil) to someone. What difference does it make who controls the wells on the ground?" Such a question is often posed by a host of misinformed journalists, commentators, and liberal pundits. Once again, the wrong question, perhaps even a false flag. Coalition or "friendly" control on the ground makes a huge difference. Remember, ultimately it's the *strategic power* of oil, not the price or profits, that rules. In the case of Middle East oil, ultimate control of the wellheads, the transport and distribution systems and networks, as well as the financial infrastructure, denominated in U.S. dollars, is not optional, nor is it negotiable for the United States.

4) FIGHTING FOR AMERICAN VALUES OF FREEDOM AND OPEN MARKETS

The columnist William Safire said in a recent article: "Mistakes have been made in this war (the Iraq War, 2003). But advancing freedom is never a mistake."

The planet's oldest democracy has done more to bless the world's people than any other nation in history. The American system of republican freedom has freed more slaves and destroyed more despots, dictators and evil empires than all other nations in history *combined*. The United States is the land of freedom and opportunity, the land of unlimited potential which people from all lands risk everything to reach.

Radical, fundamentalist Muslims, terrorists, and strongmen everywhere hate America because of her unfettered freedom, equality, and opportunity. Such values threaten their despotic plans and undermine the tyrannical status quo. We stand directly in the way of Islamic dictatorial regimes and terrorist factions, some of whom want the Americans out of the Gulf region and the downfall of the pro-American regimes there. An Islamic oil-empire is the dream of many, including Osama bin Laden, where the Islamists ultimately influence and even control the policy and prosperity of the world's nations. With such unfettered power, Global Jihad, in the name of Allah, is possible, carried to the world with an iron fist. Without it, Islam's revival and global reach is not going to happen.

Unfortunately for the purveyors of medieval Islamic madness, freedom and democracy are the ultimate global steamrollers and moral iconoclasts which are very difficult, if not impossible, to stop once the seed is firmly planted.

American values of faith in God and the universal brotherhood and equality of mankind, as documented so beautifully in the Declaration of Independence, is the inevitable heritage of the nations and peoples of the earth. Certainly there are pitfalls, many still to come. Freedom is never free. But the popular insistence of many so-called "liberals" that democracy is not meant for all people is incredibly short-sighted, perhaps even racist; such amazing arrogance and elitism, to say that any man or woman is better off in a cage, existing at the whim and will of another?

No one said it would be easy. The hurdle is that the world's elites and oppressors want to keep their slaves, their serfs, their servants. America and its enlightening institutions and liberating technologies—its ideals—are the greatest threat to their power and control. The dictatorial elites, some even living in America, believe the United States must be brought to its knees while thwarting its desire for global emancipation and free, prosperous, unfettered markets. Many are using the United Nations to accomplish this end. In the process, the United Nations, led by Kofi Annan, has already compromised itself, perhaps fatally.

God help the world if America loses heart and abandons its hope to free the struggling, shackled souls in every land. These are values worth dying for. They are eternal, they are beyond price. For a century and more American blood has been the sacrificial offering to defeat history's worst, most powerfully despotic regimes. Sadly, today, it appears we walk largely alone on this road. Sadder still, so many Americans seem ignorant of, or hostile to, America's desire to free the downtrodden.

5) PREVENTING ROGUE NATIONS AND TERRORIST GROUPS FROM OBTAINING WEAPONS OF MASS DESTRUCTION (WMD)

The next September 11th could be an attack with nuclear, chemical or biological weaponry (WMD). It is *inevitable* if we do nothing. The strike will come from some shadowy terrorist group clandestinely backed and supplied by Iran, or Syria, or fanatic groups in Saudi Arabia, or perhaps from North Korea. There are others. It will happen, unless we act. Action *begins* with Iraq and Afghanistan.

The protesters complain: Why Iraq? Why now? Why don't we eliminate al-Qaeda and Osama bin Laden first? The reason: *because they are linked.* It should be obvious by now this is not exclusively about eliminating any one person or terror cadre or faction. We are waging war on a host of radical Islamist enemies and their potential to maim and kill on a massive scale.

More importantly, we wage war on despotism. First Afghanistan, moving quickly to Iraq; we are not finished. Despotism has always been the safe harbor for assassins, state criminals, and a multitude of terrorist cadres. Tyrants hold onto their power through the effective use of the many human and non-human weapons of murder and intrigue, especially including mastering and controlling WMD. Saddam did this on multiple occasions during his reign, gassing tens-of-thousands of his own people, as well as his Iranian enemy. Saddam has wielded these weapons. No one disputes this historical fact.

Eliminating al-Qaeda and bin Laden is but a tiny, though highly visible, tip of the cancer. The growth has spread deep into many lands, amid multiple groups. Pulling the trigger on Saddam Hussein was key to eliminating a past, and likely future major supplier of some very nasty weaponry, logistical support, and safe haven to terror. I have seen his past arsenal, the many horrible weapons which he bought or manufactured to kill his enemies. He has fielded WMD on several occasions, and would have done so again if he thought he could get away with it. The U.S. military put an end to that possibility once and for all in the spring of 2003.

In addition to Saddam's WMD crimes, and linked to his potential to kill and maim on a massive scale, the Maximum Leader regularly initiated and funded terrorism, both inside and outside of Iraq. In fact, you would be hard-pressed to find a man today who has resorted more often to the many techniques of terror: a quarter-century of torture, extortion, blackmail, and death on an unbelievable, genocidal scale.

A liberated, democratic, economically stable, even prosperous Iraq, free of terrorists and weapons of mass destruction is foundational to a secure and prosperous Middle East. Only America can lead this fight. No other nation, or leader, has the material resources, the courage, or the moral fortitude to accomplish the task. No other military could have prevailed as we have.

6) CREATING INCENTIVE AND MOMENTUM FOR A LASTING PEACE IN THE ARAB/ISRAELI CONFLICT

For reasons previously mentioned, the Arab/Israeli conflict is generally *not* a cause of terrorism directed at the United States, at least not recently. That could change quickly. However, it is regionally destabilizing, as well as horribly tragic, and must be addressed.

Hamas, Islamic Jihad, Hezbollah, and the *al-Aqsa' Brigades* can only carry the battle to their Israeli enemy with the help of outside financial and logistical support. In the recent past, Iran has spent approximately $100 million *per year* financing worldwide terrorism.[23] Weapons and funding are smuggled to the above-mentioned groups within Israel, the West Bank, Gaza, and South Lebanon from Islamic factions and governments in nearly every Middle Eastern country. These include Iran, Syria, Saudi Arabia, and until mid-2003, Iraq, and from Islamic groups worldwide, some within the U.S.

Osama bin Laden is from Saudi Arabia, as were all but three of the September 11th terrorists. Their ringleader, Mohammad Atta, was Egyptian. Dr. Ayman al-Zawahiri, Bin Laden's number two man in al-Qaeda, is also Egyptian. These two Mideast countries, supposedly U.S. allies, are producing some incredibly hostile and virulent forces. From such seedbeds of anti-American hatred come religious inspiration, terror-training, and logistical support; but more importantly *cash* to fund Palestinian terrorists.

The fact that the Islamic Republic of Iran is funding Palestinian terrorism is interesting. Considering the ethnic and religious differences within the branches of Islam, major funding coming from the Islamic Republic shows just how important is the Middle East adage: "The enemy of my enemy is my friend." Iran is populated mostly by Persians. The Palestinians are Arabs. Historically, Persians have always hated Arabs, and vice-versa. Throughout much of the past they have been enemies; their warriors and assassins killing millions on both sides, even as recently as the Iran-Iraq War in the 1980s, and the subsequent mass executions of Shi'ites by Saddam in the 1990s.

However, today Iran is willing to back the Palestinians, but *not* because of Israeli treatment of the Palestinians, nor for Iranian brotherly love of their fellow Muslims. Shi'ite Persians never change their stripes. At best, they remain indifferent towards the Palestinians, who are Sunnis and by definition, "apostate inferiors." This is a political move, plain and simple. Iran wants the Islamic world to view them as powerful world leaders with a pro-Islamic, activist foreign policy.

Iran also supports Syrian-led attacks on Israel by backing several terrorist factions hosted and protected by the Syrian government, hoping to garner continued Syrian support for Iranian access to Shi'ite populations living in Lebanon. The deadly Hezbollah terrorist organization is Shi'ite, headquartered in the Bekaa Valley of East Lebanon and bordering on Syria. In true Middle East fashion of "you scratch my back, I'll scratch yours," the hapless Palestinians are merely a means to an end for both Iran and Syria. They are political pawns—window dressing—a public relations campaign, and a reason to continue the "struggle" against Israel and to lead the Muslim world to "greatness and supremacy." The Palestinians translate into political influence and control within each Middle East tyrannical regime.

As well, Saddam Hussein spent millions of dollars rewarding Palestinian terrorism against Israel. Detailed evidence will follow in subsequent chapters which demonstrate the funding mechanism and the amounts funneled to terror operations in Gaza and on the West Bank. As is the case with most Islamic leaders, Saddam wanted to appear as an "Islamic champion," leading the Muslim world in its "eternal battle" with the Israeli enemy.

Terrorism is big business and it is big politics. Lots of oil money, sometimes called "petro-dollars," (meaning the prime source of the cash comes from selling Middle East oil to the world), ultimately funds terror. Therefore, by systematically cutting off this type of deadly financial support, and pressuring host governments to end their training and inspiration to terrorist cells in and outside of Israel, *most* of the current deadly attacks against Israel will cease, lending itself to a climate where a lasting peace *may* be possible. Of course, there are other factors, but everyone agrees that eliminating the source of external terror-funding is critical. This plan begins with making Iraq part of the solution, rather than an instigator of terror and war.

QUESTION 2

- HOW CAN THE IRAQ WAR SECURE THE UNITED STATES AND BRING PEACE AND STABILITY TO THE MID-EAST AND THE WORLD?

> *"War is an ugly thing, but not the ugliest of things. The decayed and degraded state of moral and patriotic feeling which thinks nothing is worth war is much worse. The person who has nothing for which he is willing to fight, nothing which is more important than his own personal safety, is a miserable creature and has no chance of being free unless made and kept so by the exertions of better men than himself."*
>
> *--John Stuart Mill*

Your instincts were right. The March 2003 war on Iraq was not exclusively, not even primarily, waged to control Saddam Hussein's weapons of mass destruction (WMD), though WMD proliferation involving Iraq was a factor. Quoting from the President's press secretary at the time, Ari Fleischer, "It (WMD) was the only thing we could all agree on (as a reason to go to war)." Such justification doesn't come close to the whole story, of course, as the previous chapter outlines. But America and the world need more; and there is more.

As I have maintained for several years, the greatest danger was not in *finding* the so-called "smoking gun" of mass destruction weapons in Iraq, but *not* finding them. Now we appear as "the boy who cried wolf." The danger is that in the future we may not be able to convince the American people, and the world, of the growing threat of such weaponry spreading into tyrannical and terrorist regimes and factions. Those nations working feverishly to field these horrible weapons (particularly Iran and North Korea) are rejoicing over U.S. failure in finding the "smoking gun" in Iraq. America's intelligence failure buys them time, dousing the flames of fear in people's minds and giving them a freer hand. Listen to the media. Few are talking, at least effectively, about the growing danger from these weapons. As usual, our media is hawking trivia and entertainment.

Wars are seldom, if ever, fought for one reason alone. Armies, however, *always* mobilize for power. But freedom should be the highest or loftiest, most moral quest of mankind, with democracy or republican freedom the mechanism, even the inheritance, of the world's downtrodden. This is our ideal; and this is our goal.

For Iraq, our long-term challenge lies in what several world-class experts concluded are the "Three Iraqi Deficits": *Freedom, knowledge,* and *women-power,* or the lack thereof, which was outlined brilliantly in a United Nations special report published in 2002. The report was compiled by Arab scholars, among them the renowned Dr. Clovis Maksoud, Director of the Center for the Global South at the American University in Washington, D.C. This report is unique (for a United Nations' report) in that it did *not* criticize America or Israel for Arab nations' own problems; but laid blame where blame belongs—at the feet of Arab leaders and people.

Arabs are in truth slowly killing themselves when they excuse their own failure at the hands of others (a traditional, yet annoying Arab trait). Most Arab nations are faced with striking resource and demographic problems to be sure. Roughly sixty percent (or more) of all Arabs are below the age of 21 years. You cannot find another world region with such a high ratio of young people. Yet economically, Arab nations *combined* have a smaller GDP than the relatively weak European nation of Spain *by itself.* While the figures do not look good, and history seems against the Arabs, the United States is committed to the "Arab Miracle," beginning in Iraq. It will happen. Why? Because there is just too much at stake to accept anything less than success, though success won't come overnight. And failure could mean the death of millions throughout the Middle East and the disruption of the world's strategic oil supplies.

Though officially not discussed openly, the United States appears to be planning some form of tripartite government in Iraq, a Shi'ite—Sunni—Kurdish alliance with each group sharing power to some degree, allowing a measure of regional self-determination

Iraqis have never known; a federation strongly backed by the U.S. and other world nations. In order for the new Iraq to work, however, many patriotic Iraqis must step forward, men and women willing to set aside personal ambition and ethnic and religious bigotry for the good of the nation. Many have. The chain-breaking power of education is crucial, as is American and Western investment of capital and technology. Fortunately, Iraq has much going for it—vast supplies of oil, plenty of usable water, and a large, educated, capable population. But this can come only through the long-term blood and sacrifice of the Iraqi people, as well as the iron-will of America to likewise sacrifice and stay the course.

President Bush warned us shortly after 9/11 that the war on terrorism would last many years. He is speaking the truth. Sadly, history tells us the Middle East is the land of war. The preceding chapter, as well as those that follow, shed additional light on why we made war on Saddam Hussein and why we must succeed in Iraq to ensure the security of the United States and the stability of the Middle East. More specifically, they explain what is at stake for the world. Failure in Iraq guarantees that greater dangers will be left to our children.

No true and honorable American who understands our legacy of unheard of freedom, prosperity, and peace left us by our sacrificing ancestors, will in turn, through personal selfishness, leave our children a legacy of terror and war. Such an act would be tragic and history should judge us criminally irresponsible.

Follow-up Question: How can *hope* arise from the blood and smoke of war?

Hope would probably be the *last* word most people would use to describe the future of the Middle East. More likely words such as "hatred, discrimination, oppression, fanaticism," and "tragically medieval" come to mind. Over there we seem swept into a land of death where people are bent on self-destruction, or at best, endemic corruption, prejudice, and exploitation. Failure is an institution in this land. On the TV the Middle East is always bad news, armies on the move, terrorists plotting and innocents blown apart or beheaded by heartless killers with shrouded faces.

War, Middle East-style is seldom between two relatively equal military forces. Instead war is waged against the innocent, women and children, the old or non-combatants who are not fast enough to get out of the way. Mideast "warriors" wage war on those unable to defend themselves: wholesale slaughter such as Saddam rained down on civilians in the north and south of Iraq in the wake of the first gulf war in 1991, or the butchery Syria's former "strongman" Hafiz al-Assad meted out to the rebellious fundamentalist residents of Hama, Syria. It used to be considered dishonorable to attack the defenseless. Non-combatants, particularly women and children, were to be protected. Warfare was not terrorizing an otherwise peaceful population for political ends.

No more. Ask the Russians about that, hundreds of children murdered in an elementary school by Islamic thugs. Since the 1980s, more than 75 percent of war casualties the world over have been civilian. True, in Gulf War I (1991) there were few civilian casualties. As well, the recent war with Iraq and in Afghanistan against the Taliban produced relatively few non-combatant deaths. Though seldom reported in the media, our American soldiers and Marines shouldered great risks to themselves to avoid civilian losses and to protect the innocent. But overall, Middle East wars and conflicts over the past two decades (Israel-Lebanon, the Iraqi invasion of Kuwait, the Algerian wars, the wars in the Sudan and other Islamic-African ethnic butcheries, as well as the war in Kashmir and internal struggles in Lebanon and Iran) claimed *civilian* casualties in the hundreds of thousands, if not millions.

This should not be. Muhammad's fighters, the *Mujahadin*, rode fearlessly out of Arabia in Allah's holy name 1,400 years ago, throwing themselves on Christian and Persian armies like young lions. The Middle East has changed. Islam has changed. Principle and honor, it seems, have vanished like the *jinn* after only three wishes. War is no longer a test of courage and honor, but a free-for-all of savagery and rape. Truly, the Middle East has become, as former Israeli Prime Minister Shimon Perez has frequently alluded to, nothing more than a "process for war." A war process, as opposed to a "peace process," makes peace effectively impossible.

But rising with the sun, something new, something shining on the horizon, born of a new generation of educated young Arabs and Iranians who want something better. At the same time, America has determined to commit, this time, to a *lasting* solution. Now is the time; for change is rushing straight at us. During my most recent visit to the region, I saw the budding glimmer of Hope from the Nile to the Tigris—the hope of peace and prosperity, a new vision of the world, a vision mostly by the youth, that the Middle East does not have to remain the same forever.

Look into the eyes of an Iraqi child, her father and mother struggling desperately to feed and protect her. Ask an Israeli living in East Jerusalem, or the Palestinian mother fighting to nurture her children in the grinding poverty of the Gaza Strip. All are weary and all are angry at those who have built dynasties on the backs of the downtrodden. Exploiting religion to gain power, the elite often use the excuse of "honor" to refuse compromise and to confuse the issues, to cloud reality, and to make death palatable. All are weary of the terror-mongers among them who care nothing for their own children and recruit these young innocents as the foot soldiers of blood and death.

A new day has dawned and a new reality is sweeping the Land of Abraham from Marrakech to Bangladesh. Hope is the watchword, born of a vision of the potential of unprecedented peace and cooperation. The world's slaves are rising against their masters with power born of education and access to information and technology. And their old masters tremble; they are running scared.

This new generation of Middle Easterner must rise up and shoulder its rightful inheritance, too long denied by self-serving and oppressive so-called "leaders." The youth must work together for the common good and for a peaceful tomorrow. The world they create can bless their children and their children's children to the "Seventh Generation." We live in the age of hope as dictatorial leaders know their days are numbered by Allah; their sun sinking low on the horizon.

Follow-up: Why is a Middle East Free Trade Zone, as proposed by President Bush, critical for peace?

Foster goodwill in the Middle East through a free trade zone between Mideast countries, the United States and the world. In essence, this was the message spoken by President Bush on May 9, 2003, in what was hoped to be a soon to come victory in Iraq. His words, however, seemed to catch the world by surprise as commentators, experts, and world leaders scrambled to grasp such "revolutionary thinking." Everyone seemed to struggle with the concept. "Not in the Middle East, surely! A market-oriented, entrepreneurial solution to social, cultural, and ethnic hatred and war? How can this possibly work?!" Finally they opined, considering the source, "Truly such vision must be born of folly and ignorance. It's never been done that way before over there."

Of course, to the truly democratic, to the soundly free-market oriented, a free and open trading zone would be the next logical step; beautifully simple, yet powerful and far-reaching in scope. Plain as day and bold as victory itself. Once again, President Bush leaves his critics behind spinning and speculating on what just hit them.

There are dangers, of course. Arab countries, more so Iran, are skeptical or hostile to America's plans. Fearful that the United States may be plotting to construct a Trojan horse in the heart of Islam, a free trade zone is viewed as cover for increasing U.S. power and control. Using commercial penetration as a weapon to increase the seductive level of American culture, the U.S. is "clandestinely worming its way into the House of Islam," many believe. Obviously, America under Bush has them rattled.

By nature Arabs and Iranians see conspiracies under every rock and behind every burning bush. Nothing in the Middle East happens by chance. *Khalliha-ala-Allah* and *In-Sha-Allah*, "leave it to God and for God's sake." God's will controls all. Predestination is culturally ingrained. *Nothing* happens that is not God's intent. A child is hit by a truck; God willed it. A man finds treasure on his property; such are the workings of God. A woman is diagnosed with terminal cancer; God has allowed it; it is her time. And while America is certainly not considered even remotely divine, the Americans are viewed by many Mideasterners as "all-powerful." And since they are definitely not Islamic, then their power must come from the Dark Side. Hence, the "Great Satan." We might as well have buttons printed. With such overwhelming U.S. hegemony and power, the "Hand of Bush" is imagined in every shadow, at every turn and crossroads.

Nothing, however, succeeds like success. By nature people quickly move to back a winner, even if it is the Great Satan. Middle Easterners are experts at this, albeit grumbling and moaning along the way: "What have you done for me *today?*"

Conditioned by an infinite host of oppressors since "Eve got Adam kicked out of the Garden," (men have held that over women's heads ever since), Arabs believe that in vanquishing Saddam, Bush has gone a long way towards proving himself worthy. But they need more. "Arabs are either at your feet, or at your throat," goes the old maxim.

President Bush is, in effect, saying to the Middle Easterner: *Stand up and stop groveling to the terror-bosses and dictators around you. Your leaders have lied to you from the beginning. Each of you, whoever you are, deserves to freely choose your own path, free from the fear of a thousand generations of oppression.*

Fine words, but freedom is never free. It has a price, paid for by the best blood of our generation, then left to be enjoyed by those less courageous, those less willing to make the ultimate sacrifice. Many believe that Arabs are not yet worthy of democracy and self-rule, that they must always be strong-armed into line. This is insulting to those of us who see an emerging, educated, capable generation of young people who can handle it. I know it is insulting to Arabs. The time has come to remove the training wheels.

Human rights, political freedom and democracy are the inheritance of *all* the peoples of the world, and last time I checked, Arabs qualify. The challenge is that we have grown accustomed to dealing with, and profiting by, these Arab, Iranian, and Pakistani dictators and warlords. President Bush is rocking lots of boats.

When it comes down to it, it's tough to tell the difference between the Ba'athist Iraqi regime, and the Syrian variety. The al-Tikriti clan of Iraq and the al-Assad's of Syria are opposite sides of the same coin, as are the Ayatollah hard-liners in Iran. You would be hard pressed to set one above the other in the virtue department. Lincolnesque they are not.

In reality, the roots of Anti-American terror can be found not only in Baghdad, but in Damascus, in Tehran, in Tripoli and amazingly, in Riyadh and Cairo. The leaders of these nations, tyrants all, deflect internal dissent and unrest by nurturing hatred of the United States and Israel among their people, in the process distracting their citizens from their own economic and political imprisonment. When a dictator preys on his own people with impunity, and the United States seemingly condones the murder and abuse by cozying up to these royal thugs, this breeds hatred for the United States, as it should.

In the end the solution is *freedom*. Inevitably, one by one, the dictators must go. In their place the world's free nations will invest in this pivotal region, which will bring prosperity beyond anyone's expectation. If I am reading President Bush's intentions correctly, this is his objective.

Truly this *is* Vision with a capital "V." A Free Trade Zone, from Iraq to Egypt and beyond, including a free and open State of Palestine. People of every faith and creed will be electing their own leaders and building lives of their own making, backed by the power of the open market, of billions in petrodollars, and the most advanced technologies on the face of the earth. In a techno-alliance, linked to the United States, the world's greatest economic juggernaut, undoubtedly these Mideast countries will prosper.

Of course, it will not be easy. And sadly, tragically, some of the most vocal naysayers are found right here in America.

Think about it. Truly a modern miracle, if it succeeds. A Free Trade Zone, established among some of history's most virulent enemies and radical malcontents! Truly such thinking is either hopelessly foolish, or pure mastery and genius. And in the end, ironically, whether it succeeds or not will depend greatly on President Bush's ability to sell it to…America.

Follow-up: Specifically how is the United States reshaping the Middle East?

A DEMOCRACY TUTORIAL SHOP

Many years ago, a great American religious leader said: *"Put your house in order and keep your eyes on the Middle East."*[24]

While putting my house in order has always been a challenge, I've had my eyes locked firmly on the Middle East ever since.

Make no mistake we are entering a new era. Certainly many will call it the "Age of American Empire." But is it really? Are we fashioning our world after the great British Empire of the past, or the one that comes to most people's mind, the Roman Empire? Let's look at the facts.

In spite of an expanding "American footprint" in the world, America has always had as a principle, an ideal, the support of freedom. Fighting bloody wars against tyranny, we have sacrificed hundreds of thousands of American lives to free the world's downtrodden. As Secretary of State Colin Powell stated, "the only land the United States has ever sought to keep is the ground needed to bury our dead."

Dictators everywhere, even those we have supported in the past, are now on notice: "Change, or be replaced." President Bush has wisely, perhaps prophetically, placed himself on the right side of history. Having taken a stand, it appears he plans to live or die by it. Free the world's slaves! Destroy the terror-mongers! Thereby sowing the seeds of global peace and prosperity. A thousand years of peace? A goal even Biblical in nature.

Determined to end the death and destruction one way or the other, the United States has set up a "democracy tutorial shop" in the heart of the Muslim world. We are committed. Americans no longer have the luxury of ignoring global issues. September 11th got our attention. We have now determined to tackle the Middle East in ways yet untested.

Is success guaranteed? Not hardly. President Woodrow Wilson tried and failed to reshape the world following the First World War with his League of Nations. In many respects World War II was the disastrous result. Since the Second World War, the United Nations has attempted to control and prosper the globe. The U.N., however, has seen its powers steadily erode to the impotent, essentially anti-American, anti-Israeli, even highly corrupt body we see today.

The U.N. is feckless, consistently shooting itself in the foot, when it manages to shoot at all. A costly club of whiners, the U.N. has little vision and practically no power. Whether it continues to shrivel into irrelevance and a deserved oblivion will be determined by its leaders and the strategic decisions they must make. Their future lies in *their* choices.

Today America moves with power and authority. No doubt American "vision" will be painted with the broad brush of empire. "The New American Empire, *beginning* in the Middle East?" Many pundits claim this is America's ultimate goal. With more than 150,000 U.S. forces on the ground in the Gulf region, and billions of dollars of pre-positioned weaponry, equipment and military bases throughout the area, perhaps the charge may stick.

The difference, however, lies in America's historical willingness, when the time is right, to pack-up and go home. Inevitably, the Arab people, like all people, must govern themselves. Every American instinctively knows this (but few Arabs seem to, yet). In so doing, by going home, the slimy mud of "empire" will not stick to the Land of the Free. In the end, history will be kind to the president with a good heart and skilled hand; the President of the nation that paid for world peace and prosperity with its own lifeblood and treasure, just as we have always done.

QUESTION 3

- MUST MIDDLE EAST DICTATORS, SUCH AS SADDAM HUSSEIN OR OSAMA BIN LADEN, BE ELIMINATED TO ENSURE GLOBAL PEACE AND STABILITY?

> *Regardless of whether Iraq had weapons of mass destruction or not, an American expedition into far-off Iraq was necessary to accomplish what dictatorial governments everywhere have been resisting for centuries. The power of freedom, once set in motion, is like that Biblical "stone cut out of the mountain without hands," which will roll forth to fill the whole earth. Right now in history we are on the very edge of freedom's critical mass. That stone needs merely one good push.*
>
> *--Richard P. Robison*
> *Snowbird, Utah,*
> *Presentation on the*
> *Rebuilding of Iraq,*
> *August 2003*

The September 11th terrorist attacks on New York and Washington, D.C. were symptoms of a wider, deeper disease, the disease of American capitulation. Dictators and terror-mongers love natural capitulators, perpetual negotiators, and of course, hopeless appeasers.

Throughout the mid and late 1990s, the decade of trying to gently cajole terrorists and dictatorial regimes, Saddam Hussein not only used the time to physically brutalize his own people, killing *tens of thousands*, but also enriched himself by milking the United Nations Oil-for-Food Program, supposedly set up to feed Iraq's children by selling a regulated amount of Iraq's oil. Monitored by the United Nations, this program was apparently corrupt to its core, with Saddam and his cronies, as well as conspirators in other governments and lands, including within the U.N. itself, skimming *billions* of dollars diverted to private bank accounts. The U.N. investigation was carried out at a snail's pace, Saddam, it seems, perfect in his ability to suck in a variety of allies and collaborators, men willing to sell out Iraq's children for "30 pieces of silver."

The road of capitulation is the easy road, and on the surface, the politically safe one. We did it, repeatedly, procrastinating what truly needed to be done in order to avoid the pain of genuine action. History provides multiple examples of "consensus-building" and passive submission ending in September 11th-like disasters (Japanese attack on Pearl Harbor; German invasion of Czechoslovakia and Poland; U.S. diplomats taken hostage in Iran in 1979; the multiple terrorist attacks against American targets worldwide, and at home, over the past two decades).

We no longer have a choice, if we ever did. Dictators and terrorists *must* be toppled, worldwide, one-by-one, otherwise our future will be stalked by monsters wielding doomsday weapons and with little hesitation or reluctance to use them. National security is no longer an optional exercise, or a passive extension of global trade and feel-good diplomacy; neither is it solely a law enforcement responsibility, as was administered during the 1990s.

Those opposing our actions in Iraq often claim that such secular dictators as Saddam Hussein and religious fanatics like Osama bin Laden could not possibly have cooperated because bin Laden's religious convictions would not allow him to side with the very secular Saddam. Cooperation between the two men, they often maintain, was effectively "impossible."

Such thinking is dangerously erroneous for two reasons:

1) The Middle East is the heart and soul of tribal cross-dressing, which they justify as an "alliance against evil." In the "land of perpetual war," which *is* the Middle East, you cannot survive without forming some pretty distasteful partnerships. "The enemy of my enemy is my friend." (See Chapter 7 on *taqiya*.)

Even more to the point, according to Allah there is absolutely nothing wrong with such logic, if it furthers your cause. The earliest

Muslims did it, as did the Persians, and the pagans of Mecca who allied themselves with the Jews of Medina to attack Muhammad. You need a program, or manual, to keep score. Even the ancient Jews formed alliances with the Babylonians, the Egyptians, the Malekites, the Phoenicians, on and on, even adopting their Gods when it served political purposes. Today the Middle East remains unchanged: Arab nationalists ally with radical Muslims against communists or Marxists; radical Muslims cooperate with Arab communists to counter Arab nationalists, on and on. Without question the Middle East is the land of alliance, usually in secret, alliances of convenience, of profit, of blood and death, every stripe and color.

2) Osama bin Laden is *anything* but pious and morally incorruptible. First and foremost he is a hypocrite, changing into Western clothes and flying off to Beirut, there we found him with a barmaid on each arm. After partying himself ill for days bin Laden would then return home for recuperation and some serious repentance before his more religious colleagues. His past is for all to see. In the land of blatant double standards, do you really believe that Osama bin Laden was too "righteous" to turn down an offer of assistance from the likes of Saddam Hussein? Don't bet your *qafiya*[25] on it!

Yet another example, Ramzi Yusif. The mastermind behind the terrorist bombing of the World Trade Center in 1993, he planned terror operations from Manila in the Philippines where he lived the high life in the early 1990s. According to information brought forth during his trial, he had a Philippine girl friend with whom he partied in strip clubs and bars, all such activities presumably without Allah's official sanction. The FBI reported that Ramzi Yusif used Islam for his own ends, his daily life anything but devoutly Islamic.

Terrorists such as Osama bin Laden and Ramzi Yusif as well as the world's many strongmen, such as Saddam, respect only power. Religious piety is used as a weapon, seldom more.

The past decade's anemic, even wimpy peace efforts have merely emboldened Saddam, bin Laden, and others. Words spoken from their very lips, and spoken in defiance and disregard for America's might, show that these killers have nothing but contempt for the many past "peace" initiatives. For years, the United Nation's willingness to negotiate seemingly forever was viewed as neutered weakness by these men, lacking honor and deserving defeat. They have told us a much in dozens of speeches, *if* we were listening.

When the U.N. spoke, Saddam smiled, as do Iran's Ali Khamenei and Syria's al-Assad clan. Any Arab or Iranian who has grown up in the region can attest to this fact. Ask anyone who has staggered under the whip of the despot. Dictators and terrorists never fight by the rules. Certainly there are some tragically bloody battles yet to be fought. This war on terror could be the most brutal and most dangerous we have ever faced.

Follow-up: Who's to blame for pathetic Middle Eastern leadership?

The Arab World's leaders must be held accountable for a wretched legacy of corruption and self-serving brutality. Dismal Arab and Iranian statesmanship, for example, is responsible for the death of millions and for keeping many millions more in poverty and ignorance. In spite of the greatest transfer of wealth the world has ever known, *hundreds of billions* of petro-dollars have been squandered on lavish and slothful lifestyles, foreign-held treasure hordes, and state-of-the-art weapon systems. In the end such predatory and incompetent leadership, conscious or otherwise, must be accounted for.

Historically, in 1699, Europe forced the first peace treaty upon the Muslim Ottoman Empire following a significant Muslim defeat. Prior to that time it appeared Islam would roll over Europe, an unstoppable force. In fact, to that point, the Ottoman Muslims had never negotiated peace before with "infidel" nations. In all such past negotiations the Ottomans had dictated the terms and the European nations had meekly submitted.

Since 1699, the Islamic East has suffered one defeat after another at the hands of the Christian West. Battlefield victories were definitive in nature, clearly exposing not only the military weakness of the defeated, but also weaknesses in political and economic systems. Wars were fought and won in the factories, shops, schools, and especially in the homes, as well as the halls of government. Victory often revealed which god *was* God, at least in the minds of the combatants. Islam has taken a beating; Islam's pride is badly wounded. The terrorist response, to some degree, is an effort by the desperate at pay-back.

Europeans emerged from the Dark Ages in a whirlwind of technology, with faster and bigger ships and more firepower than their puny Muslim counterparts. What Arab or Turkish *dhow* or galley could compete with a Portuguese Man of War under full sail, out-maneuvering and then broad-siding the pitiful Muslim craft with impunity?

Power is vastly more concentrated in the hands of America today, as graphically portrayed in the recent Iraqi war. Even with relatively modern Russian or Soviet fighter jets and tanks, Iraqi soldiers and airmen knew immediately that directly confronting the Americans was akin to challenging the Portuguese or the British on the open seas.

Suicide.

Americans are so much more technologically advanced on the battlefield because they are light-years beyond most of the rest of the world in access to, and dissemination of, *information*. Covert intelligence, melded with superior technology, is the difference, if a single non-human factor can be identified. Historical success on the battlefield, and on the high seas, brought entrepreneurial and mercantilist domination over nearly all commercial markets worldwide. Economic and technical mastery go hand in hand with military prowess. Over time an education from a Western university or college became a requirement for every Muslim leader's son, though a gnawing resentment, sometimes jealousy, was the mantel each shouldered. Rubbing their noses in it, even the Christian religionists joined in, missionaries from one Christian sect or another proselytizing to the "heathen" the word of Christ's eternal truth. And why not? Hadn't the Armies of Christ prevailed on the battlefield, in the laboratory, and in business? Doesn't Christian culture dominate the world today? What better testimony of the rightful superiority of systems? What greater witness can God offer a disbelieving world?

But Islam does not surrender so easily. Wasn't Islam once the world's most dynamic religion, Allah's armies essentially unstoppable? Muslims have long memories. What has caused this disaster, they ponder, gazing to heaven and calling out with plaintive voices? "Why has Allah forsaken us? What did we do to deserve this?"

Generally, the blame can be laid on the narrow shoulders of Muslim leaders down through the centuries. Today, most Middle Eastern governments are in fact hostile towards religion, killing, torturing, and imprisoning its practitioners. While in the case of terrorists this may be justified or excused, in most situations these dictators use attacks on religion to remove political opponents and to pacify or control the masses, excising and expunging their leaders and keeping a sharp eye on their activities.

King Fahd of Saudi Arabia recently passed away. He had struggled physically since his stroke in 1995. In 2002 he had taken his holiday in Spain. He brought along more than 350 servants, a motor pool of about 50 Mercedes sedans, a yacht, and reportedly had $2,000 in flowers delivered to his rooms each day. Back home, in the poor neighborhoods sprawled about the eastern provinces, and around Jeddah, and Riyadh, common Saudis continued to struggle with a failing economy and a lack of jobs. The contrast between these splendid palaces and mansions of more than *30,000* royal princes, and the millions of squalid Saudi poor, is awfully hard to explain. Westerners (Europeans and Americans) struggle with how to handle these corrupt leaders who squander national treasure like it was sand in the *Rub al-Khali*, while the poor all around them gaze back in hollow pain.

Such slums are the breeding grounds for some of the terrorists who attacked us on 9/11. September 11th was also a day of disaster for the Saudi royals. They are in deep trouble. Saudi Arabia's population has exploded about 300 percent since 1970. "The Land of God's Holy Sites and God's Bounteous Blessing (oil)" is a sinking ship. Some describe the Kingdom as entering its last days, much like the Soviet Union did in the late 1980s. A growing underclass is a swelling tidal wave threatening to swamp the government and drive out the royal family.

As well, the Saudi "middle class" is hurting with unemployment reportedly at around 25% nationwide. Many of those losing jobs are losing them to cheaper and better qualified expatriates, many from India, Europe, or the United States—all *non*-Islamic countries.

Radical *imams* (religious leaders) are calling for the expulsion of all non-Muslims. This only exacerbates the problem because the Saudis alone cannot run their country's sophisticated telecommunications, banking, medical systems, and most importantly, mammoth oil industry, including petrochemical manufacturing.

How have so many of these oil-rich, Gulf Arab countries so badly hamstrung themselves beyond their poor leadership? *Careerism.* These Gulf States, highly bureaucratic in their structure, have long established state-run "make-work" programs which guarantee a government job to any young Arab citizen who wants one. Though perhaps well meaning, such "jobs" usually do more harm than good for these young workers, effectively stifling the individual's job performance and productivity.

As well, these jobs have little or no accountability. Kuwaitis, for example, come to work when they want and often leave when they feel like it. If the Arabs ever want to compete in the world they've got to eliminate these do-nothing jobs and switch employment to the private sector where accountability and performance are valued. By eliminating government jobs and shifting to and building up the private sector, everyone will benefit, especially the young Arab employee who will actually be challenged for the first time in his or her life. At last he or she will step into the real world.

Beyond the artificial, make work world of the oil-rich Gulf Arab, the Saudi Arabians, in particular, are living with a dangerous monster in their own house: the *Wahhabis*. Today the Saudis are using pay-offs in an attempt to control the beast, these very radical supporters of a medieval form of Islam. Such ties dangerously compromise the Saudi Regime, spotlighting just how illegitimate these Royals are becoming in the world. Several of Saudi Arabia's better known Wahhabi leaders have issued *fatwas* (a religious directive, of sorts) calling for the killing of Americans, intellectuals, and anyone supporting the "enemy culture."

Add to this the fact that lower-class Saudis are being squeezed financially and politically and at the same time brainwashed that their problems are *not* the result of Saudi royal family mismanagement, but due to the "Satanic Americans." Wahhabi radicals and terrorists continue to be bought off by the Royals through "donations" which were, and still are, really Mafia-like protection payments designed to keep the The Family in power.

In a major way, al-Qaeda and Osama bin Laden are products of the Saudi/Wahhabi system. In fact, Prince Sultan openly admits giving huge donations to at least two Islamic charities which support and have links to Islamic terrorism. I once heard a diplomat rail in frustration against the backwardness and support for terror issuing from this region: "Why do we sit back and let our money pour into a Bermuda Triangle of poverty, corruption, hopeless bureaucracy, and radical fundamentalism? This is ridiculous! This is insane!"

So it is. But the United States is in a terrible quandary: how to help those truly in legitimate need, and yet eliminate those groups exporting terror as they use the innocent as camouflage and human shields?

The Muslim world has lost its way. A Grand Canyon of sorts divides those who govern from the governed. The elites in these countries are doing anything and everything they can to hold onto power, including bashing the United States on one hand, and allying themselves with America on the other. Hypocrisy reigns.

And acres and acres of *denial*. Arabs wallow in it, have for generations, hoping, watching, waiting for that great warrior-general, a modern-day *Saladin*, who will ride the black horse of victory. Victory at last! *Any kind of victory.* In 1973, when Egyptian President Anwar Sadat surprised the Israelis and stormed across the Suez Canal, driving the Israelis back for several days, the entire Arab world roared their approval. At last, an Arab who stood against the West! (In the minds of many Muslims, the Israelis are just an extension [Little Satan] of the Americans [Big Satan].) Arabs celebrated in every city, calling the Yom Kippur "victory" the Ramadan or October War, even naming streets in Arab capitals after it. Though the victory wasn't a victory at all, that didn't matter to Arabs. Egyptians today still view October 6, 1973 as a "great Arab triumph." Such is the desperate, beaten-down, shamed condition of the Arab world.

Middle East countries today are awash in young people, the median age in most of these nations is below 20 years. Soon there will be a *quarter of a billion* restless, even explosive, young souls between Baghdad and Casablanca all hungrily eyeing Europe northward. Such a precarious demographic situation will impact America as well. To ensure a secure and prosperous future for the United States, as well as Europe, we must move aggressively to solve these key issues. We have no choice. More so, we cannot rely on current Arab leadership to solve such monumental problems alone. That is why, among other reasons, they must go.

Of the ten countries that lead the world in weapons purchases, *seven* are Arab. Why? Primarily because most Arab leaders are hopelessly neurotic. In a word, they think they lack *power*, so they spend billions of dollars in the vain quest to acquire it. Most are but glorified tribal warlords on a grander scale. Real power and lasting security, however, are not found in weapons systems, but issue forth from skilled, merciful, honorable, and wise minds and hearts of *legitimately* chosen leaders, leaders who willingly accept power from those *free* men and women they lead. In essence, great leaders lead great people, they are a reflection of the millions standing beside them. They are first among equals.

As Edward Said, the great Arab educator stated so eloquently in the Egyptian newspaper *Al-Ahram Weekly*, "I often think that one reason for our powerlessness is that we feel self-hatred. Otherwise it is impossible to explain how more than 200 million people with human and natural resources of a high order can continuously (wound) themselves, continuously shunning the kind of power that truly brings self-respect and seriousness of purpose. Our situation cannot be...explained away by appeals to the ravages of imperialism...or to any of the other litanies of self-exculpation. The problem is Arab powerlessness."[26]

Since World War II, millions of people have been killed in wars from Central Asia across the North African plain to Morocco. Think of the resources wasted on these wars of petty, corrupt men, the profits from the sale of *one in three* barrels of oil during this time spent on weapons of war. Envision the waste, more so the human tragedy. This fact alone should condemn every Mideast leader to the trash heap of history.

The end of the Cold War seems to have unleashed a whole

new generation of despots—the so-called Terror-mongers—into a besieged, war-weary Mideast. No other region on earth abhors a power vacuum like the Middle East. And into the void have rushed al-Qaeda, the Taliban, Hezbollah, Hamas, Islamic Jihad, on and on, more bloody "parties of death" than the proverbial "99 Names of Allah." What is important is that truly times have changed. The future is now the Middle East's, if its people can catch the vision and set aside a millennium of prejudice, greed, and hatred.

The Cold War's end has removed one huge source of past conflict in the region, the struggle between the allies of the United States and those, mostly Arab nations, who were mercenary-allies of the old Soviet Union.

With the coalition victory in Iraq, the region has been yanked (kicking and screaming) further down the path of progress. Past "realities" continue to change. Opportunities abound, incentives for prosperity are everywhere. The harsh demographic burdens of joblessness and despair for the young have, in one swift victory, opened a vast horizon of potential. Tens of billions of dollars will be spent in Iraq and the region over the next decade, providing millions of new jobs for the skilled and educated. The basic service and construction industries are ballooning, all effectively funded by millions of barrels of cheap, plentiful Iraqi and Gulf crude oil and gas.

There is no excuse for failure here. Otherwise, over the next decade millions of Arab refugees will swarm into Europe, taxing welfare programs and stealing jobs. Secretly, every European leader wants America to succeed in Iraq, though most would never admit it. Failure, for Europe, is a demographic disaster of historic proportions that could very well drag the European Union down a hole of no escape. A *quarter of a billion* Arabs staring hungrily at the ripe European plum to the north is enough to make every European (who's aware) sweat. To ensure Europe's economic stability and security, and by extension America's, Middle East nations need to get their act together. Now is the time.

At the end of World War I, Turkish president Kemal Ataturk saw the future and proclaimed: "Our task now is to catch up with

The Middle East Explained

the modern world." The struggle, at its core, is one of education, compounded by the proud, yet damning cultural "traditions of the fathers" that threaten to turn back the clock. Too many remain clutching the delusive phantom of hope, eyes shut and ears afraid to hear, hoping that somehow Allah, and the oil billions, will provide. They won't. *Kilmat ya'rayt, Ma'amaraat bayt!* (Hopeful words or wishes won't build a house.)

Yet opportunities abound. How about a water pipeline from Turkey to Syria, Israel, Palestine, and Jordan? Another water pipeline from Iraq to waterless Kuwait and Saudi Arabia? A power-generating canal between the Red Sea and the much lower Dead Sea? Or, a superhighway between Morocco and Iraq, across North Africa? A free trade zone between the United States, Iraq, Jordan, Palestine, Israel, Turkey, and Egypt, as President Bush has envisioned? Such development projects would employ tens of thousands of workers across the region. Such development would attract countless new industries from many nations. With stability and security, the goldmine of archeological-religious-leisure-adventure tourism would return, and world-class beaches, many rarely visited now, would open a vista of profit and growth. Tourists would return with a vengeance, bringing billions in hard currency to capital-starved economies.

As early as 1990, the Israeli Foreign Minister, Shimon Peres, proposed a Middle East common market or free trade zone. He even stated that "we have two choices here: "Benelux or Yugoslavia," referring to the post-World War II economic alliance of Belgium, the Netherlands, and Luxemburg, which brought much needed prosperity. Yugoslavia, on the other hand, further fragmented and deteriorated in the 1990s into war and ethnic cleansing, requiring U.S. and European intervene to stop the meltdown.

Peres also spoke of ringing the Dead Sea, on both Jordanian and Israeli banks, with resort hotels having close access to both Petra and Massada. To build up a blighted Gaza Strip, he proposed a seaport on the Mediterranean. Neither Israel nor Jordan, or any type of Palestinian entity in between can be economically viable standing alone. Some type of alliance is the only solution. Additionally, Peres foresaw that fighting over border security was the wrong approach.

"The Middle East needs *borderless* economic integration, not fences, missiles, and mistrust," he said. Red Sea waters could be desalinated and used to irrigate the land south of the Dead Sea, both in Israel and in Jordan, opening the land for settlement. There is really no limit to the possibilities. Our greatest enemy is our historical lack of vision, and the ability to present that vision, to articulate it, to the peoples of the region and the world.

It is not possible to have democracy without modernity and education. An ignorant, uncivilized, backward populace cannot govern itself. Yet, how can a people learn the skills of democracy, of self-government, if they remain sheep to worthless tyrants and technocrats? Islam, in fact, *demands* equality of governance. Leaders of the loftiest order must ultimately be subject to the same laws and standards as the humblest of citizens, man or woman. It is there as plain as day, in the Qur'ran, and in the *Hadith*, the sacred teachings of the Prophet Muhammad. Ironically, in their Islamic purity, such teachings of equality and fairness have been embraced by *America* to a much higher degree than any Muslim nation on earth. Why are Muslims the world-over not acknowledging this cold, hard fact? Why is Muslim denial so endemic and Muslim leadership so self-serving and oppressive?

Who's to blame for pathetic Muslim leadership today? The question answers itself way too easily.

Follow-up: How do Arab intellectuals approach a *solution* to national problems?

The "land of the scheme and the home of the brazen," whether in Cairo, Damascus, or Baghdad, has always struggled with *solutions*. Oddly, most seem to be fleeing from solutions as fast as they can. Middle Eastern intellectuals, however, should certainly have some loftier insights on potential solutions. Let's look at Arab society through their own eager eyes for a moment.

In Arabic, the word *hal* means "solution." Hal can also mean to take someone's position away from him; to break up an organization; to bring punishment upon someone; to regard someone as "fair game," as "easy prey"; to "seize unlawfully," to "misappropriate," or "usurp." Hal can also mean to solve a problem by force. Actually, according to the Hans Wehr Dictionary[27], "hal" has more than *one hundred* meanings or variant usages, testifying to the uncommon richness—and convenience—of the Arabic language. One can spin *hal* or solution to mean just about anything. In the Middle East, in practice, the word has been so watered down as to mean a dissolving or a *non*-solving of any given problem. Rest assured that the dictator's "solution," or the religious fanatic's *hal*, will be predatory and expedient every time.

That said, let us attempt to reach the final, only truly workable, *hal*.

The Hashemite Kingdom of Jordan is a country with few natural resources, no oil or gas, yet with a hungry, restless, very young population. Nearly every other nation in the Middle East has more wealth and resources than Jordan. Yet, the country hangs together; the people struggle, but they get by. Jordanians maximize their resources, use their heads, and to their credit they live in one of the freest and most progressive countries in the region. The reason is leadership.

From the long and effective kingship of the beloved and wise King Hussein, to the current reign of his son, King Abdullah, Jordan has made some sound political and economic decisions. The wise, open, and progressive rule of a benign, talented, educated dictator, is nearly always more efficient and prosperous than a pure democracy, which is sometimes simply "mob-rule." Of course, even great kings die, and their sons are too often rarely worth shooting. In the case of Jordan, however, perhaps the son is cut from the same cloth as the father.

Good, honest leadership is the most elusive of mankind's quests, more often than not ending in failure. So, as we struggle with the quality of Middle Eastern leadership today, where can we turn? How about academia?

Again, we come up dry as most Middle Eastern scholarship has been tainted with the same cultural baggage that has infected the ruling classes for centuries. I believe this is a cultural phenomenon, born of millennium of bureaucratic barrier-building. In essence, a survival mechanism, called "careerism" above. We see this anciently, in the halls of the Ottoman Turkish palaces, in the courts of the

Persian kings, among the Fatamids of Egypt and the Abbassids of early Muslim Iraq. An inbred, bureaucratic system of power-hording, held together by the structural congestion of Arab leadership. The more confusing the system, the more necessary the bureaucrat's job became to the king and his court. Today this is known as "job security," and can be found in America among tax accountants and lawyers, and especially within the IRS.

The best first-hand example I can offer are excerpts from a report I commissioned from a government official and academic from a Persian Gulf country that shall go unnamed. Actually, this official was an import from Egypt, brought to this particular oil emirate to handle official documentation and to interact with other foreign embassies. As you read, note how masterful he is at saying absolutely nothing for which he could be criticized, yet at the same time demonstrating his "lofty" and broad-based liberal education, which is prized by the elite regimes of the region:

"Besides the role that religion plays in legitimizing the status quo in society, in general religion plays a distinct role in backing class differences in society through rationalizing wealth and poverty since, religiously speaking, wealth is a natural phenomenon governed by divine will.

"Analyzing the relationship between the existing classes in society and their religious belief occupied an important part of the writings of Marx, Engels, Veber, Spencer, Freud, Durkheim and others, who were interested in the sociology of religion.

"Thorough analysis of the existing relationship between the situation of the classes in society and religious belief indicates that most, if not all, religious ideologies, as systems of ideas, permit and legitimizes the status quo and the interests of the different classes in society and thus helps in preserving the status quo of class differences that exist.

"In his book "Reviving Religious Sciences," Al-Imam al-Ghazali, who was contemporary with the establishment of the religious institution, we find many remarks which glorify poverty and consider it a virtue, and that justify the ruling class, among the sayings of the Prophet Muhammad, such as:

"'The poor of my nation enter Heaven before the wealthy by 500

years.'"

"'God's beloved is a poor person satisfied with his provisions.'"

"'Hunger is in God's care, only granted to those that he loves.'"

"'If you see poverty approaching welcome it, the symbol of the righteous.'"

"Such sayings create a belief among the poor that poverty is a natural phenomenon, an accepted matter and even a virtue of the believer. This belief is openly demonstrated on the behavior of the poor and their attitudes, which make them harmonious with the status quo no matter how prejudicial it is and they become so patient in facing difficulties...."

You see what I mean. Not only are most Arab regimes receiving confusing information like this every day, designed to provide job security for the advisor, the interpretation of religion is *always* skewed by the bureaucrat to protect and preserve the status quo. The Middle East is bureaucracy run amuck, pure and simple, and it's had a thousand years and more to do so! (Is this what *we* have to look forward to in America?)

One thing is certain, lacking a radical change of thinking, and more so, *action* rather than endless discussion, Arab nations are destined for decaying mediocrity, at best. At worst...? The bureaucratic mentality is literally killing them.

I'm sorry, but just one more tiny example from the same academic, finally ending the report referenced above:

"Thus, this study is based on the assumption that the relationship between religion and social change in Arab-Islamic societies is unique, complex, and multi-dimensional, and thus, analyzing this relation requires a full consideration due to the nature of this relationship and the diversity of its dimensions."

Hopeless. His words betray a man totally caught up in the show, the pomp and ceremony of an in-bred system, feeding on itself and slowly going mad. His only hope is to not only escape the box, but to smash it to pieces.

Follow-up: *Denial* is a major obstacle to peace, prosperity and freedom. So why are Arabs and Muslims so steeped in it?

I've watched my Arab and Muslim friends squirm with endless frustration, a frustration that is as much a part of Arab culture as the wind, rocks, and endless dust Arabs like to call "sand." Saddam's defeat at the hands of the Americans was a tough pill to swallow. Denial is easier.

The problem is that eventually denial catches up to you. Since the 1967 Six Days War with Israel, Arabs have felt a festering, bloating humiliation, born of snatching defeat from the jaws of victory, time and time again. Arabs never seem to miss and opportunity to miss an opportunity. They have expended considerable effort in sweeping national and cultural problems and structural weaknesses under the rug rather than actually *doing* what is necessary to correct the problem.

Virtually every Arab media outlet the world over has fallen into this trap, *especially* since America's sweeping victory in Iraq. They have resurrected every conceivable conspiracy theory and scrofulous act of American treachery and deceit. Excuses spread like cancer, while few Arab voices are willing to offer a truly accurate or worthwhile assessment of their true predicament. Denial is easier.

But denial gets people killed, or at best, guarantees failure. What was defeated in Baghdad was not simply a brutish regime, but an entire archaic system built around a Byzantine-like tyrant who fashioned his kingdom on the sands of illusion. Surrounded by "yes-men," Saddam was never told what he needed to hear in a way he could comprehend, for littering his many palaces were the bones of men foolish enough to bring the Maximum Leader the bad news. The same pattern is repeated in Syria, Iran, Egypt, the Sudan, in Yemen, take your pick. The Arab/Iranian challenge is *not* resources, native intellect, armies or weaponry, and certainly not the great religion of Islam. The problem is denial, the unwillingness to face reality, and the resistance to change.

Unfortunately this condition also blows back in the face of the innocent. It is the heart of the terrorist crisis. Terrorism is always conceived in the diseased bed of denial. Fundamentalist religion, in general, is pure, high-octane denial, packaged seductively in the wrappings of Allah and piety, tribalism and nationalism. "If the battle is for God, how can we lose?" "Myself and God: a majority of one!" These age-old mantras press young minds into the service of death, destruction, and continued failure.

If, by some miracle, Muslim fighters are one day able to prevail against the overwhelming might of the United States, *AKA* the "Great Satan," what would Islam offer the world in its place? The Islamic Republic of Iran? The Taliban? Islam, Sudanese-style? The brand of radical Islam conceived by the always creative Lebanese is called affectionately "Hezbollah." Is this what we want? Or perhaps al-Qaeda, led by the "honorable" Osama bin Laden or Dr. Ayman Zawahiri of Egyptian Islamic Jihad infamy. Remember The Jihad? The same gang of cutthroats who machine-gunned President Anwar Sadat in 1981 while he was trying to bring peace between Egypt and Israel?

Okay, my Muslim friends, here's your chance, what would *you* offer the world? Can you provide modern medicines of many varieties, and of the finest quality? Can you offer *billions* in aid to the world, in hard currency (like the U.S. dollar) which is accepted everywhere? Can you offer computerized banking services and sophisticated commercial networks that have raised the world's standard of living, freedom, and opportunity to the highest levels in history? Can you operate modern universities, public schools for *millions* of young students, local governments that are generally free of corruption and nepotism, freedom of religion for *all* peoples, and government of the people, by the people, and for the people?

Or will your offering in the end mirror the criminal Ba'ath Regime of Saddam Hussein, with mandatory Islamic religious indoctrination thrown in as a "blessed bonus?" Denial is a form of mental illness. In spite of what you may believe, my Muslim and Arab friends, most Americans would choose death before accepting such modern Islamic realities as I have described here.

The future is known *only* to God, not to Imam bin Laden, or the Ayatollah Khamenei, or to any other man. Islam may indeed triumph in the end, if God or Allah wills it, but *not* by the sword, not by the bluster of foolish, dictatorial men who talk bravely and then cower in caves and dank tunnels.

One day America may fall and an Islamic Empire may rise, but it will not be in your lifetime or mine. In the meantime, America's invincible military, lead by their Commander-In-Chief, will do whatever it takes to prevail against those bent on terror, whether Bush, Son of Bush, or any other future president, Democrat or Republican, man or woman.

Reality is the opposite of denial. Reality is truth.
Allahu Akbar.[28]

QUESTION 4

- HOW AND WHEN DID THIS CHALLENGE FROM RADICAL ISLAM BEGIN? WHAT ARE ITS ROOTS, ITS CAUSES?

CATALYST

Key events are always launched by a catalyst, whether recognized or not at the time. More often than not, such catalysts lead to major historical change. The history of the Middle East, both ancient and modern, is the history of catalyst-driven change.

In general terms, from approximately 2000 B.C.E. to about C.E. 300, the Arabian Peninsula experienced some periods when rainfall increased, providing this hopelessly desiccated land with periods of relative prosperity. One area was the *Hejaz*, or the mountain barrier running southeast down the western side of the Arabian peninsula. Following this narrow mountain barrier was the so-called Spice Trail where caravans transported commodities, mostly frankincense, from the southern hills of Arabia—modern-day Yemen and Oman—north to the prosperous markets of Egypt, Babylon, Persia, and Constantinople.

Business was good during this period, with grass more available during wetter seasons, sometimes prospering the nomads and village dwellers of the region. Trade was always lively, though risky. Arabian nomadic and town-dwelling tribes and merchant families expanded in number. Mecca, the Arab pilgrimage center, which was pagan at this time, also prospered, especially towards the end of this period.

Then came drought. Beginning in about the fourth century C.E., Arabia entered a period of drought which continued to worsen year by year. By the sixth century, when a boy named Muhammad was born, not only had the drought deepened, but the Arabian tribes had expanded their culture of raiding one another. Plunder, in women and other booty, had become an institution. With drought a catalyst, the raiders moved aggressively further and further from home, but still mostly within the confines of the Arabian Peninsula. Life and survival revolved around a culture of raiding and plunder. The relative prosperity of earlier times was being threatened, not only by the stubborn drought, but by the continued warring between tribes and the blood oaths of vengeance—blood feuds—which multiplied with each attack.

Into this uncertain world came Muhammad, who was destined to become the prophet of a new faith, Islam, and who also became a master of caravans and a successful trader. Certainly Muhammad could see the threat posed by the continual inter-tribal raiding and warfare. And he determined to do something about it.

When he was called as a prophet, by Allah (God) as Muslims believe, his first order of business was to consolidate power over the Arabian tribes and limit their self-destructive behavior of raiding one another. This was done initially in the nearby city of Medina (called *Yathrib*, at the time). Then he moved with his forces to subdue Mecca, the center of Arab pilgrimage and a wealthy trading center. Once fully in control of the Spice Trail (the Hejaz), his armies then proceeded to subdue much of the rest of Arabia, forbidding inter-tribal raiding, pillage and plunder amongst Arabs, who were now called *Muslims*, those who "submit to the will of Allah, and his Prophet."

One major problem: to the elders of these various tribes, *raiding* and *plunder* was their way of life, their reason for living, their lifeblood. However, since Muhammad now forbade it, he had to make some concessions to placate his tribesmen. So in a revelation from Allah, Muhammad divided the world into essentially two realms: *Dar al-Islam*, or the House of Islam (Submission to God), and *Dar al-Harb*, the House of War (lands not yet subjected to Allah's will).

The Arabian Peninsula, under Islam's banner, was Dar al-Islam. And since Muslims were now forbidden to plunder each other, Islamic armies had to look elsewhere. Muhammad showed them where: To the north, to the rich civilizations of the Christians and the Persians: of Palestine, Mesopotamia, Constantinople, but most importantly, Christian Egypt. Muhammad even stated, as attested by one of his wives, *Maria* (who was a Christian from Egypt), that the wealth of Egypt was not just the land and cities, but the *people*. As Muhammad told his fighters, in essence, "Do not kill the *Copts* (Christians) of Egypt, for they must live to serve you, to do your work for you, to help manage Islamic holdings." This was the genius of Muhammad's leadership, so different from the inept and unnecessarily brutal methods of other conquerors of the age, particularly the heavy-handed methods of their Christian and Persian enemies.

Now Muhammad had an acceptable outlet for the native aggression of his Arab armies, these plunder-loving, pillaging and raiding tribesmen. And as he unleashed them upon the Christians and the Persians to the north, Islamic coffers were filled to overflowing from the world's richest regions. *Fight against the (Christians and Jews) until they submit to Islamic leadership and willingly pay jizya, the Dhimmi (Christian and Jew) Tax, until they are humiliated and brought down,* is the essential meaning, in Arabic, of the Qur'anic verse Sura 9:29. Perhaps more important, however, this military expansion carried the religion of Allah into far-flung lands, amid a variety of cultures and traditions.

As history records, this expansion brought unimaginable wealth to the Muslims. Soon, however, Muhammad was dead and his successors, called *Caliph* in Arabic, pushed into Asia and Europe. In one account, the Caliph Umar, a simple man of the desert and a successor to Muhammad, heard from his governor of Bahrain that captured plunder from the north was being shipped to Medina (where the Caliphate headquartered). The amount, the governor said, was 500,000 silver dirhams. The Caliph questioned his governor if that much money even existed in all the world, and cautioned him "to sleep on it" and then report again the next day. After hearing the identical report the second time, Umar announced to his congregation these words: "We have received such an abundance of money that we are not sure how to handle it. If it is your wish we shall count for each person his share; otherwise we shall weigh it."[29] (Presumably catalog it and store it away.)

In conclusion, can we say that the Islamic expansion out of drought-ridden Arabia was, at least in part, to meet the increasingly inbred and stifling economic conditions of this desiccated land? Was the expansion a safety valve designed to let off a growing pressure from the tribes to survive? It appears so, though purists will argue that such was "God's will" regardless of climatic or demographic factors or conditions.

Still, the Islamic expansion came with a vengeance, a seemingly unstoppable force carrying Allah's religion into the heart of Christian Europe and "heathen Asia." The Islamic expansion of the seventh century was caused by a variety of factors all coming together at the right time, with this potent new religion driving the "Mujahadin," the Warriors of the Faith, forward into far-flung, distant lands. Within not much more than a century, the religion of Allah had spread from Spain on the west to India on the east and into the islands of Southeast Asia. Islam's growth would continue for centuries. Truly Europe came within a heartbeat of being completely swept up by the Islamic Banner. A key battle here, a naval victory there, the heroic leadership of men like Charles Martel and a relative handful of others. Most people are wholly unaware of the miracle that the Christian world even exists today, that Christian Europe was not in fact conquered, purged, and absorbed by the Islamic juggernaut of centuries past.

TODAY'S NEW CATALYST

When someone asks me when the war on radical Islamic terror began, I always say "in the *seventh century*." Our war with terrorism has been going on for a very long time, most of us just unfamiliar with its history. We, the Christian West, have always been fighting this war, though there have been periods of calm, usually following significant Islamic defeats. Yet, the struggle continues. The "Religion of the Last, True Prophet" is not going away anytime soon.

True, President Bush and other American leaders go out of their way to play down the fact, even deny, that this is a war of civilizations, even a religious war. But for the facts I always look to history and history tells me otherwise. In this case, ignorance is not bliss, it is lethal.

Recent events (again, history) bear this out. I make it a point to listen to people. I look at what modern Islamic leaders, like Osama bin Laden, or Iran's Ayatollah Ali Khamenai, or Ali Akbar Rafsanjani, or the Muslim Brotherhood's Hassan al-Banna, or Sayyid Qutb, and many other Islamic leaders have said, and are saying, in their speeches, in their writings, in their actions. And frankly, it scares me.

For they are talking about killing and subduing Americans, Israelis, Jews, by the millions, and in wholly and completely defeating them in the world. Beyond that, they talk of spreading the banner of Islam until it encompasses the whole earth. Even then they are far from finished. They talk of plundering countries like the United States, as Muhammad's Army of old did to the Christian Middle East, of "returning the wealth of the Americans" to the "Followers of the Prophet." In other words, accomplishing what Allah has intended from the beginning. In their minds Islamic Armies of the past failed in this Godly quest basically for one reason: "They were not sufficiently worthy." Today, according to Osama bin Laden, the Mujahadin are now sufficiently acceptable to Allah. Bring on the American plunder.

This is no idle threat. We should look no further than 9/11 for proof. For in today's world *one man*, possessing modern weaponry and technology, commands the power of great armies of the past; the "technology of the Christians to be turned back upon their own diseased heads." Listen to what the terrorists are saying! In the past it would have been impossible for a few fanatics to accomplish the goal of bringing down a great nation. Today, in our modern world, it is not only possible, but as technologies improve and spread, more and more likely. The fanatics and revolutionaries know what needs to be done.

So with climate, and other factors, contributing to Islam's expansion in the seventh century, today the catalyst driving this "clash of cultures" between the Christian West and the Islamic East is *Technology*. Modern technology is the catalyst: information technology, medical technology, weapons technology, all of it combining to stir up the Islamic hornet's nest, to empower the radicals and give them the means to attack and destroy.

This most recent clash in the war has been going on at least since the Iranian revolution of 1979 when the Ayatollahs ousted America's ally the Shah of Iran, replacing this major Middle Eastern nation with an Islamic "republic" (more accurately a highly repressive dictatorship. Iran is not, and never has been, a republic.).

Over recent decades modern medical and technological advances in the Christian West have been provided low-cost to Islamic nations, the gift of life and posterity. Coupled with the power of demographics, this new catalyst is overwhelming in its potential. It will likely, if trends continue, overwhelm Europe in the coming decades, as millions of Muslims finally accomplish their age-old goal of sweeping Christian Europe.

For centuries Islamic nations, while always having a high birthrate, would lose many or most of those children the first year after birth. So while Islamic, principally Arab, women were part of a culture which celebrated fertility, high infant mortality rates, and mortality rates in general, kept the populations in check.

Not anymore. Today, with advances in modern medicine, it is not unusual to see Middle Eastern families with six, eight, ten, even twelve children (sometimes with two or more wives, a polygamous relationship, allowed in Islam). The populations in most Islamic countries, and certainly in Middle Eastern nations, are exploding, the numbers soaring beyond projections. The median age, for example, is between the ages of 15 and 20, with approximately 75 to 80 percent of the population *under the age of 30.*

It is impossible to contain this demographic explosion within the boundaries of the Middle East and South Asia. Arab and other Islamic populations, which have flooded Europe over the past two decades, are effectively the only groups in Europe having children. Europe is on track to becoming "Islamic" in many key cities and regions within the next twenty or thirty years. Beyond what the United States is facing as our Hispanic population swells, Europe is struggling with the same type of demographic challenge, only much worse. While American Hispanics are also Christian, the dominant religion in the U.S., "Christian" Europe is struggling to assimilate these Islamic immigrant hordes who are strongly opposed to adapting traditional European civilization. Obviously the cultural discrepancy, the fundamental dissimilarities, all of it, for Europe is threatening, and in ways not yet generally recognized.

With *hundreds of millions* of young, mostly unemployed or under-employed Muslims in Middle East nations, these youth are growing dissatisfied, even desperate. Many of the most economically hopeless have turned to the Islamic radicals for "the solution." In fact, in the many mosques, the fanatics are proclaiming: *"Islam al-Hal!"* meaning Islam *is* the solution, in Arabic. And many are buying it, some even willing to "martyr" themselves for the cause, if they can take enough of the infidels with them.

The Islamic catalyst today is technology, in multiple ways. As Arabs and Muslims, for example, see modern images of Britney Spears and Madonna kissing on TV, or Janet Jackson baring her breast, the Islamic radicals use these images of an "immoral, corrupt America" as propaganda, tools of fear to recruit more martyrs, to call the faithful to Jihad! In the mosques they stand up and shout at such images from America: "Is this what you want, Men of Islam? Is this what you want your wives and daughters to become?" They wail their lament, broadcasting from the many new media outlets, and then teach in the *Madressas* (Islamic schools), which are indoctrination and recruitment centers for the fanatics, calling for death and destruction, for murder of the "Satanic Americans."

The catalyst of technology, of *the image* worldwide, the rapid dissemination of information technologies, coupled with exploding Islamic populations, hundreds of millions of desperate, hungry young people. Modern technology, including devastating weapons, empowers the fundamentalists, and in Islam there are many millions of these. This new catalyst of an Islamic population explosion, is impacting not only Middle Eastern countries, but countries in Southwest Asia, even in other parts of Asia, but especially in Europe. Add to this the radical access to technology of modern weapons of mass destruction (WMD) and the Christian West and the Islamic East are on a collision course.

For answers to just about anything, look to history first.

Recent events tell us this is a war. Some Americans agree; too many still can't (or won't) see it. From the first Trade Towers attack in 1993, soon the Kobar Towers in Saudi Arabia were blown up, killing nearly twenty American airmen and wounding scores more. Other attacks in the Kingdom followed, targeting Americans. Soon our embassies in Africa, in Nairobi and Dar es-Salaam, were demolished by huge blasts, killing hundreds. Then the USS Cole was nearly blown out of Red Sea waters, killing many U.S. sailors. Then, of course, came September 11th. How in the world are so many of us still blind to the fact that we are at war?

Since September 11, 2001, the toll continues to rise. Twenty dead in Jerba, Tunisia on April 11, 2002; more than 30 dead in Pakistan in the Spring of 2002; more than 200 dead at Bali, Indonesia on October 12, 2002; 45 killed in Morocco on May 16, 2003; more than 50 murdered in Riyadh, Saudi Arabia on May 12th, and then again on November 8, 2003; 63 were killed in November, 2003 in Turkey; then in Russia, in the Dubrovka theater 175 dead and in a Moscow subway 39 murdered on February 6, 2004. Without rest, the Islamic terror attacks continue in earnest: 190 killed in Madrid, Spain train bombings of March 11, 2004. Of course, during this period many thousands were murdered or wounded by terrorists in Israel and in Iraq. Finally, the horrible murder of about 400 in the Christian enclave of North Ossetia by radical Muslims—156 of the dead children—in an attack upon a helpless and unprotected elementary school. Also the punishing attacks on London. The barbarity is almost beyond belief.

Are the terrorists winning? From recent events one might think so. More than anything else, however, these evidences, these graphic examples, demonstrate just how challenging the war on terror is and how difficult it will be to ultimately prevail. In the end, however, the civilized world cannot allow the terror-mongers even a hint of victory or success. In the end if we acquiesce and capitulate, no one anywhere will be safe and those who have died will have died in vain. Terrorism is the heart and cankered soul of tyranny, and usually the last gasp of the desperate.

QUESTION 5

- WHAT SPECIFIC THREATS ARE THE MUSLIM FANATICS MAKING AGAINST AMERICA? WHY ISN'T THE MEDIA ACCURATELY REPORTING THESE THREATS?

To better understand the Islamic radical, his goals and objectives, let us look at precisely what he is saying:

ON OCTOBER 6, 2002, AL-JAZEERA BROADCASTED A SPECIAL MESSAGE FROM <u>OSAMA BIN LADEN</u> TO THE AMERICAN PEOPLE:

In the name of God, the merciful, the compassionate, a message to the American people:

Peace be upon those who follow the right path. I am an honest adviser to you. I urge you to seek the joy of life and the afterlife and to rid yourself of your dry, miserable and spiritless materialistic life... I also call on you to understand the lesson of the New York and Washington raids, which came in response to some of your previous crimes. The aggressor deserves punishment. However, those who follow the movement of the criminal gang at the White House, the agents of the Jews, who are preparing to attack and partition the Islamic world, without you disapproving of this, realize that you have not understood anything from the message of the two raids.

Therefore, I am telling you, and God is my witness, whether America escalates or de-escalates this conflict, we will reply to it in kind, God willing. God is my witness, the youth of Islam are preparing things that will fill your hearts with fear. They will target key sectors of your economy until you stop your injustice and aggression or until the more short-lived of us die (until either you or I are dead).

We beseech Almighty God to provide us with His support. He is the protector and has the power to do so. Say: O people of the Book! (Christians and Jews) Come to common terms as between us and you: <u>That we worship none but Allah; that we associate no partners with Him (in other words, reject Jesus Christ, God's Son); that we erect not from among ourselves lords and patrons other than Allah</u>. If then they turn back (if America repents of its ways), say ye: Bear witness that we at least are Muslims bowing to Allah's will (Koranic verse).

(COMMENT: Among other things here, Osama bin Laden is attacking Christians, particularly in the above passage "that we associate no partners with Him [Allah]," a common Muslim statement challenging the Christian belief in Jesus, the *Son* of God, as well as the Holy Spirit, and "erect not from among ourselves lords and patrons" meaning the following of any formal religious priesthood, clergy, or hierarchy.)

OSAMA BIN LADEN ON THE UNITED STATES OF AMERICA (issued prior to September 11th):

We say that the end of the United States is imminent...for the awakening of the Muslim umma [nation] has occurred.

The aggressor (the US) deserves punishment.

Do your governments not know that the White House gangsters are the biggest butchers of this age?

I tell the American people: God willing, we will continue to fight you. We will continue the martyrdom operations inside and outside the United States until you end your injustice, abandon your stupidity, and curb your insolent fellows.

Whether they try or not, we have seen in the last decade the decline of the American government and the weakness of the American soldier. We predict a black day for America.

(COMMENT: The above passage is a forewarning, a deadly threat, which we failed to heed prior to September 11th 2001. Anyone foolishly thinking we are "encouraging Islamic terrorist attacks" because of our wars in Afghanistan and Iraq, in reality this bloody war began *long* before we entered Baghdad and Kabul. Our early departure, our retreat, cannot lessen Islamic terrorism directed at Americans and American cities. It will only encourage it.)

BIN LADEN ON THE SEPTEMBER 11 ATTACKS:

Polls showed that the vast majority of the sons of the Islamic world were happy about these strikes....

When you talk about the New York and Washington raids, you talk about those men who changed the course of history and cleansed the chapters of the nation from the filth of the treasonous rulers.

The confusion caused to the enemy was sufficient to make people wake up from their slumber and rise for jihad for the sake of God. I had the honor of knowing these men. One is honored by knowing such men.

I urge you to seek the joy of life and the afterlife and to rid yourself of your dry, miserable and spiritless materialistic life. I urge you to become Muslims.

When you talk about the (9/11 hijackers') invasion of New York and Washington, you talk about the men who changed the face of history and went against the traitors.

ON THE UNITED NATION'S ORGANIZATION:

Under no circumstances should any Muslim or sane person resort to the United Nations. The United Nations is nothing but a tool of crime. We are being massacred everyday, while the United Nations continues to sit idly by.

TO THE EUROPEAN UNION (trying to prevent Europe's support for America's war against terror):

I...offer a reconciliation initiative to them (Europeans), the essence of which is our commitment to stopping operations against every country that commits itself to not attacking Muslims or interfering in their affairs - including the U.S. conspiracy on the greater Muslim world... The peace will start with the departure of its (Europe's) last soldier from our country. The door of reconciliation is open for three months of the date of announcing this statement.

ON THE MADRID BOMBINGS:

The greatest rule of safety is justice, and stopping injustice and aggression. It was said: Oppression kills the oppressors and the hotbed of injustice is evil. The situation in occupied Palestine is an example. What happened on 11 September (2001) and 11 March (the Madrid train bombings) are your goods returned to you.

ON THE BALI BOMBING:

What do your governments want from their alliance with America in attacking us in Afghanistan? I mention in particular Britain, France, Italy, Canada, Germany and Australia.

We warned Australia before not to join in (the war) in Afghanistan, and (against) its despicable effort to separate East Timor. It ignored the warning until it woke up to the sounds of explosions in Bali.

BIN LADEN ON AMERICA'S "HATRED" OF ISLAM:

It is a question of faith (a religious war), not a war against terrorism, as Bush and (British Prime Minister) Blair try to depict it.

It has become clear that the West in general and America in particular have an unspeakable hatred for Islam.

Peace be upon those who follow the right path. I am an honest adviser to you. I urge you to seek the joy of life and the afterlife and to rid yourself of your dry, miserable and spiritless materialistic life. I urge you to become Muslims.

ON FEBRUARY 23, 1998, OSAMA BIN LADEN OF AL-QAEDA, DR. AYMAN AL-ZAWAHIRI OF EGYPTIAN ISLAMIC JIHAD, AND OTHER RADICAL ISLAMIC LEADERS FROM SEVERAL NATIONS JOINED FORCES TO ISSUE A *FATWA* TO 'KILL AMERICANS, BOTH MILITARY AND CIVILIAN.' CONTENTS OF THAT FATWA FOLLOW (Interestingly the *fatwa* was issued in London. Note: a FATWA is interpreted as an Islamic judgment, opinion, or directive):

The ruling to kill the Americans and their allies, civilians and military, is an individual duty on every Muslim who can do so in any country in which it is possible to do it, in order to liberate the al-Aqsa Mosque (Jerusalem) and the holy mosque (Mecca) from their grip, and in order that their armies move out of all the land of Islam defeated and unable to threaten any Muslim in compliance with the words of Almighty God: "Fight the pagans all together as they fight you all together."

Praise be to God, who revealed the Book, controls the clouds, defeats factionalism, and says in His Book "But when the forbidden months are past, then fight and slay the pagans wherever ye find them, seize them, beleaguer them, and lie in wait for them in every stratagem (of war);

And peace be upon our Prophet, Muhammad Bin-'Abdallah, who said I have been sent with the sword between my hands to ensure that no one but God (Allah) is worshipped, (Allah) who put my livelihood under the shadow of my spear and who inflicts humiliation and scorn on those who disobey my orders. The Arabian Peninsula has never—since God made it flat, created its desert, and encircled it with seas—been stormed by any forces like the crusader armies (America) spreading in it like locusts, eating its riches and wiping out its plantations. All this is happening at a time in which nations are attacking Muslims like people fighting over a plate of food. In the light of the grave situation and the lack of support, we and you are obliged to discuss current events, and we should all agree on how to settle the matter.

No one argues today about three facts that are known to everyone; we will list them, in order to remind everyone:

First, for over seven years the United States has been occupying the lands of Islam in the holiest of places, the Arabian Peninsula, plundering its riches, dictating to its rulers, humiliating its people, terrorizing its neighbors, and turning its bases in the Peninsula into a spearhead through which to fight the neighboring Muslim peoples. The best proof of this is the Americans' continuing aggression against the Iraqi people using the Peninsula as a staging post....

Second, despite the great devastation inflicted on the Iraqi people by the crusader-Zionist alliance (this fatwa was issued prior to the U.S. invasion of Iraq), and despite the huge number of those killed, which has exceeded 1 million... despite all this, the Americans are once again trying to repeat the horrific massacres, as though they are not content with the protracted blockade (Iraqi sanctions) imposed after the ferocious war (Gulf War, 1991) or the fragmentation and devastation. So here they come to annihilate what is left of this people and to humiliate their Muslim neighbors.

Third, if the Americans' aims behind these wars are religious and economic...the best proof of this is their eagerness to destroy Iraq, the strongest neighboring Arab state, and their endeavor to fragment all the states of the region such as Iraq, Saudi Arabia, Egypt, and Sudan into paper statelets and through their disunion and weakness to guarantee Israel's survival and the continuation of the brutal crusade occupation of the Peninsula.

All these crimes and sins committed by the Americans are a clear declaration of war on God, his messenger, and Muslims. And (the) ulema (Islamic scholars) have throughout Islamic history unanimously agreed that the jihad is an individual duty if the enemy (comes to) destroy the Muslim countries. Nothing is more sacred than belief (Islam religion) except repulsing (the) enemy who is attacking religion and life.

On that basis, in compliance with God's order, we issue the following fatwa to all Muslims:

The ruling to kill the Americans and their allies—civilians and military—is an individual duty for every Muslim who can do it in any country in which it is possible to do it, in order to liberate the al-Aqsa Mosque and the holy mosque (Mecca) from their grip, and in order for their armies to move out of all the lands of Islam, defeated and unable to threaten any Muslim. This is in accordance with the words of Almighty God, "and fight the pagans all together as they fight you all together," and "fight them until there is no more tumult or oppression, and there prevail justice and faith in God."

We—with God's help—call on every Muslim who believes in God and wishes to be rewarded to comply with God's order to kill the Americans and plunder their money wherever and whenever they find it. We also call on (the) Muslim ulema, leaders, youths, and soldiers to launch the raid on Satan's U.S. troops and the Devil's supporters allying with them...so that they may learn a lesson.

Almighty God said "O ye who believe, give your response to God and His Apostle, when He calleth you to that which will give your life. O ye who believe, what is the matter with you, that when ye are asked to go forth in the cause of God, ye cling so heavily to the earth! Do ye prefer the life of this world to the hereafter? But little is the comfort of this life, as compared with the hereafter. Unless ye go forth, He will punish you with a grievous penalty, and put others in your place; but Him ye would not harm in the least. For God hath power over all things. So lose no heart, nor fall into despair. For ye must gain mastery if ye are true in faith."

WHAT CONSTITUTES A LEGITIMATE FATWA?

Osama bin Laden has issued, or been associated with several *fatwas* in his long career, using various fatwas to justify his holy war against the United States and others. According to the *Usul al-Fiqh*, Islamic Principles of Jurisprudence, a fatwa is legitimate and binding only when *four conditions* are met:

1) The fatwa must be in line with legal proofs, deducted from Qur'anic verses and correct Hadiths, or traditions or sayings of the Prophet Muhammad;

2) The fatwa is issued by a person (or group) having proper Islamic training and knowledge, and meeting with "sincerity of heart";

3) The fatwa is free of individual or group political or financial opportunism or corruption;

4) The fatwa is "adequate with the needs of the contemporary world." (Obviously lots of room for personal and group interpretation is inherent in this process.)

THE JOHN MILLER INTERVIEW WITH BIN LADEN, MAY 1998:

John Miller of ABC television interviewed Osama bin-Laden on May 26, 1998 in the mountains of Afghanistan. Bin Laden issued a very specific threat to the American people in that interview: *"Leave Saudi Arabia or die."* In essence, Osama bin Laden claimed that Allah had ordered him to purify Muslim lands, especially the Arabian Peninsula, of all non-believers. He went on to say that they do not differentiate between American military and civilians, that they are all targets.

Bin Laden likes to claim that his fighters will be deadly against the Americans by referring often to America's failure and retreat in Somalia in 1993 at the hand of ragtag, poorly armed militiamen:

"The youth (of Somalia) *were surprised at the low morale of the American soldier and realized more than before that the Americans are 'paper tigers.' After a few blows, they ran away in defeat...."*

DR. AYMAN AL-ZAWAHIRI (al-Qaeda, 2nd in Command):

Bush, reinforce your security measures...the Islamic nation which sent you the New York and Washington brigades has taken the firm decision to send you successive brigades to sow death and aspire to paradise.

Mujahadin fighters in Iraq have turned America's plan upside down.... The defeat of America in Iraq and Afghanistan has become just a matter of time, with God's help. Americans in both countries are between two fires. If they carry on, they will bleed to death. And if they pull out, they lose everything.

Since the U.S.-led invasion of Iraq, al-Zawahiri has called upon the *Mujahadin to attack and devour the Americans and bury them in the graveyard of Iraq.*

ABU MUSAB AL-ZARQAWI

We will carry on our jihad against the Western infidel and the Arab apostate until Islamic rule is back on earth.

AKRAM DIYA AL-UMARI, Professor at the Islamic University of Medina, Saudi Arabia, explains the goals of Islam in the world, as he interprets the Qur'an and other teachings of the Prophet Muhammad:

Jihad is an Islamic term meaning to fight in the way of Allah in order to...realize the aims of Islam on earth. This was to facilitate the spread of Islam by removing any obstacles placed in its path...to give the Muslims the upper hand in the world. In this way no one would be able to persecute the believers wherever they were or make them renounce their faith. This directive may be clearly seen in the following verses from the Qur'an:

"And fight them (the enemies of Islam) until there is no more tumult or oppression, and there prevail justice and faith in God altogether and everywhere" (al-Anfal Surah 8:39).

"Fight those who believe not in God nor the Last Day, not hold that forbidden which hath been forbidden by God and His Apostle, nor acknowledge the religion of truth (even if they are) of the people of the book (Christians and Jews), until they pay the jizyah (the special tax required by Christians and Jews) with willing submission, and feel themselves subdued" (al-Tawbah Surah 9:29).

Al-Umari concluded: Jihad is one of the most important religious duties in Islam. It clarifies the major aim which Muslims strive to achieve, namely the freedom of all people in all parts of the world to embrace Islam, and the formation of the political and military power needed to support this freedom and to protect the new (newly 'converted') Muslims.[30]

Finally, in answer to the original question of this chapter: *Why isn't the media accurately reporting these threats?* In essence, it appears an unmistakable and unfortunate combination of personal and professional bias on the part of those who should be the vanguards of truth. Also, a factor may be a certain lack of professional expertise in the region, and perhaps a dose of laziness, neither reasons an acceptable excuse in my view. Finally, in some timid cases, there may be a concern over appearing inflammatory or politically incorrect in a highly charged environment.

Bottom line: media organizations in general have done America a terrible disservice in not accurately focusing media resources on the threat to all Americans originating from Islamic radicals, particularly over the past decade as attacks have escalated. We were blindsided on 9/11. We should not have been.

One day I am certain history will conclude that our media of today was highly derelict. And from that future 20/20 vantage point, Americans will sharply condemn our media moguls, stars and starlets, both domestic and foreign. Considering the mountains of information available from a myriad of sources, as time passes the actions of today's journalists are going to appear increasingly inexcusable, perhaps even treacherously laced in some extreme cases.

QUESTION 6

- WHAT DO THE RADICALS, THE TERRORISTS, TRULY WANT? WHAT IS THEIR HIDDEN AGENDA?

LIVING IN THE LAND OF OZ

The following is a list of the recent demands made by Osama bin Laden, Ayman al-Zawahiri, Abu Musab al-Zarqawi, and others, principally representing the al-Qaeda Organization and allied terrorist factions, worldwide. In essence, this is what they demand in exchange for "peace":

1- All U.S. Forces, as well as any "significant" U.S. commercial interests or enterprises, must leave the Middle East immediately.

2- All corrupt Mideast regimes, as supported by the United States, must be removed from power and driven from Islamic Lands. These are deemed "un-Islamic" and an abomination in Allah's sight. A new Islamic Caliphate must be established, centered in Arabia and the Middle East.

3- The United States must cease its support for Israel, stand back and watch the butchery of the Jewish State without interference.

At least for the moment, the radicals claim the above is all they want. Simple and straight-forward enough, right? Hardly. Actually, this is what we can refer to as the "A-List." The Islamic terrorists, blackmailers, and extortionist's demands have no end...until America and Israel cease to exist. That is precisely why, no matter the cost, we cannot grant or capitulate to even *one* demand. The moment we do, we are finished. For the terror-mongers will know at that moment we can be beaten; perhaps in stages, but in the end beaten down and destroyed nonetheless.

Without much imagination, one can predict what the Islamic radicals' future demands will likely be. Try these:

1- $75 to $100 dollars per barrel oil. Of course, as we know from previous chapters, future oil supplies for the world's vital needs will be available and found in principally Mideast Islamic countries.

2- No limits or restrictions on weapons' technology purchases by Islamic nations, including nuclear, chemical and biological weapons (WMD).

3- Blanket security and protection guarantees for Islamic Terrorist (they call them "Warriors of God") Training Centers throughout the Islamic World. After all, they will demand, "we have the right to defend ourselves."

4- Preferential treatment for Muslims residing in Europe and the United States to allow them full and free movement, as well as no restrictions on fundraising, the building of mosques and *madressas* (Islamic indoctrination centers for children), and the proselyting of non-Muslims. Of course such rights and freedoms are NEVER offered to Christians, or any other religion, especially Jews, living and residing in the Middle East or in most Muslim Lands.

5- No restrictions on Muslim countries in their weapon, missile, and war technology trade with North Korea, China, Europe, and Russia.

6- United Nations recognition for the coming New Islamic Caliphate, the super-alliance of most (or all) Islamic nations which the radicals are pushing for, including "special standards" for judging human and civil rights abuses, i.e. "special Islamic standards" regarding the restrictions on women, and the punishment of dissidents and "criminals."

7- The New Islamic Caliphate must have a permanent seat on

the U.N. Security Council, of course, and with full veto rights over America and her allies.

8-Finally, official U.N. status and recognition for brutal Islamic organizations such as Hamas, Islamic Jihad, the Islamic Salvation Front, and of course al-Qaeda, to be given offices at the U.N. and afforded all rights, honors, and privileges bestowed on other established, legitimate international agencies.

If you believe that "appeasement" and "cultural understanding" will protect you from the very real, and very dangerous, clandestine objectives of these radical factions, cells, and rogue nations, you are living in the Land of Oz.

Follow-up: Then, isn't this truly a war pitting Islam against Christianity?

In essence, yes, though more generally a clash of cultures and ideals, but most of all a war for power and dominion. Throughout history, Muslims have seldom sought the direct and total destruction of Christianity, only hegemony or dominion over Christian and Jewish populations. Actually a large body of subservient *dhimmi* (Christians and Jews) makes a highly useful, well-taxed service sector in traditional, *jihad*-oriented Islamic societies. In fact without the dhimmi close at hand, past Islamic empires and caliphates have eventually faltered.

Today, in spite of American victories in Afghanistan and Iraq, the war continues, the clash has been off and on since the seventh century, whether or not our leaders will admit it. While the war has not always been a hot war, Islam and Christianity have been at odds. You do not believe me? Ask any one of millions of Christians who have fled Muslim countries over the past century. Their stories are eerily similar. Ask the Armenians of Turkish or Azeri lands. Ask the Copts of Egypt, or the Assyrian or Chaldean Christians of Iraq. Ask the Bosnians, the Kosovars, or the peoples of Durfar (the Sudan). While such genocide may have resulted from local or regional power struggles, or the fight for resources, religion has been the traditional fault line.

When Islamic terrorists chose a target in North Ossetia in the Russian Caucasus, they picked an elementary school in this *Christian* enclave, 700,000 citizens, almost all Orthodox Christian. It was there that these Islamic fascists carried out their slaughter of more than 150 Christian children. Look at the ethnicity of the dead and tell me this is not a religious war.

In the Darfur region of the Sudan, untold thousands of mostly Christians have been murdered and upwards of two million displaced from their homes in a horrific example of modern genocide, with systematic rape and plundering of these Christian regions by soldiers of the Islamic government of the Sudan. In spite of pleas by international organizations, the Sudanese regime continues to push to depopulate this key oil area of their southlands, with hundreds of reports of Christian girls being taken to the Islamic north of the country as slaves and concubines, some sold in other Islamic nations, including Saudi Arabia.

In 1996, seven Christian Trappist Monks in Algeria at Tibherine had their throats cut by Islamic rebels who demanded protection money from the monastery, yet who also demanded that all Christians and foreigners leave the country.

All over Islamic lands you will find similar incidents and tragic encounters. Certainly this is a clash of ideals, of power and control, but with religion a catalyst of the untold depredations. Once more, Islam seeks global reach, and a lofty level of power due "God's truth faith." To accomplish this, America, along with Europe, must be reduced to the status relegated them in the Qur'an, that of the "dhimmi." From the Holy Qur'an: *Fight against those who believe not in Allah, nor in the Last Day, nor forbid that which has been forbidden by Allah and His Messenger* (Muhammad) *and those who acknowledge not the religion of truth* (i.e.-Islam) *among the people of the Scripture* (the dhimmi, meaning Christians and Jews), *until they pay the Jizya*(the dhimmi tax) *with willing submission, and feel themselves subdued.*[31]

Follow-up: Why is Europe, which seems to cater to the Islamists more and more these days, not only becoming increasingly anti-American, but accepting the classic role of the submissive "dhimmi?"

The Continent of Europe has a serious problem: Islam. Europe hosts more than *16 million* Muslims, living mostly in concentrated enclaves throughout the continent. Western European governments struggle as they cater to these relative newcomers. European Russia is under attack by Muslim rebels. Mosques are going up everywhere in "Europa." The *burqa*, the veil, sometimes called "chador" can now be seen in all European cities. The call to prayer is heard everywhere. The Europeans, it seems, are bending over backwards to appear pacifist, except when criticizing America, of course. The trend is clear: Europe is no longer Europe, many are claiming. It is a growing northern province of Islam.

Actually, Europe is acting out a role it once was forced to act, that of the "dhimmi," when the Christian Continent was threatened during the Middle Ages, for over hundreds of years, by Islamic invasion, from the Arabs, the Moors, and the Turks. In fact, Muslim warlords controlled vast regions of the continent for centuries, from Spain to Eastern Europe. The dhimmi, which is Arabic for "protected," was the name given to Christians and Jews who lived in the Islamic empire or in Islamic-controlled lands. Indeed, they were "protected," but were more accurately a "kept people," not quite slaves, but hardly a rung above.

Islam provided (in fact encouraged) conquered Christians and Jews to keep their religion, but for the "privilege," were required to pay special taxes, the dhimmi tax called *jizya*, as well as land taxes, for the right of maintaining ownership of lands now conquered by "God's Army." The dhimmi, the smart ones anyway, kept their heads down and their mouths shut. In this fashion, they sometimes survived and occasionally thrived, though they existed under highly restrictive laws, laws that applied only to them.

The dhimmi, the protected ones, are also called in Arabic the "People of the Book" or *ahl al-kitab*. This differentiates them from the "heathen," or pagans or polytheists, who during the Middle Ages were widespread in Africa, Asia, and even Europe. As dhimmi, these Jews and Christians could never marry Muslim women. As well, they could not build churches or synagogues. In many cases, they were not even allowed to repair existing ones, but had to let them fall into disrepair. The largest and best know churches the Muslims often converted into mosques, which made it impossible to ever convert them back again because Islamic law states that once a building has been used as a mosque, it cannot be used for any other purpose.

The dhimmi were not allowed any outward manifestations of worship such as the ringing of church bells or public processions of the cross, or the public sale of religious articles. The building of new churches was widely prohibited because it would require the occupying of new land, lands conquered by the Muslims and therefore now "sacred Muslim ground."

The dhimmi (*ahl al-dhimma*) pay the *jizya*, or Christian and Jew Tax, which is paid directly to the Islamic State. As well they were responsible for any property taxes that could be assessed. According to the Qur'an, Muslims must "fight the Christians and Jews until their members pay tribute, one by one, humiliated."[32]

The Qur'an also stipulated that Christians surrender their weapons and avoid riding horseback (because of the power a horse-mounted soldier has over infantry troops). A dhimmi must dress in a special way to signify his religion, not be allowed to testify against a Muslim in a court of law, and especially forbidden to take the daughter of a Muslim to wife. Christians were never allowed to keep Muslims as slaves, or to act as guardians to underage Muslims.

Restrictions continued, such as harsh penalties for trying to convert a Muslim to Christianity, which could result in the penalty of beheading or hanging. All such restrictions essentially asphyxiated occupied Christian and Jewish communities, leading to either emigration northward to European Christian lands, or conversion to Islam just to survive. Those unwilling to convert were marginalized to the point of slowly fading to dust, in most cases, unable to get a decent job, excluded from any kind of government administrative position, and kept from joining the military. The dhimmi lived a life of endless discrimination. The inequity and bigotry continues today in many Muslim lands.

Throughout its history, Islam has been far more concerned about controlling lands and wealth, the means of economic production, as well as armies, police and intelligence networks (to maintain power) than in killing off Christians and Jews, which would have been a foolish waste of the most important resource available to them. This explains how a relatively small, yet smart band of warriors was able to conquer and hold these large and established Christian lands and empires.

Certainly, the founders of Islam were "wise as serpents" understanding from the beginning that "approved" religions, like Christianity and Judaism, were not a threat as long as the Muslims controlled the government, the military, the courts, and the means and ability to tax these conquered peoples.

The Muslims believed in the beginning as well that since the Jews and Christians belonged to an inferior order, they were often deemed non-threatening to God's "true" people. Besides, Islam has never recognized the concept of nation and citizenship, but only the Islamic community, called the *umma*. A Muslim may live in any location, but is still part of the religious community of believers. The *Dar al-Islam*, or House of Islam, is everything. And those not a part, the "outsiders," are to be exploited. In fact, they are essential; as Muhammad taught, "treat them well and they will be your workers," freeing Muslims to worship their God (Allah) and to continue *jihad* into far-off lands. Certainly Muhammad and his early generals were wise and capable holy-imperialists.

Today, this ancient form of submission by Christians and Jews to Islam is once more being resurrected in Europe, often called "dhimmitude." As modern dhimmi, Europeans are once again keeping their heads down, as good, quiet, intimidated vassals, and paying their hemorrhaging taxes to support their many Islamic immigrants. They are, in some cases, actually bribing or paying off terrorist groups with their "donations," and waving the flag of Anti-Americanism like good dhimmi should. By submission and being servile (by coincidence that's what the word "Islam" means in Arabic…hmmm.), they hope to avoid a confrontation, and perhaps even profit by their passivity. Yet, it seems that the Christian scriptures have something to say about the proverbial lukewarm, the fence-sitters, the pathetic "moderates" who sell their souls for a little perceived security.

QUESTION 7

- WHAT IS AMERICA'S MOST CRITICAL QUEST IN ACCURATELY UNDERSTANDING THE MIDDLE EAST?

THE ORACLE AT DELPHI

In the ancient world of the Mediterranean, and in much of the Middle East, when seeking an answer both warrior and king would travel hundreds of miles to consult the Oracle at Delphi in the mountains of Greece. Legendary are the insightful answers offered by the sibyl, the female *Pythia*, the priestess on the temple mount at Delphi. For nearly 2,000 years, the sacred Oracle was esteemed by millions as the "Gateway to the Gods."

Today the virgin priestess of the Oracle is gone, though some say her spirit can still be felt amid the rocks and ruins of the ancient temple mount. Greek, Roman, Persian, Christian, and then Muslim empires have risen and then faded from view in this incredibly innovative, revolutionary land we call the Mediterranean basin, which extends into the Middle East. Modern America is, in no small way, both the heir and the creation of this genesis of religion, philosophy, and global conquest rolling out of the region 3,000 years ago. In the same vein, who we are, or who we have become, can be traced to prophecies uttered at Delphi, which inspired the kings and armies of the past.

Today America faces supreme challenges once again originating in the Middle East. And today we continue to consult the "oracles," so-called experts who claim special insights. We see them on cable news programs. We read their commentary on the Mid East in magazines and books, and on-line. These modern sibyls are prolific creatures, ranging far from craggy Delphi, racking up frequent-flyer miles and hotel vouchers in nearly every land. Many are good at what they do. But they are not good enough. As I travel and speak I find most Americans increasingly confused over our objectives, our role, and our purpose over there. In the Age of Information this must be a failure in education, in communication, and in detached objectivity on the part of our media sibyls.

The greatest obstacle most face, especially the "experts," is *they are asking the wrong questions*. "Ask, and ye shall receive, knock and it shall be opened unto you." The greatest challenge in life, not unlike the supreme challenge facing the ancient king who was approaching the Oracle for answers, is *to know what question to ask*. Answers are usually easy; it's the questions that trip us up. The difference between the amateur and the professional is often in the quality of his or her questions.

The core frustration of the human condition is our inability to know everything. To counter our native ignorance we should, from our children's earliest ages, impress upon them the importance of learning how to inquire. This quest, I believe, is the essence of genuine humility, and the beginning of wisdom. Through a combination of research, hard work, experience, and good judgment (which comes from experience), the right questions can be ferreted out. Then—and this is critical—listen carefully to the answers and *vett* (verify) those answers through other experts or sources. Such a quest requires uncommon humility and dogged determination, but will pay huge dividends.

In the Middle East, we've seen far too many mistakes by the "experts" who should know better. Unfortunately, mistakes over there have gotten Americans killed in large numbers in recent years. Understanding *exactly* what the questions are today is beyond critical. It means life or death.

For example:

"Why can't the Arabs and Israelis just get along?"

This straightforward question has been asked many times. Unfortunately, it has nothing to do with understanding *why* Arabs and Israelis are butchering one another, sending the seeker in the wrong direction. The more accurate question should be:

"What, or more accurately, *who*, is encouraging, supporting, and bankrolling these deadly attacks and why? What do the terrorist leaders hope to gain by blood and death?"

Or more specifically:

"What powerful group, or groups, *benefit* by supporting

ongoing sensational bloody violence and terrorism against Israel?"

Now *that's* a question you can sink your teeth into. It's the kind of question that gets the powers-that-be squirming. Everything that happens has a reason, especially in the Middle East. The trick is to discover, through research, investigation, and qualified sources, who gains and who loses by any given act or deadly attack. There are usually powerful benefactors, deeply and necessarily veiled, lying just beyond our sight. Identify them and then defeat them.

Another typical false-flag question:

"Why did we make war on Saddam Hussein? Do we want to take Iraqi oil?"

This is perhaps the most naïve foreign policy question ever mustered. The real question should be:

"How does a powerful U.S. military move against Iraq, and in the Persian Gulf region, further U.S. goals of guaranteeing peace, freedom, stability and prosperity in the world?"

Or, with even more relevance:

"How does a U.S. Military presence in Iraq help assure future U.S. global leadership, improved security at home, and greater prosperity for the world?

This is the true question, the heart and soul of the issue, sending us down the road of genuine understanding and covered in detail in the following pages.

Remember those in power often find skilled ways of actually molding or influencing, in advance, the questions they are asked, thereby telegraphing the answers they want us to hear. You walk away thinking everything is out in the open, clear and concise. Such manipulated and slyly crafted questions are really non-questions, false flags or red herrings, designed to misdirect the public—you and me—at the critical moment.

Some very fine political careers have been built on the professional clouding of issues or so-called "spin." Of course, *spin* is really only well-packaged dishonesty and deception. In this Age of Information, however, our only excuse if duped by such leaders is laziness, and a willingness to accept whatever information is paraded before us without vetting it. With the finest sources in history at our fingertips, our enlightenment is merely one question away.

Follow-up: Why is it important to understand how Middle Eastern youth truly view U.S. Mideast policy?

Arab youth are the key. They are an excellent, yet essentially untapped, barometer of Middle East trends. Though not a scientific poll of a balanced cross-section of young people, some interesting insights emerged from my January 2005 visit to the Arab world. I found that within understandable cultural limits, many Arab youth are very well focused and informed on current events, probably better than their American counterparts. And they are certainly more malleable, or flexible and open, than their eternally-rigid parents.

Let us consider some socio-political realities:

- The Middle East, North Africa, and Southwest Asia are literally bursting at the seams with young people, the population nearly doubling over the last two decades. The majority of the population is well below 30 years of age, literally hundreds of millions of young, impressionable minds. Potential soldiers…or terrorists.

- These youth, 60% of the population and more, are exceedingly restless and mostly poor. The 22 Arab countries *combined* have a lower GDP than the country of Spain alone. Never has a generation of young people faced a more uncertain future. What's more important, and even more dangerous, they know it.

- This is the Madonna, Michael Jackson, and *Bay Watch* generation, translated into Arabic of course. It is Disneyland, Las Vegas, and Fantasy Island. Arab youth admire, no they are *infatuated* with America. America is wealth, power, security, and most importantly, freedom. For young men, America is fast cars, fast women, and easy money. For young women,

America represents glamour, dating (generally forbidden in Muslim lands), and marriage for love, rather than by family arrangement or mandate.

- Arab youth respect, admire, and even crave power, especially the males. Power is virility, pure masculinity, and it is "wasta" (total influence, but so much more), the ability to sweep aside the weak and impotent ones as does the grand *mufti* or mighty sultan, conquering his enemy and taking the defeated man's females for himself. Most youth I've talked with—and I've interviewed many hundreds over the years—are torn between admiring unlimited American might and prowess, and rejecting what that power is perceived to be doing in Muslim nations. "Myself, my brother and my cousin, against the stranger" is an old Arab saying. Arabs often feel a brotherly loyalty to other Arabs, or even to other Muslims. However, such loyalty and sympathy is not as strong or universal as often portrayed in the media.

- While Arab youth wrestle with current political issues, they can be won over to America's side. Many are. American victory must be followed by grand American magnanimity, portrayed as a fearless sacrifice to free the oppressed, as well as plenty of warrior poses with happy and well-fed Arab children playing safely at the American soldier's feet. These priceless images will filter through the masses, especially the youth: the wonderful, potentially overwhelming power of the TV and video image. And in the end, *In-sha-Allah* (God willing), their anger towards America will be softened.

Follow-up: Why did the U.S. military call our initial attack on Iraq "Shock and Awe"?

"I want to see American F-16s pound Saddam on TV with my own eyes," the 18 year-old Jordanian said to me, excitement flashing from his raven face. "I love war very much!" He added, grinning. "Saddam must go. He is not good for Iraq or for Jordan."

The teen, who worked selling souvenirs to tourists at a Jordanian archeological site just before the 2003 Iraq War, was alone with me for the moment. Though working a "dead-end job," he was an educated kid, like many of the struggling, under-employed in Jordan. Alone with me, and unafraid, his words came easily.

I asked, "Do you love America?"

Immediately his smile faded. He did not answer. Some peers, all souvenir-hawking associates had just arrived, pressing up into my face. (Arabs have an entirely foreign concept of personal space.) He glanced about nervously and I knew that now I was wasting my time. Honesty in a group situation is just not possible. The moment Arab minds meld, irrationality and ego take over.

"Bush, bad," one young fellow blurted in his best English, his comrades grunting "Aw," meaning "yes," in street Arabic. "Bush want Arab oil, Bush want Arab land," another chimed in. "Why America want to take everything from us?" One shouted, the enthusiasm sweeping everyone, electrifying each of the youth standing before me. Suddenly everyone was speaking at once, a classic Arab moment. Apparently it didn't dawn on them that Jordan had no oil to take, nor did America wish to occupy Jordanian land. Of course, they were not Jordanians any longer, but Arabs and Muslims.

I held up my hand and they quieted politely for the stranger, (another Arab trait that I admire). I said, "If you were strong and unbeaten like the Americans, would you not protect your interests and your people?" I asked in Arabic. Suddenly the bunch seemed confused, then turning somber and thoughtful.

"Besides," I added mercilessly, "America pays Muslims well for their oil. And they *always* pay. Does Saddam pay? Does Arafat? Do the Saudis pay? They are very rich, but do they share their wealth with you? How about the Russians or Chinese? Can you trust them? America is rich enough. It has no need to steal your oil. America is powerful, it can afford to be generous; and in victory, can afford to be merciful."

Having doused their spirited affront, they suddenly became pensive. It is impossible to argue against a logic on which you, yourself, have been raised: the logic of power, the sense of rightful hierarchy, the just reward of the conqueror, the way it's always been.

These youth, like all youth everywhere, are smart. As I weighed their collective reaction to my arguments, it was obvious they understood, perhaps better than American youth (and even many adults), the realities of survival in a hostile world. Middle Easterners respect the warrior who demonstrates honor, who wields his sword with a measured hand. True, the victor must conquer. That is what victors do. But he must also judiciously avoid hubris, that unrighteous arrogance which taints the champion's triumph.

In the world of the Arab and Muslim, in spite of all the rhetoric to the contrary, overwhelming power *must* be wielded *absolutely*, otherwise the enemy will perceive you as weak and respond lethally. With skill and finesse the battle ax must be brought down hard, the enemy crushed...but never completely.

"I love war very much," the Arab youth had said to me. And to the Middle Eastern male war *is* pure romantic fantasy; what true and virile men do in a threatening world. In the Arab mind, men who cannot or will not make war when attacked are "women" or eunuchs, undeserving of respect. "Peace at any price," seemingly the new-age religion of many today in America, in Hollywood, and in Europe, is the ultimate shame to the Arab. We *had* to hit Iraq, and hit it hard. We should have done so long before we did. And if we back down now, *500 million*-plus bright, discerning Muslim youth from Marrakech to Bangladesh will get the message. Future massive terror attacks on America's cities will be deemed "deserved," the just reward of the shamefully weak and impotent.

I realize this concept is hard for Americans to comprehend. It seems pure barbarism. Yet, I cannot emphasize strongly enough the harsh reality of America's predicament in the Middle East. *Listen* to what Saddam Hussein, and Osama bin Laden and al-Qaeda, have been proclaiming now for years! An emasculated America, the land of American eunuchs, of "whining women," as the terror-mongers have painted us over and over, deserves its punishment in their minds, an America to be justifiably whittled down and destroyed.

Our only choice was to act and act overwhelmingly, for the sake of America's future security, and for the world's freedom. We even gave it a name the Arab, and Muslim, would understand:

"Shock and Awe."

Follow-up: At its heart is this blood feud inevitable?

Unlike other major religions in the history of the world, Islam and Christianity have always been on a collision course, though many are yet unwilling to acknowledge this fact.

From the inception of Christianity, most practitioners of the faith could not deny the prophesied, inevitable triumph of Christ Jesus the Nazarene sent by his Father to spread the word of his gospel. Until when? Until every knee shall bow and tongue confess that Jesus is the Christ, the Son of the Living God.[33] The Religion says nothing of it being superceded later by Allah and his desert Prophet. "Strait is the way and narrow the gate that leads to eternal life and few there are that find it," Jesus said. And in the end, just prior to his millennial reign, most Christians believe Jesus will return from the heavens in power and majesty.

So, how does Islam and Muhammad's version of all this fit the Christian mold? Simply, it doesn't.

The Prophet Muhammad was born about A.D. 570 in a backwater of the Middle East, in Western "Hejaz" Arabia. There is nothing wrong with being born in a backwater. That is what Jerusalem, or more precisely its suburb, *Bayt Laham* or Bethlehem, was during the height of the Roman Era.

Still, Muhammad's Islam, revealed to the pagans of Arabia, could have easily fallen into obscurity and died with his own death in A.D. 632. However, those who came after Muhammad would not allow it, particularly *al-Khulufa al-Rashidun*, the Four Righteous Caliphs who carried the word of Allah into distant lands, converting and plundering as they moved.

Incidentally, almost from its inception Islam grew at the expense of long-established Christian communities—in Egypt, in Palestine, in North Africa, what is Turkey today, and Spain, and then clear into the heartland of Christian Europe. It is interesting to hear Osama bin Laden and others of his kind rail at past (and present) Christian Nations "invading" "Muslim Lands" when these lands were originally stolen from Christians by attacking, plundering Islamic armies. Once conquered, the Christians were systematically oppressed and subjected to Allah's way. Judged by that measure, the Christian Crusades were technically *not* invasions, but wars of liberation, as brutal and misguided as they usually were.

From its beginning, Islam has skillfully implemented the Prophet Muhammad's edict that "there is to be no compulsion in religion."[34] This was done, speaking generally, by special Christian and Jew taxes (*jizya*), discriminating against these under-classes of occupied peoples, effectively making conversion to Islam a wise economic, political, and security move. Yes, there is generally "no compulsion" per se, just some very serious incentive. Give them credit. The Muslims were smart. They knew how to conquer and control an empire.

From both beginnings, Christianity and Islam have competed for much of the same lands and peoples. During the Renaissance and Age of Discovery the tide turned against the desert Prophet's faith and Islam's formerly unbeaten armies suffered one significant defeat after another, even finding most of their lands occupied fairly easily by invading Christian forces.

In Egypt, Napoleon took the entire country from the Pasha's soldiers in but a few days leading only a small force of French dragoons. In humiliation, the Islamic Empire was systematically chopped up and divided among Christian conquerors. It was not until this recent century that the Christian West (Europe) began to relinquish control back to local, mostly Arab, warlords and dictators, so-called "ruling families."

The wounds remain. Today the United States has shouldered the mantel of the conquering West, a modern "Crusader army," at least in the minds of most Muslims. Obviously in the hearts of the radicals the struggle continues. Muslims realize they cannot abandon the quest of the Prophet to bring the world under the Banner of Islam. Such an admission of defeat would effectively acknowledge Allah's failure and the dilution, or eventual destruction, of the Faith. Allah is God and God is never defeated. Listen to what Islamic leaders are saying, in the mosques, in their writings, on their websites. The Faith, the required submission to Allah, *must sweep the world*. It is Allah's will. To accomplish this both the Jews (Israel) and the United States (the Christians) must be brought down and humbled. The radicals believe that many Americans, if not most, must be killed in order to accomplish this task. Then all remaining Americans will submit to Islamic rule and pay the *jizya* tax, as required by Islamic Law.

You tell me, my friend, that there is no modern conflict existing between Islam and the Christian West; that all faiths and peoples can live together in peace? There are none so blind as those who will not see. Open your eyes, your life and the lives of your children and grandchildren depend on it. *You* are the "Great Satan." And in the eyes of the radicals, you are therefore marked for destruction.

Follow-up: Specifically who is the Great Satan?

In the mind of Osama bin Laden and others the United States is the world's Great Satan, though others sometimes qualify. On 9/11 his minions spearheaded an attack into the heart of the beast, hoping to kill as many Americans as possible and bring down the American economy. From evidence we have, 9/11 was only the first wave planned against the American homeland. Those future attacks have not yet been scaled back as far as we know, but expanded to the eventual use of nuclear weapons on American cities. "The Great Satan yet lives." Therefore, the war continues.

Bin Laden was not the first Muslim leader to use this phrase. Iran's Ayatollah Khomeini, from at least the 1970s, referred to America as the Great Satan and Israel as the "Little Satan." But Khomeini had a more Qur'anic, more focused, take. In the Qur'an, as in the Bible, Satan is usually described as "the Seducer" quietly going about his business in the shadows, whispering in his victim's ear words of seduction. He is not described as the leader of a superpower nation, commanding powerful armies and out in front leading the destruction of mankind. No, he remains in the shadows recruiting others to accept those powerful, highly visible roles. In essence, Satan is a quiet, cunning, whispering seducer.

This is precisely how the Ayatollah once described the Christian West, led by the United States. We are a "seducer," providing a tempting image to the Muslim World such that no one can resist—the video or TV image of overwhelming wealth, "loose" women, lax morals, and unrestricted freedom. *This* is the reason Khomeini has branded us the Great Satan, for no power in history can compare to the seductive "Image of the Whore" (Europe and America) presented to the Islamic World by the fundamentalists. The Muslim radicals fear that such an image will erode Islam until it has been thoroughly corrupted and made over in the image of America and Hollywood.

To Khomeini, Osama bin Laden, and others, this is the Last Great Battle to see if Allah and his *Mujahadin* (Warriors of the Faith) or the Beast, led by the United States and Israel, will emerge victorious. The loose morals, hedonistic lifestyle, and liberal ways of America must be fought and destroyed, so say the radicals. That said, it amazes me every day when the American "Hollywood Left" spout off that all we need is "a little mutual understanding" and not all this "Bush warmongering." Truly amazing when all the facts are considered. Don't Susan Sarandon, Alec Baldwin, and Michael Moore realize that if the Islamic beheaders had their way it would be *them* first in line?

QUESTION 8

- WHAT ARE THE PRINCIPAL FACTORS DRIVING UNITED STATES' MIDDLE EAST POLICY?

The Bush Doctrine on Terrorism
"Our war with terrorism begins with al-Qaeda, but it does not end there. It will not end until every terrorist group of global reach has been found, stopped and defeated. ...And we will pursue nations that provide aid or safe haven to terrorism. ...Every nation, in every region, now has a decision to make. Either you are with us, or you are with the terrorists. From this day forward, any nation that continues to harbor or support terrorism will be regarded by the United States as a hostile regime."
--President George W. Bush, September 21, 2001

The United States' military move on Iraq significantly altered the global equation. And in victory over Saddam, America gains much more than simply the end of a dangerous enemy. A swift and successful American operation against Iraq further marginalizes the Europeans, though the United States has never had that as a goal. In essence, Europe has shot *itself* in the foot. Lacking viable military reach, political courage and will, the Europeans (with the notable exception of the British) are at last being exposed to the world as the weak-kneed, non-players they have become. Simply, they lack global vision, a moral standing, and worldwide reach and influence; so by extension they are increasingly viewed as powerless, more so, impotent and spineless.

Adding to their troubles, several key European leaders were paid large sums of money for cooperating with Saddam, who was skimming tens of millions of dollars from the United Nation's Oil-For-Food Program. This program was set up to help the starving children of Iraq. True to form, Saddam "let them eat cake."

The Maximum Leader dangled the promise of future oil contracts in front of the predictably greedy Europeans, and lucrative weapon system's sales (including weapons of mass destruction technology). No wonder European opposition to the U.S.-led invasion arose from the start, particularly issuing from the self-serving French and Germans.

For their own good, however, and the good of the world, the Europeans need to understand that United States' successes in the Middle East have long-term security and prosperity ramifications for everyone. That is why we are there—period.

Mercenaries to perfection, European leaders are certainly aware of this, though their native arrogance and self-centeredness gets in their own way. Not only will a successful, pro-U.S. government in Iraq expose how weak and indecisive the Europeans have become in recent years, the Peoples' Republic of China, and greater Asia, will witness the power the United States has in controlling principal sources of their energy imports. At the same time, the Saudis, leaders of the Organization of Petroleum Exporting Countries (OPEC), will find their global influence waning when these enormous new oil reserves in Iraq come on line, though such will take time.

With a powerful move into Iraq, and into the greater Middle East by the Coalition, led by the United States, the strategic marginalization of mainland Europe is inevitable. Increasingly the Middle East will depend on the United States as massive commercial and industrial expansion takes place in a region stunted in the past principally due to security issues and endemic, native corruption and mismanagement.

Today Iraq is in a mammoth rebuilding and stabilizing phase. Other Middle East nations will join in. With American franchisers moving in, and lucrative joint-ventures consummated every day between Arabs and Americans and their allies, the future appears bright, in spite of the drum beat of negativity in the media.

In the end there is nothing more certain than change. Iraq is destined for greatness, for power and influence in the world. Security and prosperity are the mighty dual-drivers behind U.S. Middle East policy.

With regional military dominance, markets are naturally more easily and successfully created, developed, protected, and secured. Profitable commerce is the eager mistress of the conqueror. Capital huddles for safety behind the most powerful player on the block. Perhaps better than any other people on earth, Middle Easterners understand this. They respect a winner; they flock to power, they long for security. They have sought a mighty conquering warrior since the days of *Saladin*, the great vanquisher of the Christian Crusader, Richard the Lionhearted. A loser is shameful, lacks honor, and cannot be trusted. When honor is compromised, the death of one's own security and prosperity can't be far behind. The shameful and weak deserve death; in fact, it is considered a mercy killing. Arabs understand this. For some reason Americans don't. The victor retaliates harshly against his enemy to set a precedent. Anything less brings the enemy back, often stronger, and with an eye to vengeance.

In summary, the Middle East holds so much more than merely lakes of crude oil for America's future prosperity and security. To focus strictly on oil for oil's sake, or to line the pockets of American oil companies, merely cheapens the equation and vastly undersells the implications. We are far beyond that.

THE SEVEN (OFTEN SHROUDED) TRUTHS BEHIND AMERICA'S MIDEAST POLICY:

1- The *strategic power* of Middle East oil, and the struggle to protect and control these primal resources, is *the* insurance policy for continued U.S. global leadership, power and control, and ultimate long-term global security. It's not the *price* of oil, but the *strategic power* of that oil which matters.

2- *No Middle East dictator*, regime or rogue nation beyond the influence of the United States (except Israel, of course), will be allowed to acquire and field *weapons of mass destruction* and the means to deliver such weapons against American targets, or against our allies.

3- The *radicalization of Islamic fundamentalists*, and their desire to integrate and coordinate terrorist acts with other hostile cells and/or nations, will not be tolerated by the United

States. Any nation harboring or supporting such activity will be in America's sights and reap the whirlwind.

4-The *Arab-Israeli conflict* over control of "holy lands" while important, is in effect, a sideshow. The true objective is in the Persian Gulf region and the Caspian basin, and is centered on strategic oil resources and the control of, or hegemony over, those resources. Sadly, the Palestinians are pawns in this global game, used by their Muslim "brothers" for larger political ends on the broader regional and global stage. For example, al-Qaeda did not need the Palestinian issue as an excuse to attack America. September 11th would still have happened with or without the Palestinians. Only *after the fact* did Osama bin Laden begin talking about the downtrodden Palestinian people. Only then did he decide he needed additional justification for his mayhem and mass-murder, an excuse that would play well in the Arab streets, and among the intellectual Left in Europe and the United States.

5-A prime factor in Middle East unrest and anger, particularly among the huge population of mostly young and poor, is the continued *unequal distribution of Middle East lands and resources*. These nations are dictatorships, usually controlled by individual families, which are increasingly viewed by the disaffected masses as corrupt, inept, and wholly self-serving, which they are.

6-The *unequal distribution of Middle East political power* is a constant smoldering flashpoint in all areas. The call for democracy is partly due to the endemic corruption and nepotism of these tribal rulers and warlords. The demand for democracy is growing with each passing day. In fact, it is unstoppable.

7-America's cultural, economic, and military *penetration* into Muslim lands, and accompanying rapid technological advancement, is causing disruption and unrest. The Middle East is being wrenched, overnight, from the dark ages into the modern world. This disruption is playing into the hands of the terrorists.

Follow-up: Why is it impossible to understand U.S. Middle East policy without considering the "China card"?

Iraq is a high-stakes game, driven by U.S. national security interests and cannot be separated from the war on terror, or from strategic challenges coming from China, Europe, and elsewhere.

For example, from 1980 through 1990, China's gross domestic product (GDP) growth averaged 10.1% annually. Over the following decade, 1990 through 1999, China's growth increased to 10.7% per year, the highest in the world. Over the past few years the rate has fallen somewhat to about 8% or 9%.[35]

Obviously, China's economic expansion continues at unprecedented rates in the world. The future is China's and the Chinese know it. The question slapping us in the face is: Will China be friend or foe as its political and economic power in Asia expands into nearly every area?

Hardliners within China's Communist Party view the United States as the principle roadblock to superpower status and inevitable Asian, then world, dominion. With the U.S. firmly in control of most Middle East oil, China cannot sit back and allow others to manipulate or stifle its domestic and foreign policy agenda. Obviously, China cannot allow the Americans to control their most important source of foreign, imported energy.

For decades China has sought energy self-sufficiency and security. In 1990, China *exported* almost 5 times as much crude oil and oil products as it imported. But since the early '90s, their world has turned upside down. By 1997, oil imports, mostly from the Middle East, had *doubled* the amount of oil China was exporting. Past self-sufficiency in oil is now history. Proven in-country oil reserves may run out in 14 years, so the Peoples Republic is moving aggressively to secure future suppliers. Iran is now China's second-largest source of imported oil.[36]

The realities of supply, availability, but mostly cost, have forced China to look in the direction of the ultimate source of oil, the Middle East. As already discussed, these market realities are squeezing China into energy insecurity and economic and military vulnerability they are struggling to overcome.

CHINESE ENERGY GOALS

According to recent news reports China is looking at acquiring UNOCAL, a California-based energy conglomerate, among several other key global energy sources, technologies, and means of production. From Canada to the U.S., from Latin America to Asia and Africa, China is moving powerfully to secure itself on the energy front.

The hot Chinese markets are firing their parched thirst for oil, including rabid economic and industrial development previously discussed. Such growth requires an infusion of energy supplies to maintain the growth. China imported 122.72 million tons of crude oil in 2004, up a whopping *34.8 percent* over the previous year![37]

One little recognized byproduct or advantage for China resulting from this break-neck commercialization is that market forces are forcing China to rapidly acquire key skills, including global banking, acquisition skills, and the accompanying legal expertise in a variety of regions and disciplines. Called management and acquisition skills, or M&A, the Chinese are mastering these with calculating effectiveness.

They are also pursuing oil sands development in Canada. The high price of petroleum is driving the interest in formerly marginal energy sources such as tar and oil sands, increasingly cost effective with oil hovering around $50 per barrel. As well, newly developed technologies are making these formerly pricy sources of energy doable and profitable.

Recent restructuring of Russia's oil industry giants has once more raised Chinese interest in possible investment there, perhaps as a minority partner in the development of several well-located Siberian fields, though many hurdles remain for significant investment and return in Russia. As well, Chinese investment in coal-to-oil technology is moving forward.

Obviously the Peoples' Republic is moving forward aggressively in an effort to secure other sources besides those from the Middle

East. While China imports most of its finished oil products from South East Asian suppliers, in reality these Asian refineries are using "feedstocks"[38] from the Persian Gulf. China does not like it, but it remains one of the world's largest oil importers and consumers. As well, China's own refineries remain inefficient and with poor capacity. Oil refineries must be re-tooled to handle various grades of crude, from so-called "sweet crude" to the "sour" or heavy varieties. Asia-Pacific countries as a whole are averaging a 66% dependency rate on foreign imported oil. The number is rising and the greatest factor is the dependency on Mideast oil feedstocks. While Asia is being hit particularly hard, this growing Middle East dependency trend is worldwide. The Saudis and Kuwaitis, in particular, view China as their potentially largest future market. Others, including Iran, have landed lucrative contracts, including refinery deals and weapons-for-oil swaps, as well as other capital investments from the Chinese.

The bottom line: China is hooked on Persian Gulf oil and the Gulf Arabs, as well as Iran and Iraq, are intent on keeping the product flowing eastward. The Chinese are experts in the use of oil as a tool of foreign policy to influence the actions of Middle East countries. But right in the middle are the always vigilant Americans who also understand this, their hands safely within reach of the all-important Gulf oil shut-off valve.

Like all nations, China worries over "chokepoints," such as the Malacca Strait, through which all Middle Eastern oil reaches Asian countries. This is the likely reason behind China's ratification of the U.N. Convention on Law of the Sea, which guarantees uninterrupted, free-flow of legal shipping on the high seas. They had previously opposed this convention prior to their Mideast oil dependence.

The Peoples' Republic is one of the world's largest oil consumers and importers of crude. In fact, in the not-too-distant future China will import more oil than Japan, Australia, and New Zealand combined. Lack of an efficient infrastructure has raised the cost of supplying needed energy to all regions. However, Communist government controls have kept artificial caps on prices, further clogging the system, making it costly and without critical market incentives. Most infrastructure development is in coastal areas, further entrenching the Chinese dependence on foreign oil and gas shipped in by supertanker.

Existing Chinese Far Eastern offshore oil cannot satisfy more than 10% of demand. China's old stand-by, the Tarim Basin oil field, is dilapidated and needs massive capital outlays to increase dwindling production. The distance between large industrial regions and the key cities is another factor. In sum, China has been "forced" to connect with cheap Middle East oil, usually offered at a discount to world prices. On the one hand, China views the United States as key to its economic success, because the U.S. buys so many products from China. On the other, they see the U.S. as a danger to their energy security and prime obstacle to eventual Chinese superpower status.

Having learned much from the highly vulnerable Japanese model of energy dependence, China is now demanding a prominent place in the "energy food chain." For their own security, as well as to be a respected, global force, they must become a prime energy player in the Middle East. China's greatest obstacle is that the U.S. wants to effectively bridle them. Herein lies the challenge, with the Persian Gulf region playing the principal role. Chinese forays into the Middle East, principally with Iran, and in the Sudan, have been to trade weapons for oil. China is watching and waiting and will do whatever it takes, within reason, to limit American influence in this vital region.[39]

For example, China has sent Iran entire factories for the production of chemical weapons, selling the Iranians tons of industrial chemicals which could be used to manufacture nerve agents. Leaked U.S. intelligence reports claim that China may have sold Iran equipment and vaccines for biological weapons production. As well, they have shipped nuclear equipment and technology that could be used to manufacture nuclear weapons, though claiming the technology is for Iran's civilian nuclear program. Chinese technicians traveled to Iran to build a new uranium conversion plant, and have been reported working along side Iranians in missile production plants and facilities.

China sells weapon systems to Iran for primarily two reasons: to enhance political ties with this key oil producing Gulf nation, and to provide badly needed foreign exchange for the Chinese weapons industry. Obviously, maintaining close ties to Iran is a priority, as most other Gulf oil producers are now strongly influenced, even controlled, by the United States.[40]

Global economic success and world leadership is at the *heart* of national security and the continuance of Communist Party control in China. These primal issues also drive American Middle East policy absolutely, and, by design, are veiled. Thus President Bush and his team of specialists are not executing the sinister nor nefarious. They are skilled in what they do and are acting in America's, as well as the world's, best interest. Many dictators and terrorists are salivating over control of this pivotal Gulf region, and most are not nearly as pleasant as Bush, Cheney, and Rice. They are found scheming in Tehran, in Beijing, and in a dozen and more lands and nations.

Hunting down and killing terrorists not only makes us feel better, it has, in some cases, slowed down the murderous ones for a time. However, even more important is that continued U.S. presence in Muslim oil-lands of the Gulf lessens the organized and coordinated threat from nations sponsoring and financing terrorist attacks. Though poorly understood by most Americans, oil access and control, military power, and global security, peace, and prosperity are all vitally linked, as detailed above.

Make no mistake, America is at war, and we are fighting for our lives. Just don't expect the Europeans, the Chinese, and especially the Ayatollahs in Iran to be even marginally understanding. The stakes are just too high.

QUESTION 9

- WHY IS THE ISLAMIC REPUBLIC OF IRAN AT THE TOP OF THE PRESIDENT'S EXCLUSIVE "AXIS OF EVIL" HIT-LIST?

If history teaches us nothing else, it demonstrates over and over how a few good men and women driven by faith, conviction, and vision, can change the world.

The land of Persepolis, of the Magi, the game of chess, the cradle of government bureaucracy, and the land of ancient warriors, Iran is a magical land. Iran is majesty and beauty, the mystery of the harem and a heartland of a great branch of the religion of Islam. Tragically today, however, Iran is dying.

For *2,500 years*, Iran or Persia was led by a *shah* or king of the Pahlavi Dynasty. But in 1979 the oldest continuously reigning dynasty on earth was driven out of Iran. Since then the nation has been ruled not by reason or justice, but by religious fanaticism. These fundamentalist Ayatollahs, masquerading as "prophets of God," call themselves "Imams of the Sacred Line," representing a God who seems determined to beat his loyal subjects into submission.

These fanatical Ayatollahs should study their history. The bleached bones of countless dictators scatter the historical landscape, when the abused and neglected serfs and slaves have finally had enough. That day will come; and when it does Iran's tyrants, too, will not survive the cleansing.

Democracy and freedom are inevitable twin victors over humankind. Since the 1970s, when my cousin took his family to Iran to be the Shah's banker, I have held a fascination with this ancient land, once called Persia. As a boy I heard about the 300 Spartans under the inspired leadership of King Leonidas. He led the desperate battle to defend Greece from the mighty warriors of Xerxes, son of Darius, whose Middle Eastern slave army (numbering perhaps 250,000), came very close to conquering Europe. Had Xerxes prevailed, the foundation of a distinctly evolving European culture, the seedbed of republican freedom, and the later age of discovery and exploration, would have been crushed before it could flower. The great British historian Ernle Bradford tells us: "For over a thousand years the East challenged the West, and the most crucial of all these challenges was that which was now set in motion by Xerxes. Had it succeeded, the Zoroastrian[41] creed might have been imposed upon the...Greeks. There would have been no fifth-century Athens, and all European history would have been very different."[42]

The tyrant government of Xerxes' Persia, however, could never subjugate and hold a freedom-loving people such as the Greeks. The Spartans in particular lived and died to defend their way of life. Xerxes' enormous force conquered and killed King Leonidas and the 300 Spartans he led that day at the Battle of Thermopylae (480 B.C.), Leonidas' dying words: "Go tell the Spartans that we remain here, loyal to our law and to our word."

The following year, remembering King Leonidas' sacrifice for his homeland, *40,000* Spartans, the finest warriors on earth, decked out in red cloaks (to hide their blood from the enemy), including many more Greek allies, met Xerxes' army on the plains of Plataea and utterly annihilated their Persian foe. The unselfish sacrifice of their Spartan king, Leonidas, had served to rally Greece to victory. Once driven from Europe, the Persians never returned...until today.

Europe, 1997. After several years of official hand-wringing, the German high court finally handed down a verdict indicting the Iranian government for at least *sixty* assassinations of Iranian dissidents seeking refuge in Europe. Although the United States had for years been trying to convince the Europeans that Iran was secretly carrying out these killings on their soil, European governments, mostly for mercenarial and political reasons, turned a blind eye to the murders and ignored U.S. government warnings.

According to the German high court in their long-delayed judgment, the assassinations were ordered by Iran's "Committee for Special Operations." This committee included the then President of Iran, Ali Akbar Heshemi Rafsanjani, Secret Service Chief Ali Fallahian, Foreign Minister Ali Akbar Velayati, and Iran's spiritual leader, the Ayatollah Ali Khamenei. In other words, these assassinations were ordered at the highest level of Iranian government. Of course such top-level government criminal activity issuing from

Iran was no surprise to the Americans. And if they would be honest about it, it was probably not to the Germans, either.

Following the indictment, the Iranian Ayatollahs pressured the Germans by reminding them of how "helpful Iran had been" in the release of German hostages held in Lebanon by Hezbollah, a vicious Iranian terrorist ally. In other words Iran was saying, "You play our game, or we hurt you. And all you Westerners (Europeans and Americans), because of your freedom and openness and your global business and diplomatic activities, you are *most* vulnerable to our wide-ranging assassins. Our terrorists are 'everywhere you want to be,' so back off...or else."

This pattern of Iranian blackmail and extortion, with the alternate "carrot" of possible lucrative oil and weapons contracts in Iran, continues today. The Europeans, Russians, and Chinese appear particularly susceptible to such "incentives." French officials resist imposing restrictions on the Islamic Republic of Iran, stating that "commercial and political issues should be kept separate." When it comes to lucrative commercial contracts the French are always short on scruples and long on greed.

Of course, many Europeans believe that eventually Iran will be the key player in the Gulf and a regional power that must be dealt with. These analysts believe it unwise to alienate Tehran, its secretive, fundamentalist regime, and its many terrorist allies. A good example of Iran's arm-twisting and thuggish methods can be seen in the 1990 French presidential pardon of Anis Naccache, a terrorist convicted of the attempted murder of an Iranian dissident living in France. To force the French to pardon Naccache, Hezbollah, Iran's Shi'ite ally in Lebanon, offered to release French hostages taken for that very purpose. Obviously the French got the message right away and buckled, fearful that Iran and her Shi'ite allies could strike anywhere, anytime.

Certainly the Spanish received just such a message on March 11, 2004, when multiple bombs went off almost simultaneously on Spanish trains, killing 201 people, and wounding 1,500, apparently executed by Islamic extremists tied to al-Qaeda.

Once again, as in ages past, the West (America and Europe) is locked in a conflict with forces attacking from the Middle East, its deadly terrorists, its assassination squads and killers for hire. Perhaps the motivations have changed over the centuries, and so has the weaponry, but the danger is still very real for both America and Europe. Once again the West needs a Leonidas, a leader willing to sacrifice himself or herself, if necessary, to drive the enemy back and seek out and annihilate its shrouded assassins.

In 1997, the United States Information Agency (USIA) reported that: *"Tehran is trying to prevent the 'illegitimate influence' of the United States in the Persian Gulf, the Middle East, Central Asia, the Caspian Sea region, and the Caucasus, and is unwilling, like Russia, to accept the expansionism of the United States and some of its allies in these regions. Tehran welcomes the promotion of relations between countries such as China and Russia, in order to fight against Washington's hegemony in regional and international calculations...such relations could increase Russia's capacity to gain its historic position against the West and could help Iran increase its capacity to maneuver against the United States...*[43]

In the mid-1990s, 19 U.S. airmen were killed in a powerful blast in Eastern Saudi Arabia at the Kobar Towers. 500 were injured. Though the Clinton Administration promised to investigate fully, the results were never officially released, and the Administration at that time apparently was concerned over letting the cards fall where they may for fear of actually having to respond to the attack and hit back. Though the FBI investigation led straight to Brigadier General Ahmad Sharifi of the Iranian Revolutionary Guard, the Administration refused to act, perhaps hoping that what they thought were the beginnings of democracy in Iran "might be harmed if the U.S. appeared hostile."

According to hard FBI evidence, however, Sharifi had selected the American target in Kobar at the behest of the Ayatollah Ali Khamenei, with Iran providing the explosives and equipment, and then training the attackers. What would become a pattern throughout the 1990s, the United States failed to respond to the many attacks of that decade, thus emboldening the terrorists. President Clinton did write Iran's President Khatami asking for his help in the investigation. Khatami wrote back stating that he didn't know what Clinton was talking about. In frustration, the then FBI director Louis Freeh decided to wait for a change of administrations in Washington (in 2000). Since 9/11, President Bush has had his sights on Iran, which has been for a number of years the number one backer of terrorism in the world, receiving top billing on his "Axis of Evil" hit list.

Effectively living as they are in the Middle Ages, the Ayatollahs of Iran are destined for destruction, to the dust-bin of history, unless they change. The modern world, with its sweeping information and technology, will wash over the Ayatollahs and cleanse the ancient land of Persia far more effectively than a phalanx army of Spartan warriors. It is inevitable, in fact. In the end, I predict, the Islamic world will finally accept democracy and openness, "discovering" that this was the kind of government the Prophet Muhammad "had wanted all along and from the beginning."

Before we reach that shore, however, I fear we must traverse treacherous seas. Men, women, and children will die to placate the tyrannical Ayatollahs' lust for power and their drive to capture the "prize" of the Gulf and spread Allah's faith worldwide.

Follow-up: About the Iran threat: What did we know and when did we know it?

On September 21st, and again on October 5th, 2000, the 106th Congress of the United States held special hearings on the threat from Iran, which was (and is) aggressively building ballistic missiles and weapons of mass destruction, including nuclear weapons. Iran's principal suppliers: Russia, China, and North Korea.

Since this was prior to September 11th 2001, the hearings appeared, at least from reading the transcripts, less than urgent, particularly when considering the hopelessly naïve assessment of the Iranian threat as reported by State Department "experts" in attendance. From the transcripts, in fact, it appeared that the majority of Senators on the committee were not even in attendance.

Of course, this was an election year, George Bush and Al Gore were locked in a heated contest, the margins razor-thin. Still, considering the nature of the building storm rising from the Islamic Republic of Iran, such bureaucratic passivity seems irresponsible at best. Historically America has coddled or ignored a variety of tyrants, stroking, often rewarding these thugs who mean to do us ill.

America has always been slow to anger.

For example, in response to a senator's questioning, Ambassador Robert J. Einhorn, Assistant Secretary of State for Nonproliferation said, referring to Russian and Chinese assistance to Iran's weapon's program: "Clearly, many of the remaining problems involve shortcomings in the relatively new Russian system of export control. Even with greater resources and the best of intention, it would be hard for Moscow authorities to detect and stop all attempts to circumvent Russian controls, but equally clearly, part of the problem is a lack of determination (on the part of the Russians).

"We are convinced that if Russian leaders gave the matter sufficient priority, Iran's nuclear and missile procurement efforts in Russia could be stopped... We do not doubt the Russians when they say their interest would be harmed at least as much as ours by Iran's acquisition of these capabilities, but if the Russians believe that (their) nuclear and missile cooperation (with Iran) now underway will not actually contribute materially to and accelerate Iran's acquisition of such a capability, they are engaging in wishful or short-sighted thinking."

Too often our *own* leaders have been likewise wistfully engaged. Sometimes we want something so badly, or we cannot envision the pain it will require to correct the situation, that we find ourselves "hugging the delusive phantom of hope," as the American patriot Patrick Henry once warned.[44] The Russians have no intention of halting such profitable arms deliveries. As well, they are gaining unprecedented access to a key Persian Gulf nation. In sum, they are "in the game."

The Ambassador continued: "Recently we have seen some encouraging signs. At their July (2000) meeting at the Okinawa G-8 summit, President Putin assured President Clinton that he would take personal responsibility for ensuring that Russia's laws and commitments with respect to these nonproliferation issues are carried out faithfully... We *hope* that this action will be a forerunner of concrete and decisive steps to halt assistance by Russian entities to missile and nuclear programs in Iran."

Hope? There's that word again. President Putin is a former KGB officer. In the KGB you live or die by your wits. The Russians exist in a shrouded world of pay-offs (and payback) and of course broad-based, endemic corruption. Even if Ambassador Einhorn believes that President Putin is telling the truth, Putin's "truth" will be sufficiently doctored to meet Putin's political needs. The fact is Russian leaders *do not want* to stop selling the Iranians anything and everything lucrative and profitable and by the metric ton.

Finally, Assistant Secretary of State Einhorn concluded: "By the standards one must judge nonproliferation efforts, our policies with respect to Iran have been effective. They have succeeded in slowing and complicating Iran's programs and driving up their costs. They have closed off many of the world's best sources of advanced technology to Iranian procurement efforts and have forced Iran to rely on technologies less sophisticated and reliable than would otherwise be the case and, critically, *we have bought additional time*."[45]

Tragically, that is all we have done. We are in a race against time as the Islamic Republic continues to acquire these horrible weapons, and to train personnel, including a host of terrorists, on how to use them against *us*. To Ambassador Robert J. Einhorn's credit, he does hit it on the mark explaining the Iranian motivation for their weapon's program: "Even if democracy succeeds in Iran (referring to the "election" of Iran's president, Muhammad Khatami), there is little to suggest that its quest for weapons of mass destruction and missile delivery systems will end… it's own non-conventional programs *bolster its aspirations for influence in the Gulf region*, and *leadership in the Islamic world*…(and) to persist on the dangerous course on which it is now headed."[46]

Perhaps the best example of the Clinton Administration's past willingness to cater to and accommodate the Ayatollahs in Iran— Clinton's so-called "strategy of accommodation"—and the U.S. Government's willingness to overlook obvious signs of growing danger, is found in the Spring, 2000, edition of *The National Interest*, by Ray Takeyh. Outlining the Ayatollah's devious and unmistakable passion to acquire weapons of mass destruction, and to drive the Americans from the Persian Gulf region, Mr. Takeyh concludes: "But for Iran, the intensely coveted aim of regional mastery requires as its precondition the retraction of U.S. power in the Middle East and the marginalization of America's leading ally, Israel. *Iran and the United States are, in short, two states competing over the same territory.* And this is where an (American) strategy of accommodation falters. For no degree of internal liberalization (in Iran) is likely to alter this fundamental clash of interests (between Iran and the U.S.)."[47]

In sum, the United States government has known for more than twenty years that the hard-line Iranian regime is determined to expel the U.S. from the Persian Gulf region and move powerfully to control Gulf lands and oil resources. America's deliberate move into Iraq and Afghanistan is designed, in part, to further encircle Iran and counter the Ayatollahs' overarching objectives in the Gulf. Obviously the United States has been engaged in a high-stakes game of strategic chess with Iran for more than a quarter of a century. The great, but deadly game continues.

Follow-up: What is Iran's Council of Guardians and why is this body important in the War on Terror?

Today Iran is controlled by what is called the Council of Guardians. Iran has but a single political party, though they arrogantly insist that the will of the people is always considered. They even have "elections" periodically, electing a president by "popular vote." Of course the list of candidates must be approved by the Guardians, the 12 ruling Ayatollahs, with the council having ultimate veto power on any electoral decision.

The ultimate source of power in Iran is the Ayatollah Ali Khamenei, appointed supreme leader when the Ayatollah Khomeini died in 1989. The challenge for the Islamic Republic of Iran's regime is the challenge of legitimacy. The Ayatollahs squash student and workers' riots and demonstrations from the intellectual left and commercial groups from the center and right. Most political factions feel wholly estranged from the Ayatollah's hard-line leadership, which they are. This is a theocracy, a purely religious dictatorship.

For governments to remain in power over time, however, they must be effective. They must meet the needs of the people. But since the heady days of the revolution, Iran has been in decline. The Ayatollahs blame the 1980s war with Iraq, or the sanctions imposed by the United States. Still Iran flounders, stirring the desires of ordinary Iranians for better, more responsive government. For America the danger is that in this political limbo the Ayatollahs feel threatened. Indeed, when they are dangerously vulnerable, they are *dangerous*. As a result, they have stepped up support for several terrorist factions outside Iran, as well as buying weapons systems mostly from Russia and China and developing a nuclear weapons program.

In years past, the United States used Saddam and his Iraq as a bulwark against, and counterbalance to, Iran. With Saddam's elimination, the United States is taking a more direct, hands-on approach to containing Iran. America is the only force capable and willing to stand in the way of Iran's long-sought goal of winning regional power and control over not only two-thirds of the world's oil reserves, but the *best* oil and the cheapest to produce.

Following the death of the Ayatollah Khomeini, America hoped for what was called a "Tehran Spring." At first, Iran's leader, Ali Akbar Rafsanjani, appeared somewhat progressive and willing to work with America. In reality, what he wanted were Western loans, which he promptly used to finance massive weapons purchases, acquiring billions of dollars worth of Chinese, European, and Russian equipment. Even to the most optimistic, it was soon obvious Iran had not moderated with the death of Khomeini. Since then, the situation has become more precarious.

Citing sources such as the CIA and the U.S. Department of Defense, an April 2003 report from MSNBC stated: "Iran is branded as the most active state sponsor of terrorism…. State institutions, notably the Revolutionary Guards Corps and the Ministry of Intelligence and Security, are thought to be involved in the planning and execution of terrorist acts and continue to support a variety of groups that use terrorism to pursue their goals. Iran supports and encourages Hezbollah and the Palestinian rejectionist groups—including Hamas, the Palestinian Islamic Jihad, and Ahmad Jibril's Popular Front for the Liberation of Palestine, General Command—with varying amounts of money, training and weapons. Tehran also provides safe haven to elements of Turkey's Kurdish separatists, PKK, and support to terrorist groups in North Africa and South and Central Asia, including financial assistance and training."[48]

During the 1990s, Iran's Council of Guardians appeared almost eager to confront the United States over control of the Persian Gulf region. Many speeches by Ayatollah Khamenei, Rafsanjani, and their recent president, the "moderate" Muhammad Khatami, demanded that the Americans leave the region. Ayatollah Ali Khamenei, in his usual bellicose fashion, called upon Muslims everywhere to rise up and drive the Satanic Americans from the Persian Gulf. He has made use of the "Satanic" label on multiple occasions. At the December 9, 1997, worldwide meeting of the 55-member *Organization of the Islamic Conference,* held in Tehran, Khamenei called upon Muslims to unite so that Muslim countries of the world could take the initiative to oust United States forces from the Persian Gulf, the Islamic Sea. "Isn't the time ripe for the world of Islam to respond to this spirit of arrogance?" He demanded.[49]

Turning aggressively to the Russians and Chinese for weapons help, including weapons of mass destruction, following the first gulf war in 1991, Iranian leaders continually blamed the U.S. military presence in the Gulf as "wholly incompatible with peace and stability." Leading the resistance to American influence in the Gulf, as they have for most of two decades, the Council of Guardians has engaged in secret contacts with some of the world's most dangerous terrorists. U.S. Senatorial hearings have stated that the Council remains determined, eventually, to displace the U.S. in the Persian Gulf region.[50] Such insight into the Council's psyche and objectives prompted experts in the region to comment: "It is difficult to see any future scenario in which Iran doesn't dominate the region, either as a threat, or a power. The alternative is perpetual conflict."[51]

In other words, in the end, *two-thirds* of the world's most strategic and cheapest oil supplies will be controlled by either the United States or the Islamic Republic of Iran and its terror-backing allies. Literally, it is that simple. And driving the clandestine effort to wield terror and force the Americans from the Middle East will continue to be the Council of Guardians.

Follow-up: Iran is a Shi'ite Muslim dictatorship. So how does Iran present a unique challenge for the United States, beyond what was discussed above?

For more than a thousand years Shi'ites have been a people

who mourn: men flaying themselves with whips and chains, heads and faces with blood smeared; ritualistically a small boy is raised high to the crowd, drenched in blood as women wail and men shout their allegiance to the *Shi'a i-Ali*, or Ali's Partisans. This is the holy month of *Muharama*, the Month of the Martyrdom, of Hussein, the grandson of the Prophet Muhammad who was murdered by Sunnis as he held his infant son in his arms at Karbala in A.D. 680.

The religion of Islam is divided into two principal branches: Sunni and Shi'ite. The Shi'ites are found principally in Iran (ethnically Persian), Lebanon (ethnically Arab), Yemen, in the south of Iraq (ethnically Arab), and in the Eastern oil provinces of Saudi Arabia, Bahrain, and to some extent, Kuwait. Most of the rest of the Muslim world, from Morocco on the west to the Philippine Island of Mindanao on the east, is Sunni. Amazingly, the largest Muslim nation is Indonesia, located thousands of miles from Muhammad's homeland in the Arabian Peninsula.

Shi'a Islam's legacy is one of sacrifice, blood, and injustice. Among the Shi'a, cultural baggage is stacked to the ceiling. The Shi'ites are the picked-on and abused cousins of Islam which should have received, they believe, the highest honors from mainstream Muslims, because the Shi'a claim descendancy directly from the Prophet Muhammad.

Essentially, Shi'ites differ from Sunnis in their understanding of rightful Islamic heritage and earthly authority. Shi'ites claim divine license through Ali, the cousin and son-in-law of the Prophet, and believe that the House of Islam should follow a legitimate, direct descendent of Muhammad.

Sunnis, on the other hand, maintain that authority to lead the Islamic community is found in the Holy Qur'an alone. Sunnis believe that religious leaders, called *"imams,"* should be chosen by Muslims based upon consensus, as well as their individual piety, strength, and wisdom, and the high level of respect freely given by their followers. The prophet's grandson, Hussein, was murdered by the consensus oriented Sunnis, producing the split in Islamdom that continues to this day. Hussein was killed near Karbala, an Iraqi city south of Baghdad, and a most sacred shrine for past and present Shi'ite pilgrims.

Iraq contains two of the world's holiest Shi'ite pilgrimage shrines. The Americans now have control over these ancient prizes, which are proudly situated near some of the world's largest and most important fields of oil and gas. The United States has a tiger by the tail.

This rift in the faith of Islam has continued for 1,400 years as the Shi'ites cling to their separatist beliefs. Of the 1.25 billion Muslims in the world today, nearly 90% are Sunni, with about 10% Shi'ite. Following America's disastrous experience in Lebanon with the Shi'ite during the 1980s, Shi'ites became known to America as fanatics, assassins, terrorists, and suicide bombers. It is a deserved reputation, one they have earned.[52]

Since the 1990s, however, the principal enemy, the one inflicting the most damage on America, has been radical Sunnis, products of predominantly Saudi and Egyptian Islamic hotbeds of American hatred. While there is evidence of cooperation between the two sects against the greater enemy (America), generally Sunnis and Shi'ites tend to hate each so much mutual assistance is out of the question. However, there are times when 1,400 years of animosity may be set aside. It is no longer safe to believe these sects will not unite to kill Americans. Actually they have, several times we know of, over the past decade.

With the overthrow of the Shah of Iran in 1979, the Gulf's Sunni Arab princes have lived beneath the always threatening shadow of The Great Imam, Ayatollah Khomeini. This threat has drastically altered their method of governing the indigenous Shi'ite locals residing along the "Pirate Coast." (The Pirate Coast, the area between Southern Iraq and Oman in the Persian Gulf, traditionally a cauldron of Shi'ite raiding, smuggling, assassination, warfare and terrorism in the name of Allah—opportunistic trader one day, then pious pilgrim, finally bloody pirate, depending upon the type of victim, er...*customer* at hand.)

Knowing this, the Arabian Sunni rulers live cautious lives. Feeling a bit heathen by comparison to their zealously religious cousins in Iran, Sunni leaders have attempted to match Shi'ite fervor by outward displays of religiosity, supporting Saudi *imams* who change school textbooks to include wholesale "Death to America" chapters and verses. Both sides are attempting to "out-religion" one another. Sheik Salman al-Awdah, a leading Saudi Islamic teacher, wrote in a much circulated text: "America—we urgently call upon God Almighty to destroy its economy and society, to transform its states into countries and turn them against each other and to make it an example to all nations."[53] Americans everywhere are justified in asking: "Why do they hate us so?"

So, the competition for "Allah's favor" rolls forth. The Shi'ites who reside in the al-Ahsa Province, the so-called "oil province" of eastern Saudi Arabia, number about 500,000. Closely monitored by the Saudi police and military, they are forbidden to celebrate important Shi'ite religious ceremonies during holidays. They live frustrated, angry lives. Many seek a scapegoat.

The 20th century was the age of the oil boom. The Shi'ite villages in Arabia are located near the richest oil fields. Many Shi'ites were hired to work the fields by ARAMCO, the Arabian-American Oil Company, a joint venture between the Saudi rulers and the Americans. Following the Shah's expulsion from Iran, the Shi'ites in Arabia, with Iranian backing, revolted. In November 1979 the Saudi National Guard brutally suppressed the Shi'ite uprising. The rulers of modern-day Saudi Arabia, followers of the Wahhabi sect from the interior of Arabia, rule a rebellious land of oasis cities, not unlike an archipelago of islands in a sea of sand.

With the American war in Iraq and the ousting of Saddam Hussein, Shi'ites are once again in the spotlight. Numbering about 60% of the Iraqi population, the Shi'ites will command significant power in an emerging democracy. The once downtrodden Shi'ite community, commanding a solid majority, may want to exact some type of revenge on their Sunni overlords, so long protected by Saddam's military and security apparatus. Only the Americans stand in their way.

Many Shi'ite leaders who remained in Iraq through 25 years of Saddam's brutality cannot accept those Iraqis returning with American forces, such as the Iraqi leader-in-exile, Ahmad Chalabi, who is Shi'ite, but has not lived in Iraq for 45 years. Iraqis living safely and comfortably in the United States or Europe, while Saddam raged, and during the bloody eight-year Iran-Iraq War, are the brunt of jokes and criticized by locals as waiting safely to cash in on the spoils. Many believe such brazen arrogance on the part of these exiles, and on the part of the Americans, guarantees their failure. Local clerics preach time and again from the pulpit of local mosques that only those who lived with and survived Saddam's butchery have the *right* to lead Iraq.

Early in the U.S. occupation, Sheikh Kadim al-Abade, a lesser cleric leader in the Shi'ite enclaves of Baghdad, spoke to a Friday gathering of about thirty-thousand worshippers. Accusing the Americans of wanting to take over and steal Iraq, he claimed that the Americans were using their night vision goggles to see through Iraqi women's clothing; that Iraqi women were being abducted by U.S. forces to use as prostitutes; and that children were given candy wrapped in pornographic pictures. He closed his sermon advocating that Muslims carry out terrorist attacks against the Americans.

Rather than arresting and punishing such sources of lies and disinformation, U.S. forces asked more moderate clerics for assistance. Other, senior clerics, countered the statements made by al-Abade, after U.S. troops allowed Shi'ite leaders to look through night vision goggles and assured them that no Iraqi women were being kept in such a fashion.

Other leading clerics censured al-Abade and now require that all speeches be cleared by senior religious leaders in advance. And while many moderate clerics apologized to the Americans for the rash comments, the struggle continues, the daily necessity of relaying the truth to the people and countering the ongoing lies. This is a war of education as much as anything. Most Middle Easterners are politically savvy and accustomed to being bombarded by rumors and falsehoods. They know that every leader is bias, never completely trusted. With the right approach, the United States can win this war of truth verses lies, but it will take much skill and time.

America cannot allow a radical Shi'ite state, patterned after Iran, to be established in the land between the two rivers. Such a nation would immediately become a haven for terrorists and control prime oil resources and nearly unlimited funds to back terrorist operations and weapons acquisition.

Following the U.S. military move on Afghanistan in the

fall of 2001 to root out the Taliban and al-Qaeda, intelligence increasingly showed that al-Qaeda terrorists, in large numbers, were seeking refuge in Iran. In fact, several senior al-Qaeda leaders are reportedly hiding there, presumably with the knowledge of the Iranian government. While Iran claims to have arrested a number of al-Qaeda fighters, little information on those arrests was provided to the U.S. or its allies. Most experts assume these "arrests" were simply more window dressing.

So, where does Iran stand? What are Iran's goals following the powerful U.S. move next door into Iraq?

My greatest fear is at some future time America will be blindsided in a devastating way, more so than 9/11. For located near the U.S. naval base at Manama, Bahrain, the headquarters of the U.S. Fifth Fleet, led by an aircraft carrier task force, is a place called "al-dahna." *al-dahna*, in *Gulf* Arabic, means "pearl." America's next Pearl Harbor may be coming in the treacherous waters of the Persian Gulf, *if* we are not extremely vigilant.

As an Iranian businessman once warned me, a man with much experience in the region (see the book *The Middle East War Process* by the author, Chapter 1): *One night out of the fog of the Gulf, ten sleek attack boats will speed, each driven by a zealot, a member of the "Islamic Sons of Jihad," an as yet unknown fanatical faction (a fictitious group, used here as an example only), each boat equipped with a small, tactical nuclear weapon.*[54] *And while most suicide boats are destroyed in the water before they reach their target, one pushes through and detonates near our aircraft carrier. And in one horrible moment, ten thousand U.S. sailors, soldiers and airmen are sacrificed on their ships and in port facilities.* At that moment, if you are the U.S. president, what do you tell the American people? How do you explain the catastrophic and horrid loss? Can you envision the national political upheaval? Can you imagine the uproar in the American media? "What are we doing over there?" They would shout. "All the oil in the world is not worth the life of a single U.S. serviceman or woman!" The commentators would wail and lament. "They've got to sell the stuff (oil) to someone. Why are we even there?" On and on they would rage; and whomever happened to be president at the time would be finished. If he did not resign, he would be impeached, or certainly voted out in the next election.

Of course, after the attack the Iranians would immediately deny any connection to the "Islamic Sons of Jihad," claiming they are an "independent rogue faction." With enough distance, Iran believes it could avoid U.S. retaliation, also believing that a "weak and vacillating" American populous will demand the U.S. immediately pull out all remaining forces from the Persian Gulf and flee the Middle East entirely. Americans, the Islamic fanatics believe, have "forgotten how to die" and are weak and politically divided at home. Quoting the zealots' own words (al-Qaeda or Hezbollah, as examples; there are many others) "America is a land of women and rich, spoiled children. America can be beaten because Americans fear the sight of their own blood. More so, they are a godless, cowardly people, hiding behind their wealth and technology."

Obviously Islamic radicals have made the fatal mistake of lumping all Americans into the same boat. As well, President Bush's strong response in Iraq and Afghanistan has set this line of thinking back a bit for the moment, though most terrorists still actively promote the notion of American weakness in every Muslim mosque and *madressa*. Past, and certainly future, terrorist attacks will be conceived, directed, and executed on the belief that this assessment of American resolve—or lack thereof—the Michael Moore Syndrome—is on the mark and accurate. Therefore, it will take much more American determination to stay the course and once and for all shatter these erroneous notions of American weakness. To our advantage (perhaps) the terrorists have forgotten Omaha Beach, Little Round Top, and Bunker Hill.

I only hope Americans have not.

Follow-up: Who are the most deadly, and most effective, terrorists in the world?

Recently Deputy Secretary of State Richard Armitage described Hezbollah as the "A-team of terrorists." His words seemed to place this Shi'ite-inspired clandestine army above the al-Qaeda Organization of Osama bin Laden in its well-known death-skills.

America's track record with Hezbollah, the "Party of God," is tragic and abysmal. Hundreds of Americans have lost their lives to these suicide warriors. Best known are the 243 American Marines killed in Lebanon on October 23, 1983 when a dump truck loaded with Iranian-supplied explosives crashed into their barracks and blew up. That one loss at the hands of Hezbollah, it seemed, was enough to drive the Americans from Lebanon and set a precedent, an image of American timidity we have been trying to shake ever since. Many within the U.S. military establishment believe that Hezbollah deserves payback and that inevitably it will come.

The A-team of terrorists? Perhaps. Such assessment has merit when considering sheer numbers of fighters, past track-records of deadly attacks, training, and most importantly, Iranian backing. For now, however, Hezbollah appears to have adapted a wait and see attitude regarding American intentions in Iraq and the Gulf. Besides, it is, for the most part, out of their region of influence.

Commanding broad-based support throughout Lebanon, Syria, and in other regions, Hezbollah is a complex creature. In Lebanon, the heart of Hezbollah territory, the organization is viewed as essential to Shi'ite survival. The organization receives millions of dollars in support—cash, weaponry, medicine, training, and equipment—from fellow Shi'ites in Iran and elsewhere. Hezbollah is regarded as anything but terrorist in the poor Shi'ite regions of South Lebanon. There the organization runs hospitals, schools, orphanages, and the equivalent of soup kitchens, as well as providing security forces for crime prevention and peace keeping in the streets. They even have a construction team which quickly rebuilds Shi'ite homes, businesses, schools, and clinics damaged in fighting.

It would be virtually impossible for the government of Lebanon to attempt to dismantle Hezbollah. Sheikh Hassan Nasrallah, spiritual leader of the group, addressed a gathering of thousands of followers in Beirut in 2003 to celebrate the end of the Shi'ite sacred month of Muharama. He announced that "today was the beginning of the end of the American era in Iraq and the region." The Sheikh seemed to claim "special inspiration" on the topic of America's coming "death" in the Middle East and the world. Coming from Hezbollah, this is troubling.

The well-known yellow flags of the "Party of God" are found in Lebanon, Southern Iraq, Syria, Yemen, and of course, Iran, the motherland, bankroller, and inspiration of Hezbollah. The Party's humanitarian efforts are viewed by outsiders as Hezbollah's attempt to win the hearts and minds of Muslims to accept the "real work," that of terrorism and armed resistance against the enemy of the Shi'ites. This is Jihad, or Holy War (struggle). Hezbollah discovered that the collection of donations through outwardly legitimate humanitarian front-organizations is one of the best ways to do it. As "cover-for-action," such humanitarian work can be the finest smoke screen to cover terrorist operations.

Hezbollah continues to stockpile weapons and ammunition in Shi'ite controlled areas of South Lebanon. For what purpose? Shi'ite fighters will be ready when and if Israel (or anyone else) determines to return. Israel was driven out of Lebanon in 2001, principally by Hezbollah suicide fighters. These commandos and insurgents operate camps in Lebanon, training members of the Palestinian terrorist groups Hamas and Islamic Jihad; they also maintain contact and cooperate clandestinely with al-Qaeda. Hezbollah supports cells in many major world cities, including within the United States and Canada. They control several regional TV and radio stations and operate a number of websites.

In Lebanon, Hezbollah is a reality the U.S. and Israel must prepare to deal with. Short of a massive and brutal military campaign, and the total elimination of millions of Shi'ites in the region, South Lebanon will remain Hezbollah country. This deadly and motivated Islamic army will continue as a threat for some time, both to Israel, and to future strategic objectives of United States in the Middle East.

Hezbollah's principal backer and motivator and the key to controlling this deadly group is found in Iran, Hezbollah's spiritual headwaters. And as the United States and the Islamic Republic of Iran face off in the Gulf over control in Iraq and control over oil resources, Hezbollah prepares for martyrdom.

QUESTION 10

- TAQIYA—"WHEN A LIE IS NOT A LIE"—WAS A CRITICAL CHAPTER IN YOUR PREVIOUS BOOK. WILL YOU REVISIT IT HERE?

> *Hadrat Ali, cousin of the Prophet Muhammad, once said that on the battlefield one could not observe the highest standard of truth as a Muslim has been exhorted to do in matters of religion. For example on the battlefield one has to "hide facts and outwit the enemy."*
> —Hadith Sahih Muslim, Vol. 2, #1446

ISLAMIC IMPERATIVE

Taqiya is the necessary, even required, deception of God's enemy in order to protect God's true religion and His true believers. A lie is not a lie when executed in Allah's name and for His protection.

In dealing with Islamic fundamentalism, it is essential to comprehend an ancient Middle East practice of protecting, and then spreading, radical religion. In Arabic the practice is known as *taqiya*. Though often credited to the Shi'ite branch of Islam, taqiya is not exclusively Islamic. It is an ancient practice found in nearly every sect, creed and religion of the region.

One of the most important chapters of my book, *THE MIDDLE EAST WAR PROCESS: The Truth Behind America's Middle East Challenge* (AuthorHouse Publishers, USA; 2003) introduced the practice of taqiya, or the cloaking of the truth for "worthy" ends. Taqiya is dissembling in all its forms. Understanding taqiya is absolutely critical in comprehending the danger America faces today from many terrorist groups worldwide.

Without a doubt taqiya (sometimes spelled *taqqiya* or *taqiyya*) is the product of religion under siege. In our comfortable, prosperous and secure America we struggle to comprehend what it would be like:

a life under constant attack, trying to exist with a brutal, predatory government breathing down our necks, a world of absolutist dictators, of endemic insecurity. This *is* the Middle East. Perhaps what Americans felt the morning of September 12th 2001 gave us just a tiny taste. But most nations of the Islamic world have known little beyond a deadly struggle for survival throughout history. From ashes of hopeless insecurity, destruction, and exploitation creeps this virtual yet all-encompassing institution of taqiya.

Taqiya is more effective perhaps than any weapon on earth when used against a free and open society. In the United States where the assumption of innocence before guilt is the standard we live by, it is easy to see how America could be sucker-punched as we were on 9/11. Since taqiya requires the deception of the enemy in order to protect Allah and his loyal followers, all bets are off when dealing with the Taliban, or with al-Qaeda, or the many Islamic terrorists, strongmen, or dictators. Check your civilized rules at the door. Taqiya is all-out warfare in the name of God, no holds barred.

To Muslim fundamentalists and terrorists, America and the West (Europe) are populated by "deadly conspirators" and non-believers. To protect the security of the Islamic faithful when confronted by the non-believer, it is perfectly acceptable to practice this form of skilled, clandestine deception. Taqiya is not only sin-free, it is mandatory. "He who has no taqiya has no religion."[55]

Of course, motive is everything. Ideally taqiya is to be used *only* in defense of Godly things, and to protect the virtue and honor of women, the family, as well as household and personal belongings, lands and possessions. Unfortunately, to the ever rationalizing and often desperate fundamentalist mind, God can be found in every dusty, dirty hovel, and in every worldly pursuit. Religion can be a most flexible shield, and an always compliant (and pliable) excuse. In the Middle East as a whole, *especially* in Iran, Iraq, and Lebanon among the Shi'a, we forget taqiya at our peril.

Some of my Muslim friends have argued that, yes, among the Shi'ites taqiya is very much a part of the religion. However, among the majority of Muslims, meaning among the *Sunni* majority, taqiya is not valid.

This statement is untrue. Historically, numerous examples exist of the use of taqiya by the Sunni mainstream of Islam, by Sunni leaders and scholars, as well as by the Prophet Muhammad himself. According to important research by a leading scholar at the American University of Beirut, Dr. S. Makarem, historical evidence proves taqiya was practiced not only by Shi'ites, but also Sunnis and the Khawarij, as well as Islamic philosophers and various Sufi sects.[56]

An example, as revealed in the Hadith, tells of a believer, Ammar Ibn Yasir. Following the Hijra, the migration of the followers of Muhammad to the city of Medina (Yathrib), some of the followers of the Prophet were captured by Muhammad's enemies in Mecca. Ammar Ibn Yasir and his parents were taken and tortured in an attempt to force them to renounce Muhammad. Ammar's parents refused to denounce Islam and were tortured to death.

In order to escape, however, Ammar told his captors that he no longer believed Muhammad's words and had left Islam and accepted idol worship. Upon his release he fled to the Prophet. Approaching Muhammad, Ammar lamented his deeds and his lack of faith before the enemies of Islam. Ammar asked the Prophet if he had sinned for claiming disbelief in order to save his life. Muhammad assured Ammar that he had done his duty to survive and escape, no matter what he had said, if he was still loyal in his heart. Muhammad then revealed the following verse, which is in the Qur'an: "Anyone who, after accepting faith in Allah, utters unbelief, *except under compulsion, his heart remaining firm in faith*, but such as open their breast to unbelief, on them is Wrath of Allah, and theirs will be a dreadful penalty."[57] (Italics added.)

And from the Sunni Muslim scholar Sahih Bukhari's research on the Hadith, the sayings of the Prophet Muhammad: "Following the conquest of the city of Khaybar by the Muslim army, the Prophet was visited by Hajaj Ibn Aalat who asked: 'O Prophet of Allah, I have (remaining) in enemy-held Mecca some of my excess wealth and property, and some family members. I would like to get them back. Am I excused to bad-mouth or denigrate you in order to escape persecution (and get back my property)?' The prophet allowed him to do so, telling him: 'Say whatever you have to say.'"[58] Sahih al-Bukhari added that "it is acceptable to smile at a person while your heart curses him."[59]

Quoting from the al-Islam encyclopedia.org: *It has been demonstrated under the section of "Sunni Sources In Support of al-Taqiyya" that it is permissible to lie to save oneself, as al-Ghazzali asserted; and that it is legitimate to utter words of unbelief as al-Suyuti stated; and that it is acceptable to smile at a person while your heart curses him as al-Bukhari confirms; and that al- Taqiyya is an INTEGRAL part of the Quran itself, as has been shown under the section of "The Quran Speaks: al-Taqiyya vs. Hypocrisy;" and that it was practiced by one of the MOST notable companions of the Prophet (PBUH&HF), none other than 'Ammar Ibn Yasir (May Allah Reward him GENEROUSLY); and we have seen that al-Suyuti narrates that al-Taqiyya is permissible until the Day of Judgment; and that a person can say anything he wants, even to badmouth the Prophet (PBUH&HF)if he is in a dangerous and restrictive situation; and we have also seen that even the Prophet (PBUH&HF) himself practiced al-Taqiyya in a manner of diplomacy that served to advance good relations among the people. Furthermore, the Prophet did not disclose his mission for the first three years of his prophethood, which was, in fact, another practice of al-Taqiyya by the Prophet to save the young Islam from annihilation.*[60]

Though most Americans have never heard of it, taqiya is as formidable a weapon today as it was in ancient times. Today scholars identify taqiya as the equivalent of deception or disinformation, covert action, or techniques often associated with intelligence organizations in the modern world. Here it is unique due to its very ancient religious origin and prophetic sanction, yet many modern Muslims, certainly many mainstream American Muslims, are perhaps not yet aware of its existence.

It is obvious that for those terror groups and Islamic factions fighting tooth and nail to kill Americans, as well as Israelis, Europeans, and many others, every possible weapon must be used. Of the true believer, Iman Jafar Sadik, a Shi'ite Muslim Iman, reportedly said: "Taqiya is of my religion and of the religion of my forefathers. One who does not keep taqiya he has no religion." On a different occasion, Iman Sadik added, "Fear for your religion and protect it with taqiya."[61]

Over the centuries Muslim scholars have pointed to the Qur'anic verse: "Let not the believers take the unbelievers for friends rather than believers, and whoever does this, *he shall have nothing of God, except when you have to guard yourselves against them for fear.* Allah cautions you to remember Him; For the final goal is to Allah. Say: *'Whether you hide what is in your hearts or reveal it, Allah knows it all...'*"[62] (Italics added.)

As the *al-Tawhid*, "the Unity" or the Islamic conquest of the Arabian Peninsula swept forward, and then the *Fatah*, "the Opening" or Arab penetration into the Christian Lands of the Middle East (Egypt, Palestine, Lebanon, Syria), effectively taqiya became institutionalized. Its ancient cultural roots were sanctified and blessed by a Muslim's divine mission to spread Allah's word at all cost. It was, in effect, mandated and canonized. Taqiya became a tool, perhaps more accurately a *weapon*, as acceptable as the scimitar or lance. After all, the lands of the enemy were titled "Dar al-Harb," the House of War, by the Holy Prophet, to be conquered, bought-off, neutralized, and subdued without fail.

In spite of today's many Muslim pundits and apologists (including President Bush) lauding and extolling the "peaceful origins" of the faith, history and the facts testify otherwise. Fundamentalist, highly expansionist Islam is anything but "peace promoting." Most fundamentalists claim that as "God's true religion," in the end Islam *must* be spread throughout the world. As in medieval Christianity, the sword was, and is, all too often the preferred method; though clandestine deception is more likely utilized by the radicals, a highly effective and complimentary weapon when used in conjunction with the sword.

According to the Hans Wehr Dictionary of Modern Written Arabic[63] the root word for taqiya is *ittaqa*, "to fear God (more than man)." The meaning of *taqiya* is: "fear, caution, prudence and the dissimulation (hiding, cloaking) of one's religion under duress or in the face of threats." Also related is the word *muttaqin*, meaning "god-fearing."

Taqiya is also practiced within factional and heretical movements of Islam, as well as modern Islamic terror organizations. Expectedly minority sects and terror groups *require* a strong doctrine of cloaking and dissimulation to survive. As has been stated, Shi'ite Islam requires it. Shi'ism is built around the prophecy of the Guardianship of the 12 Holy Imams, descendents of the Prophet Muhammad. One, in fact, known as "the *Mahdi*," is "in hiding" (cloaked) and many believe will return one day soon to exact Allah's revenge against the Americans and Israel and those who stand with them for their oppression of the faithful. The Mahdi will establish a "New World *Islamic* Order," honoring and blessing faithful Muslims for their long-suffering sacrifice and loyalty under duress from the "diseased hand of the infidel."

Sunni Muslims, as well, cannot escape their past use, even outright promotion, of taqiya. (In effect today they are using taqiya in order to deny that taqiya exists!). Perhaps Islam's greatest theologian, Imam Abu Hammid al-Ghazali, said: "If a praiseworthy goal is attainable through both telling the truth and lying, it is unlawful to … (lie) because there is no need for it. When it is possible to achieve such an aim by lying, but not by telling the truth, it is permissible to lie if attaining the goal is permissible."[64]

Certainly among mainstream Muslims, particularly in the United States, such a forced global Islamic "crusade," built upon secrecy and deception, and spread through the use of terror and horrible weaponry, is *not* of God and not what most American Muslims desire or promote. However, these modern Islamic moderates are *not* who we fear. In fact, they are effectively non-players, as long as they remain on the sidelines unwilling to voice their opposition to the murderers and terrorists. This is the heart of the tragedy: a great world religion allowing itself to be hijacked, prostituted, and brutalized by hired killers and zealous fanatics.

Truth is light and openness. If an idea must be cloaked, denied, or "spun" to the world in order to keep it alive, it is probably a false idea and better off eliminated. This is why entering the shadowy mind of the radical, those adopting the Taqiya Principle to more effectively kill Americans, is so critically important to us right now. This is why the religious hierarchy of elders, the radicals of Iran and their Mujahadin (Hezbollah, Hamas, Islamic Jihad, and even al-Qaeda) allies in many lands pose such a threat to America and to the world.

It is imperative we understand that they are *not* motivated by the same set of core-values as are we. "They hate us more than they love their own lives," as repeatedly stated in interviews by the Middle East expert Thomas L. Friedman. This is a war that may be with us a very long time. As the Sunni Islamic scholar al-Suyuti once said: "Al-Taqiya is permissible until the Day of Judgment."

When conciliatory sounds are heard issuing from Tehran, or Karbala, or Riyadh, or Cairo, or from any Islamic leader or mullah, we must first insist on *proof* and then demand *action*. "By their fruits ye shall know them." And if their fruits are rotten? Then it is mandatory on *our* part: Show no mercy.

Obviously the days ahead will require extreme vigilance. Although taqiya is a bald-faced lie, it is a lie often subtle, easily misunderstood by Americans. Truly taqiya is one of the most poignant realities of Middle East-born terror, and a weapon, even a weapon of mass destruction, we may be missing.

(For additional information see *THE MIDDLE EAST WAR PROCESS*, by the author, Chapter III, page 44.)

Follow-up: What other unique cultural challenges exist in dealing with Middle East societies?

BLOOD VENGEANCE

A leading Arab businessman in Irbid, Jordan once spoke to me of Blood Vengeance. Utterly fascinated, I spent much of the evening just asking questions.

As my friend put it: *An oath once sworn can never be forgiven, until executed in God's name and with His holy vengeance. A covenant once spoken can never be forgotten; once uttered, both Heaven and Hell bear record. Only blood satisfies the obligation.*

At the very core of the Arab is the concept of *honor* and *shame*. A man lacking honor is nothing before both God and men. Shame is the mantle of the weak and impotent. Honor killing, the murder of one's own daughter or sister caught with a man who is not a member of the close family, is shrouded in this honor and shame mystique, manifest in the requirement to cleanse the wrong, the shame, with blood. Only blood satisfies the obligation. (For more detailed information see Question #16 [Chapter 16] of this book.)

Obviously these are ancient customs; or more accurately, curses. Still, they exist and are important factors in our understanding. However, more than a few Hadiths of the Prophet (his sacred sayings) state unequivocally that if a man determines an oath is detrimental to his family, or if he finds a better path to follow, he should use his God-given wisdom to choose the better path and renounce his oath. Unfortunately, today, ancient cultural ways, and modern expedience, too often take precedent over God's word, pushing the Prophet and his wisdom to the back of the bus. Blood vengeance is still very much a part of Middle East culture and drives many terrorist acts.

THE ISLAMIC MESSIAH

Many Muslims, particularly the Shi'a, believe the *Mahdi*, or "the one led by God to truth," will soon be revealed. Miraculously, as God's Redeemer, he will convert the world to Islam; he will be the Expected Deliverer, an "Islamic Messiah" of sorts.

"Al-Mahdi" is his title given by Allah, just as many Christians believe that Jesus Christ, when he comes again, will bear the title "Messiah." Muslims do not agree exactly on the nature or purpose of "The One Led by God to the Truth," and Muslims, some who practice the Sunni sect, do not believe in the Mahdi at all. But throughout the Muslim world the name "Mahdi" has power which fires the imagination and brings hope for a Godly future of peace and justice for the world.

For those millions who do believe, the Mahdi will appear in the period of anarchy and destruction which is expected just prior to the end of the world and before the coming of God's (Allah's) kingdom. Evil will abound and *al-Dhazhal* (which in Arabic means "the Deceiver," the equivalent of the Christian Anti-Christ) will rage in the world. The blessed Mahdi will kill *al-Dhazhal* and restore all things to a disbelieving world, though many will not accept the faith taught by God's Messenger and many will be destroyed. One early Muslim writer, Ibn Kathir, predicted that in that day the Qur'an will be disregarded and alms-giving and fasting, both key tenets of Islam, will be forgotten by a disbelieving world. Men will refuse to worship in the mosques and leave the churches empty. God and his greatness will be ignored.

The Mahdi and his coming in power and glory is essential. Many believe the birth of the Mahdi will be miraculous, and the child will demonstrate Godly powers and divine understanding even as an infant. When he assumes his throne, he will reign for 70 years. The Mahdi, whom some Islamic historians claim will be called Muhammad Abdullah al-Mahdi, will appear in Mecca on the day of Ashura, or the 10th day of the Muslim month Muharama. This is the Day of Hussein, commemorating an important Shi'ite martyr's death at the hands of his enemies near the town of Karbala in Iraq more than a millennium ago.

Ibn Khaldoon, an important Sunni historian also talked of the coming of the Mahdi, "at the end of time," and that he would be a descendent of the family of the Prophet Muhammad. Such traditions, like similar ones among Christians and Jews, are important in understanding the "messianic" and apocalyptic nature of these ancient faiths and the Middle East as a whole. All three major religions originated in relative close proximity to one another.

Understanding the message of Mahdism and his anticipated coming before the end of the world is critical to comprehending the mindset of many fundamentalist Muslims, and more so, terror factions and radical groups. Initially the Mahdi's principal mission is to vanquish the Anti-Christ (who is really more anti-Muslim) in a "great and final battle." Then he will "turn his wrath upon the non-believers and those practicing treachery against Allah's people."

When fully considered, such apocalyptic anticipation is ominous, and goes a long way towards explaining some of the terrorist attacks seen of late. In the minds of the fanatics, who view themselves as the emissaries or "trailblazers" of the Mahdi, America *is* the Anti-Christ, usually translated or described by the media as "The Great Satan." The Mahdi's mission, therefore, will be to defeat and destroy the United States of America.

CONSPIRACIES HAUNTING THE MIDDLE EAST

The Middle East has always been the land of smoke and mirrors. Mid-Easterners love a new conspiracy theory, and they live to speculate on the latest "sighting." This hopeless "conspiracy climate" ties closely with President Bush's unfortunate unwillingness to reach out to these people, allowing a void or vacuum of truth and information throughout the Arab world. Into that void rushes a host of disembodied, even weird and wacky, conspiracies. In very fact, the Middle East is one great conspiracy theory in progress.

I have never seen a region or a people more prone to swallow just about any tale or yarn that comes along, a new one almost every day. The Arab rumor mill is truly unique. No, call it a rumor *factory*, the only heavy industry found in the Arab World.

Perhaps it is the nature of the region, grounded in Byzantine Christian, Islamic, Persian, and Mongol history. Things don't "just happen." Everything must be "orchestrated by the powers above." For example:

Rumor One: These deadly terror attacks in Iraq have been carried out by Mossad (the Israeli Intelligence Service) in order to further galvanize public opinion against both Saddam's loyalists and against the Islamic fighters. The "big terrorist" al-Zarqawi is a ghost. He doesn't exist, except as a specter, a bogeyman, to further the goals of the United States and Israel by having an embodied, evil terrorist on which to lay blame. (In other words, those *Islamic* beheadings we all witnessed on camera never happened.)

Rumor Two: The new CIA chief, Porter Goss, is a "diabolical Jew," wholly in bed with the Israelis in his desire to destroy the Muslim and Arab Worlds and establish the "Israeli Empire" from the Tigris River to the Nile.

Rumor Three: The Bush Administration and the CIA have determined that Islam must be destroyed, so it has infiltrated both the Christian and Muslim Communities in the Middle East and is the cause of recent stirrings up between the two communities, causing the deaths of many.

Rumor Four: Secretly the so-called "neo-cons" in the Bush Administration have decided to wage a clandestine war against the Muslim community worldwide. Part of that war is to get the Coptic Christian community involved in secretly resisting and fighting Islam throughout the region. The CIA and the Copts are working clandestinely. This is but one front of many the Bush Administration has established to destroy the religion of Islam.

Rumor Five: Both Osama bin Laden and al-Zarqawi have been captured by the CIA. They are being held in a secret location to glean further information from them by torture (with help from the Israelis, of course) and to wait until the optimum time to let the world know of their capture.

QUESTION 11

- BY TOPPLING SADDAM HUSSEIN HAVE WE MADE THE REGION SAFE FOR THEOCRACY, RATHER THAN DEMOCRACY?

> *Mankind is buoyed by a personal spiritual connection to a heavenly being, without whom people often, in fear, embrace a strongman or a radical movement—in effect, a counterfeit deity—whose basic tenet of faith is violence, war, and indiscriminant terror to achieve its ends.*
>
> *--Richard P. Robison*
> *Iron Blossom Resort*
> *Presentation on the*
> *Rebuilding of Iraq,*
> *October, 2004*

ISLAMIC FUNDADMENTALISM: A FORM OF MODERN FASCISM

By toppling the Saddam Hussein regime, have we made the region safe for radical *theocracy* rather than democracy? Time will tell. According to a Sunni Imam I knew in Egypt, radical Islam sprang first from a desire of Muslims to take back their world, whether along the Tigris, or the Nile, to turn back the clock. And they will attempt to use American actions to their advantage, if they can.

The radicals' message is usually well received, my friend told me, because it offers resistance to the rock music, the American fast food restaurants in every Middle Eastern city, and Hollywood movies which increasingly disrupt and overshadow Muslim culture. The loose morals, disrespect for elders, and above all, blatant feminism, are threats which accompany the "poison" of American pop-culture. Music, TV, movies, even technology, especially things marketed exclusively to women to free them from home and family, all are feared, all represent a cultural assault. Topping the list today is the internet and computers—the world-wide-web and the overwhelming power it projects. In the zealot's mind, such cultural pollution must be resisted totally, even to the shedding of blood.

The second reason my Egyptian friend cited was that Mid East countries are dictatorships where political parties are not allowed. The local mosque and the speeches of these clerics, called *imams*, are the only legal political outlet for the masses. Confined within the mosques, such political activity is easily monitored by the government and safely regulated to protect existing regimes. In such an environment, local clerics become increasingly powerful and influential, especially in poor, desperate neighborhoods. In reality, these imams are working as government agents to keep their people in line by giving them a controllable outlet for their frustrations.

Dictators quickly discovered that local preaching in the mosques against America or Israel was just fine. In fact it distracted the masses from seeing the many deficiencies in their own governments and corrupt leaders. Dictators, including our friends the Saudis, Egyptians, and Jordanians, allowed the Imams, the mosques, to speak against the Americans, always relieved when it was not directed at them. These governments actually encouraged the anti-American diatribes in an effort to diffuse public anger over lack of jobs, poor healthcare, roads, water, everything. "Yes, the treacherous Americans are to blame!" "If it wasn't for an evil, scheming America, everything would be fine in the Middle East!"

Since the mid-1970s, in an effort to counter the radicals, the United States has pumped about *$50 billion dollars* into the Egyptian economy! In effect, we have used massive "donations" of U.S. taxpayers' dollars (are taxes under *any* circumstance a "donation"?), trying to counter the inept, nepotistic, and corrupt Arab leadership in a land that should be prospering. In true bureaucratic fashion, we have thrown money at the problem hand-over-fist, but to no avail. Why? What is our strategy here? Losing Iran to the Ayatollahs in 1979 was bad enough. The loss of Egypt to the zealots and the establishment of an Islamic Republic along the Nile would be a major foreign policy disaster, just like Iran was for the Carter

Administration. Egypt is key to maintaining stability and moderation in the Islamic world. Sunnite Egypt contains the oldest and most important Islamic university in the world, *al-Azhar*. It is the heart of Islamic scholarship, and a potential hotbed of radicalism no world leader, not even President Bush, wants to tackle. So we continue to allow the Egyptians to shake us down, our protection money today as much a part of the scenery as the pyramids, money the Egyptians have come to expect. And as addicts to American dollars, they have long-since stopped thanking us.

While the Mubarak Government in Cairo has brutally kept the pressure on the radicals, still they continue to operate. The brains of al-Qaeda's operational wing is essentially Egyptian, key former leaders from the bloody Egyptian Islamic Jihad organization. They are the same group that assassinated President Anwar Sadat two decades ago. Al-Qaeda's number two man and head of operations, Ayman al-Zawarhiri, is a leader of Egyptian Islamic Jihad. As was Muhammad Atta, one of the leading 9/11 suicide hijackers. Undoubtedly Egypt is relieved these capable terrorists are focusing on non-Egyptian targets, at least for now. Egypt has witnessed horrible attacks in recent years, despite nation-wide crackdowns and mass arrests.

The bombing of the World Trade Center in 1993 was inspired by the so-called "Blind Cleric" Sheik Omar Abdul Rahman, an Egyptian currently being held in a U.S. prison. The Muslim radicals want to cut Egypt loose from U.S. financial aid and prevent tourists from visiting the country. Egypt earned billions of dollars a year from tourism prior to several effectively-placed and deadly terrorist attacks. Cutting off tourism, the zealots hoped, would bring down the economy allowing the Muslim radicals to take over. Their efforts are working. Egypt's economy is a basket-case, sinking by the day. Islamic Jihad warned foreign firms in the country to "liquidate their investments and leave or be targeted." The threats continue.

Egypt is rotting from within, and body-slammed by the eighth Egyptian plague: Islamic Fundamentalism. With sixty percent of the population under the age of 20, unemployment and hopelessness is the modern reality. Some try to survive on less than a dollar a day. Cairo is more than seven times as crowded as New York City. Many

Egyptians lack even the basics in housing, living beneath stairwells, on roofs in plywood and cardboard hovels, even in old cemetery tombs. Life is brutal.

For years President Mubarak has sworn to hunt down the zealots with a swift, sure hand. Hassan al-Banna, the founder of the activist Muslim Brotherhood, came from Egypt. "The Brothers" have funded and inspired much of the radical, nationalist Arab and Muslim movements throughout the Middle East and the world, backed by Saudi money.

Though an aging political movement in Egypt, the threat from The Brothers continues (and spin-off groups), and the Egyptian government, under Mubarak, continues to make arrests and infiltrate these radical factions. While President Mubarak has succeeded to some extent, his harsh measures have merely driven the zealots abroad, to attack softer targets, targets easily struck amid the free and open societies of Europe and the world. Mubarak's methods of arresting or driving out indigenous terrorist factions, however, have not halted Egypt's slide towards anarchy. The radicals and fundamentalists believe that "Patience is of Allah; haste of the Devil." The terror-monger believes time is on his side. We must respond wholeheartedly and eliminate these groups in every nation, no matter the cost. Above all, we cannot allow Egypt to slide further into the web of the radicals.

It should be obvious by now that fundamentalist Islam is principally a political, rather than a religious, movement. Simply, it is a grab for power. Extremists use religion as a cover-for-action to implement their own lust for political power and wealth. In reality, fundamentalist Islam is a form of modern fascism.

Follow-up: Specifically, why is modern, radical Islam such a threat to world peace and freedom? Can't it be safely contained with vigilance, with sanctions?

Radical Islam is essentially fascism. Fascism will always be a threat to peace and freedom.

The United States is an exceptionally open society, the perfect environment to plan, fund, support and execute a variety of deadly terrorist operations. So is Europe, perhaps even more so, but for different reasons. In a free and open society like the United States, you cannot "contain" anything effectively.

Interrogations of al-Qaeda and other terrorists reveal how they have studied America closely and then tailored their operations to use our freedom and openness against us.

Successful operations usually require a team of specialists. Initially the targeting groups arrive as tourists, students, or guest workers who benignly videotape a wide selection of potential target sites. Then security men move in to evaluate whether the potential target is "soft" or "hard" (measuring the target's ease or difficulty of attack), followed by a more senior team that brings in the required cash to procure the weapons and/or explosives. This team then rents a safehouse in the area as a base of operations and secures a sterile storage facility, which can be abandoned quickly. Finally, just before the attack, when everything is in place and the target is ready, and with absolutely no hint of compromise in the wind, the actual attackers casually roll into town. To the typical Muslim fanatic or terrorist-wannabes, these men are superheroes, rock stars, the "Mujahadin," Warriors of the Faith. It is a heady business, one that appeals to millions of young, adventurous, idealistic Arab and Muslim men from Morocco to Malaysia.

Many cities and towns in Europe, the Middle East, and Asia, even America, are home to undetermined terrorist group "connectors," safehouse operators, and sympathizers. The "Lackawanna Six," the young Muslim men in New York State who were arrested and pled guilty to various charges related to supporting terrorism, may have been one of these "sleeper cells." Recruited by al-Qaeda, they traveled to Afghanistan in 2001 for military and terrorist training, in some cases meeting with Osama bin Laden and listening to his speeches. Supposed "connectors" aided their journey to Afghanistan, the former "Disneyland of Terror."

Many terrorist foot-soldiers are recruited in the hopeless Arab and Muslim slums, within the thousands of *madressas*, or Islamic schools found in every Muslim country. Such schools' prime curriculum is the honoring of Allah and his Prophet, and the systematic brainwashing of these young, impressionable minds ensuring eternal hatred for the United States. Such a poisonous program is largely funded by our old friend Saudi Arabia. Why? The Saudi royals continue to deflect the hatred of their own oppressed peoples against the Saudi regime onto the broad backs of the Americans. The Saudis underlying message to their *Wahhabite* radicals: "Do what you want to the Americans, just leave us, the Royal family, alone. Leave us to live out our privileged lives of ease and opulence." Saudi leaders know they are walking a fine line, though *staggering* is probably a better description. Depending heavily upon the Americans for their security and prosperity, the royals continue to want it both ways. Saudi leaders have even been heard to say to the numerous Americans working in the kingdom: "We want you to be like the wind. We want to feel you, but we don't want to see you."[65]

Muslim fundamentalist leaders today, however, want their holy warriors with their *brains* in America, but their *hearts* in Mecca. Terrorists are becoming increasingly sophisticated, lethally efficient and professional, an inevitable process and trend in the Age of Information.

Middle Eastern dictatorial states, and some European nations as well, take the easy, though somewhat expensive road, and buy off these killers. It's a temporary fix for the Saudi Royal Family. They are playing with fire. So are the Egyptians, who since the 1950s and earlier, have pumped money into fundamentalist Islamic parties to buy them off. Dancing amid the flames, the inferno blew-back in the face of President Anwar Sadat in 1981, leading to his assassination by the very fanatics he had nurtured. Morocco's King Hassan II, father of the current king Mohammad VI, also built up religious parties and factions as a counter-balance to the communists and other Arab nationalist groups. The early summer 2003 multiple terrorist attacks on western targets in Morocco, carried out by the *Assirat al-Moustakim*, or the "Straight, or Righteous Path" was the result. Even the United States is tangled in a similar web, funding and training countless Muslim fighters in the 1980s to attack the Soviet occupying army in Afghanistan. That training is now being used by al-Qaeda's leaders to train and equip modern Mujahadin to attack America. (In hindsight, it looks pretty foolish on our part, though at the time everyone thought it was a good idea. And at the time, it was.)

Jihad, a term nearly everyone is familiar with these days, cannot be defined accurately as "holy war" in the sense of fighting for, or spreading, the Islamic faith, at least not directly. While jihad may eventually *result* in the spread of the Islamic religion, the specific purpose of jihad is the capturing of Islamic power and control of lands and people. Whether the individuals living under Islamic governments embrace the faith or not is secondary to having total and absolute control by Muslim leaders or conquerors over political and military institutions. This has been the objective of Islamic movements from the beginning, and the objective of al-Qaeda. This is why the spread of radical Islam is primarily an activist political movement, such as the Ayatollahs in Iran, or the Taliban in Afghanistan. The real goal is *power*.

Islam is God's law, called *Shari'a* in Arabic. Within Islamic systems there can be no separation of church and state, which is a wholly Western concept. Islamic law contains many secular parts which must be enforced by a secular government. Naturally such government must be in the hands of Muslims who will enforce the law. Presumably non-Muslims would fail to enforce Islamic principles. Therefore, to control a nation, a state, and a people, Muslim leaders *must control territory*. To win and hold territory, Muslims must declare and fight wars. To fight wars in Allah's name is, by this definition, *jihad*.

The drive for Islamic power is not an option for radical Muslims. In a true Islamic state, whether ancient or modern, non-believers, referred to as *kafirs*, must never rule. Such would be an abomination to Allah. These rulers would quickly corrupt Allah's law and destroy the Islamic community. Kafir rule is an attack on God. In Muslim governments all non-believers must be removed from power, by force if necessary. Such was the case with the Shah of Iran in 1979, or with Egypt's Anwar Sadat.

The distinction between believers and non-believers, or the House of Islam and the House of War, is crucial here. Islam does not compel people to join. *"Let there be no compulsion in religion."*[66] The Prophet Muhammad was most specific on this point. While the "People of the Book" or *Ahl al-Kitab* (specifically identified as

Christians and Jews) were generally allowed to maintain their beliefs and many of their religious practices, they paid higher taxes to their Muslim conquerors for this privilege and lived under restrictions some would define as slave-like.

One could argue that their second-class citizenship effectively coerced many "Ahl al-Kitab" (Christians and Jews) to convert. Yet, it appears true that they were not forced at the point of a sword to conversion. In fact many Jewish and Christian sects maintained their unique identity in Middle Eastern countries throughout the centuries of Muslim rule until the present day.

Polytheists, or those who believed in multiple, usually *pagan*, gods, were not so fortunate. Such beliefs were and are considered an abomination by Allah. A polytheist had three choices basically: Flee Islamic controlled lands, abandon such multi-god beliefs and practices, or die. Most, however, chose a fourth, more practical path: total conversion to Islam. Few pagans were willing to sacrifice life and limb for gods of stone, wind, and fire.

Forced conversion to Islam of the conquered was never the *primary* purpose of Islamic conquest, although conversion was a worthy byproduct. The purpose of Islamic penetration of Christian and pagan lands and peoples was to politically, economically, and militarily subjugate all peoples under Muslim governmental control. Only then could God's Law be implemented as Allah intended.

Allah and government meld as one in the "true" Islamic world order. Fundamentalist religion and government are interdependent in Islam; they use power equally to control the masses. Islam in its original, medieval form was propagated, nurtured, and enforced by bureaucratic tyrants. Islam is Law, and "law is not left to individual interpretation." Individualist, "anything-goes" culture is what is causing moral rot in America today, Islamic leaders like Sheik Osama bin Laden have said time and again. To "save" America, they conclude, the only solution (*al-hal*) is Islam. But radical Islamic government and modern Western-style freedoms are wholly incompatible; they are native enemies. In the end one side will conquer, the other defeated and eliminated. Western-style freedom and radical Islam will always be rabid enemies, just as freedom and fascism cannot co-exist.

Follow-up: Does Islam really provide for a cadre of "religious police" to perpetuate Islamic control in society?

Cane-wielding religious police are a regular feature in Saudi Arabia, especially visible in areas with greater concentrations of Americans and foreign workers. They are the enforcers. The *Mutawa* were originally created in 1932 as part of the Department for the Preservation of Virtue and Prevention of Vice, by Saudi Arabia's founder, King Abdul-Aziz.

The Mutawa are often seen in Dhahran, the oil city near the Persian Gulf coastline where many Americans and other foreigners live, and in Riyadh, the capital. Should a Western woman be tempted to expose too much skin, on her arms or legs particularly, the Mutawa will not be far away to mete out punishment. They frequently prowl malls or shopping areas, markets, theaters, and parks.

They can demand that people stop for prayers five times a day, as the Qur'an requires. Those unwilling to comply may feel the sting of their preferred weapon, a three foot length of bamboo cane. Video sales and rental shops are often searched for movies showing nudity and if found the tapes or DVDs quickly confiscated. Oddly enough obscene language in movies is seldom, if ever, a problem to the Mutawa'iin (plural form of Mutawa). This is likely due to the fact that most Mutawa do not speak English.

For years the Mutawa have been a source of irritation not only to Americans and other foreigners trying to work in the Kingdom, but also to the local Saudis who spend an inordinate amount of time looking over their shoulders when out in public, ever watchful for the "friendly neighborhood religious police."

Follow-up: Distilled to its essence, what distinguishes Islam from Christianity and which system is better positioned to benefit by modern global trends and changes?

Though originating from the same Middle Eastern religious seedbed, Islam and Christianity have taken two very different philosophical paths. At the heart of Christian culture is the concept of personal choice, sometimes referred to as "agency." Though "God knows all," including outcomes and choices men and women will make, still "it is given to mankind to choose." Personal choice is a foundation of Christian belief. And since that choice is critical to mankind's growth on this earth, choice cannot, it *must not*, be set in stone.

In other words, history was made, and the future altered, by dynamic choices taken each and every day. History *is* choice, the actions (or inactions) of men and women. History is not events. Events are a byproduct of human choice. Even in the case of the city of Pompeii, buried by the eruption of Mt. Vesuvius in A.D. 79, the founders of Pompeii *chose* to build their city at the foot of a volcano. Obviously there are exceptions, but they are just that, exceptions.

Islam, on the other hand, maintains the foundational belief that "everything is Allah's will," that mankind cannot alter the will of God and it is dangerous to try. Islam is predestination in its perfect (or imperfect) form. Most Muslims end each sentence of a future intention with the well-worn phrase *"In-sha-Allah,"* God willing. In fact many Muslims believe that Americans are hopelessly arrogant in *not* using such a statement in their own speech, as if anything can happen without God's will and sanction. Herein lies the heart of the challenge—the challenge of reconciling two religions which are as different in their core philosophies and cultural compositions as oil and water. From the start, these two philosophies set each individual believer on entirely different paths.

On the surface such differences may seem trivial. They are not. If everything is predestined by God, why wear your seatbelt when speeding into traffic? If you are destined to die that day, no mere seatbelt will save you. "It is God's will." If your company is going to prosper, that too is Allah's will and happens by His hand, alone. If you are going to cure the common cold, or cancer, in essence it will be Allah's doing, so do not spend your time worrying, or scheming, or struggling over this problem. It is in God's hands; in his due time.

Perhaps this is why so little gets done in the Arab world, and why the total economic output of all 22 Arab nations is *less* than the rather meager output of the single nation of Spain. *Khalliha-ala-Allah*, Leave it to God, the common phrase of the native Arab procrastinator.

Logic tells us that religious and cultural proclivities matter. Christian choice (personal agency) will always out-perform, and offer far greater individual opportunity, than Allah's pre-destiny or "Allah's will." History bears this out. Predestination, which is so deeply ingrained in the various Muslim cultures, has stifled generations of individuals, many hundreds of millions of shackled souls over countless generations. Such standards have clogged Muslim countries economies and cultural development (in slowing or halting the emancipation of women, for example), and obstructing their progress at every turn.

Christianity, as is Western (American and European) culture, is built on personal freedom and choice. Most Christians believe that freedom is the God-given destiny of mankind, if there is a "destiny." Freedom is to die for. Allah's pre-destination, which tears at the heart of Christian freedom of choice, in reality places Islam on the wrong side of history. Pre-destination can never compete with freedom and personal choice in the modern world. The future, which is *not* set in stone, will belong to those who believe that they alone, through daily choices and actions, determine their own success or failure.

The path of pre-destination, on the other hand, is highly defeatist and damning. It destroys nations; but more importantly to Christians, it destroys *individuals*. The happiest people on earth, psychologists tell us, and the most successful and productive, are those who rise every morning knowing their future will depend on *them*. They are driving. That is why our American Forefathers fought so tenaciously for individual freedom. Freedom allows choice, and correct choices lead to the greatest happiness. As well, freedom has made America the greatest, most prosperous nation on earth, the Shining Light on the Hill, and the long-time envy of the down-trodden the world over.

Follow-up: Why is Europe so critical in the conflict between Islam and the Christian West?

Many answers—and dangers—in dealing with radical Islam lie in Europe. European nations have millions of Muslims, more than 5 million in France alone, arriving in Europe over the past decades from mostly Middle Eastern-South Asian nations. In Europe, Muslim young people struggle with their identity, the process made particularly difficult by the culture gap between European liberalism and harsh Mideast Islamic tradition. In France, the popular, secular culture is essentially void of spiritual values, often clashing with the conservative values of Islam. Young Muslims struggle to find a middle ground. The "third way," some call it, is serving to fill that void.

Perhaps the most prominent leader of this movement is Tariq Ramadan, a young Swiss-born, ethnically-Egyptian professor and grandson of Hassan al-Banna, the radical founder of the Muslim Brotherhood who fought the British occupation of Egypt in the 1930s and 40s. While such activist family credentials concern European authorities, many of Europe's Muslims are enamored by Ramadan.

Genealogy is important to Arabs. Who your ancestors are is often all that is required to legitimize a person's right to leadership. Ramadan is certainly capable; he not only has taught at the College of Geneva and the University of Fribourg, but travels all over Europe lecturing before groups of mostly young Muslims, the children of immigrants. He has also taught in the United States. His message to youth is to return to their roots, to the Qur'an, and to find ways to maintain their spirituality and Islamic principles while living amid secular European societies.

To the young Muslims of Europe, the charisma and charm of Ramadan is irresistible. Muslims have sought fervently for centuries for capable, genuine, charismatic leaders with the ability to inspire and to lead with strength. This young professor not only has the genetic qualifications, but presents himself with the sincere dedication of a great religious stalwart, and the stage presence of a rock star. Undoubtedly, Tariq Ramadan will be a future force in the growing power of the European Islamic community. Whether he will advocate accommodation or militant resistance is yet to be seen. He is a leader to watch and to remember. Perhaps he is a leader to fear.

Europe is a fertile seedbed. In the Middle Ages it was the cradle of the coming age of discovery and exploration. It was the ground from which Christianity sprang to conquer and convert much of the world. Europe was the cradle of democracy, republican government, and civil freedom. Out of Europe came Mother Teresa and Adolf Hitler, Joan of Arc and Joseph Stalin. Two world wars were handed us exclusively by the Europeans, as were the Auschwitz and Srebrenica atrocities of mass murder and ethnic cleansing. And now, this continent may become the fertile ground for a type of Islam with massive appeal, a 21st century compatible-brand of the faith which could sweep much of the world. However, this European version could just as easily turn militant. Islamic objectives, as we have seen, are too often dangerously cloaked.

As a passionate student of history, I view the future of the Middle East with hope, but also with a gnawing fear. The Middle East for a thousand years and more has been steeped in medieval thought and practice. It is slow to change. Too many cultural snags and historical baggage. Activist Islam in the modern age is on the ropes. To survive, it must change, it must mutate. September 11th was to the religion of Islam what Pearl Harbor was to the Japanese. Tragically I don't believe most Muslims, particularly the radicals, yet comprehend the power of the combined forces rushing straight at them.

On September 11th this major world religion was revealed, and what we saw was not a great religion, but indiscriminant terror and mass murder. Islamic leaders in the Middle East, Africa, Europe, and throughout Asia further compounded their problems by not speaking out strongly and quickly against the 9/11 atrocities. In many instances they seemed to support them! Even American Muslim leaders' responses were collectively weak, at best, or more often non-existent. Apparently, Islam has been hijacked by a loosely-allied band of fanatics. And killer-fanatics cannot survive in our modern, secular world, in spite of God's supposed "will." The powers that be, especially the world's only Superpower, will never allow it. America's response was seen in Afghanistan, then in Iraq. The war is far from over.

Again, the hope for Islam, I believe, is found in Europe; but *not* from those who incite hatred and violence. Such a harsh example is found in Belgium, a country in the heart of the European Union with an immigrant Arab population of 500,000; one that is swelling in numbers every day. Among these European Arabs is a man named

Abou Jahjah, a Lebanese immigrant who received Belgian political asylum in 1991. Abou Jahjah has since pushed himself to the head of the class of Arab-European activists. Known for a confrontational style, the handsome young founder of the Arab European League (AEL) is sometimes called the "Belgium Malcolm X."

Accused of inciting the November 2002 race riots in Antwerp, many Europeans fear his growing muscle in Arab neighborhoods. Following the September 11, 2001 attacks on America, Abou Jahjah received widespread criticism when he stated that "people were now smiling" in the Arab homes and neighborhoods of Europe. These radicals seem to *want* to fight the bloody, hopeless wars of the Middle East in their own cities, in their own ethnic neighborhoods of Europe. The modern world, however, a world of technology, security, and global investment, will not tolerate such blatant hostility. Men like Abou Jahjah are medieval, they are dinosaurs, and only European timidity to this very point allow these Arab activists to continue their destructive game of power-politics. Such passivity is suicide in the post 9/11 world, though America and her allies have had to pick up the slack for the timid Europeans. But unless Abou Jahjah suddenly becomes more subtle in his approach, and more effective at playing the game, he too will not survive the global war on terror.

Islam desperately needs a Western catalyst, it needs freedom and openness. It has popular appeal and the political legs to stand proud. What it lacks is a modern realism, an understanding of global trends and major forces and how best to capitalize on those trends.

Though often accused of arrogance in presuming I can predict the mind and will of Allah, I draw your attention again to history. God does not change, but the history of mankind is *the* history of choices and change. Religions built on truth, justice, social inclusion and equality, which are willing to adapt to a changing climate, *sometimes* survive. Those that do not…well, how many thousands of great religions of history are now dead religions? Sadly, almost every one, and we do not even remember their names.

September 11th marks either Islam's declining moment, or a powerful turning point. Appropriately, this choice will be made by Muslims; not by their enemies, nor by any others. Despite the medieval Muslim false dogma that "everything is predestined," in reality, in the end, Muslims will choose their own fate. In effect, God gives men the opportunity to choose a moral, peaceful life, and to reject the acts of evil leaders. Such a path leads eventually to prosperity, freedom, and justice.

Choice is everything; the very essence of freedom. Also, if we choose, God gives us the freedom to turn our backs and walk away into historical oblivion. It is really that simple.

I hope Muslims choose wisely.

QUESTION 12

- WHAT ARE SOME ESSENTIAL, YET LITTLE KNOWN, MIDDLE EAST CULTURAL INSIGHTS WE MUST UNDERSTAND?

THE DAY THE WHITE OX WAS EATEN

An Arab parable, called *Three Oxen and the Lion*, tells how Lion came one night to kill his dinner, attacking White Ox, Red Ox, and Black Ox. But the three oxen stuck together, kicking as one against Lion, overpowering him and driving him away. No matter how hard Lion tried to kill one of these oxen as long as they stuck together it was not possible.

One day Lion, not usually recognized for his ingenuity, devised a plan. He sent a message through the fennec fox to White Ox, who whispered in the ox's ear telling him that Red and Black Ox were spreading shameful lies about him. At first White Ox didn't listen to the fennec, but eventually the lies wore him down and he refused to associate with Red and Black Ox anymore. His honor and his pride were wounded and he wanted nothing to do with them.

As soon as the oxen were separated Lion attacked, killing and eating White Ox.

Then, the fennec visited Red Ox.

Predictably, because oxen are not known for their intelligence either, Red Ox would have nothing to do with Black Ox and, standing alone, Lion killed and ate him, too.

Finally, when he was hungry once more, Lion went to kill Black Ox. As he approached, Black Ox faced Lion and proclaimed loudly to all the world, "*Akilt al-youma okila al-thoor al-abyad!*" Meaning "*I* was eaten the day White Oxen was eaten."

The above parable has always played well in the Middle East—the importance of sticking together no matter what. Unfortunately for most Arabs, it's a cultural ideal seldom realized. Arabs in general have an annoying habit of talking much, yet doing little, often failing to rise to the ideal, perhaps finding the sacrifice or the danger too great. It's not that the intent isn't there. It usually is. Yet historical and cultural shackles always seem to block the way.

I say this not to denigrate an otherwise great people, but to state a fact. (Every culture has its weaknesses, including our own.) Oratory, or at least oral pontification, is an age-old Mid East art, not merely a cheap form of entertainment. Being able to stand and opine before the world and before God is an important cultural obligation. "The world must know that I am a man!" Such a masculine verbal outlet is especially prevalent in societies which are culturally and politically limited and oppressed. The ratio between talk and accomplishment is often directly dependent upon a society's inherent personal freedoms.

From an early age, every boy and girl is taught what is, and is not, acceptable. Such bounds or "chains" have a direct relation upon the "can-do" or "can't-do" make-up of a culture. This is why a country blessed with a legacy of pure, broad-based freedom usually accomplishes so much. In Mid East society women especially have their cultural bounds, mostly limited to admonishing, often antagonizing, their husbands within the confines of the home. However such wifely admonishments must always remain within the home, never outside for the world to see. This is shameful.

In spite of their best efforts, most of the time men and women fall short. The parable of the Three Oxen and the Lion is an ideal only. Every Arab would like to believe they are tied to Arabs everywhere by an invisible bond which is not only physical but also spiritual: "What happens to an Arab, in any land, will sooner or later happen to me." In practice, however, Arabs rarely let the ideal rule the practical. They must protect self and family first, though they will talk about Arab solidarity all the time if for no other reason than to "let the world know that I am a man who stands for something!" This is what men do.

Follow-up: How can the relationship between men and women offer important cultural insights we may be missing?

The wedding was a grand affair. I watched from the back of the ballroom within the heart of the Shepherd Hotel near *Midan Tahrir* in the center of downtown Cairo. The bride was dressed in an elaborate white gown and veil, as fine attire as any I have seen in the

States. Both Egyptian families of the bride and groom stood nearby as the newlyweds entered the dining hall. The festivities continued well into the night. Though there were Islamic and cultural elements of the wedding which emphasized the Divine nature of the union between man and woman, much of the celebration could have taken place in Peoria or Rapid City. Obviously the family wanted a "Western" wedding, the kind they had read about in bride magazines or seen on TV. Though traditions are important, in practice more and more personal preferences tend to rule the day for brides and their mothers, even in Cairo.

It is hard to separate God from marriage. Even among people who are not particularly religious nearly every bride wants a "church wedding." God adds a legitimacy few will openly challenged. Even among some Arabs who are not generally religious, why risk alienating God (Allah) unnecessarily? Why insult the pious elders and matriarchs of the family by slamming the door in the face of a host of venerated ancestors? Though Great-uncle Abdul is resting peacefully in Allah's arms, he may be susceptible to any perceived slight from the land of the living.

Islam teaches that men are the creation of an omnipotent God. Regardless of whether we believe it or not Islam says we belong to Allah and inevitably, must submit. Muslims maintain the universe is a chain of command. The world too is a hierarchy; as is a nation, tribe, and family. God, in the mind of most Muslims, is strongly masculine. Women are expected to answer to men, as men answer to God. Who has the right to change what God set in motion from the beginning?

Even in daily cultural practice, men still establish their rights as men, and stake their claim on their woman through and by the wedding vow and through gifts. From the earliest age in the Middle East, giving a woman jewelry, particularly at her wedding, announced to the world that she was now his. When a man adorns a woman with his wealth, he is proclaiming to other men that she now has his material protection and, more so, physical security; that he will protect "his property" with his life, demonstrating to potential rivals by his vow that he is an honorable, capable man.

Historically, this is what the gifting of jewelry from a man to a woman represented. Superficial adornment was but a minor aside. A woman, and her father who "gave her away," were most concerned about her security. With the transfer of a portion of the groom's wealth to her (or to her father) in the form of jewelry, usually gold, precious stones, land or livestock, came also the groom's commitment of protection and support. He now had a stake, an "investment" so to speak; his commitment not to be taken lightly by other men.

Though we may live far away from the Middle East in time and distance, our cultural roots remain largely Middle Eastern, though we may not recognize them. Too many in modern America today reject our heritage as worn-out baggage, best discarded. But remember, many people the world over still strongly value their traditions. To some, they are worth dying for.

It is crucial we understand why people behave the way they do. The ultimate submission of a wife to her husband is not unique in Arab culture. It is universal among patriarchal societies. The origin of this ancient cultural practice is grounded in religion, but more so in tribal survival. Such foundational notions will always be slow to change.

Islam is a highly tenacious religion built upon submission to God, or Allah. This means submission to Allah's Law, the *Shari'a*, and to the *Hadith*, or the sacred words and traditions of Muhammad. They teach that only those willing to humble themselves and submit will find happiness and peace, possibly in this life, but certainly in the Heaven (*al-Janna*) or Paradise to come. Such is the true path, the sign of the believer.

Therefore, for a woman in marriage, submission to both God *and* her husband is divinely linked. One without the other is "satanic," and, to the "true Muslim," destructive in its intent. To Muslims, man was meant to worship and obey God, and woman to follow the man in God's path. Anything less, tradition tells us, is divisive and evil.

Muhammad taught, however, that in marriage if a man does not serve and protect his wife *more* than she serves and provides for him, he is neither a man nor a Muslim. The Prophet Muhammad taught this by example, realizing that men and women were hardly perfect, but had the potential to rise above the pagan traditions of their forefathers, from the so-called "days of ignorance" or *Jahiliyya*,[67] in

Arabic. People must, however, choose for themselves, for *"Let there be no compulsion in religion."*[68] Since marriage is a critical part of God's Plan, then one could take it a step further and say, "Let there be no compulsion in *marriage*."

The importance of this necessary change in established traditions can be seen in what is unfolding in the Middle East today. Islamic absolutism regarding the Law of God is destroying Islam. I will say it again: *Islamic absolutism is destroying Islam* by restricting or damning Muslim people. Why did the Taliban fail to create a prosperous Islamic State in Afghanistan? Why are the harsh, totalitarian Islamic governments in Iran and in the Sudan hopelessly floundering? The answers are obvious: Lacking freedom to choose, these Muslim governments are killing innovation, robbing productivity, and most of all, stifling the freedom necessary to succeed and prosper.

In the relationship between men and women, how can one oppress the other without damning both? Spiritual maturity goes hand in hand with spiritual freedom, the freedom to make choices, the marital *partnership* of loving cooperation. Radical Islam will fail because it divides and enslaves men and women, rather than empowering a marriage partnership.

In the relationship between men and women, where harmony must reside, there remain many hurdles. Some couples rise to incredible heights of personal and family achievement, success, and unselfishness; many more use their freedoms to corrupt themselves in self-serving and destructive ways. Muslim men must stop getting in the way of the education and opportunity Muslim girls and women deserve. The man who shackles those around him is nothing more than a common jailer.

One final word of advice, ladies (as the father of five daughters I can say this): Beware of Arab men, or *any* men, bearing gifts.

Follow-up: What is the Islamic institution of the "Temporary Wife," "Wife of Pleasure," or "Wife of Convenience"? How can such practices exist in the modern world?

In essence, such practices have always existed. I'll explain. But first:

The woman (or sometimes her father, if she is a virgin) names her price, the man counters, and her final cost is established. The agreement is sometimes put in writing; more often, not. Money is paid up front and the man then has all sexual rights to her as in a normal marriage.

As is the custom in most Middle Eastern societies, the male dominates the relationship for the life of the contract. However, he is not obligated to provide his "wife" with shelter, medical care, or food. This is the institution known as the "temporary wife," sometimes referred to as "wife of pleasure or convenience." The practice, legal in Shi'ite Islam—called *sigheh* in Iranian and *mut'a* in Arabic—also has a Sunni version called *misyar*, which has become increasingly common in Arabian Gulf States and in Egypt.

Among the Sunni population, temporary contractual marriage, or *misyar*, was legalized in Saudi Arabia recently by a *fatwa* issued by Sheikh Abdel Aziz bin Baz. In 1999, misyar was also legalized in Egypt by the Sunni Imam Sheikh Mohammed Sayyed Tantawi, the Grand Sheikh of al-Azhar Islamic Center. The primary difference between mut'a and misyar marriage is that misyar, while temporary, does not specify a date or time when the marriage will terminate. Misyar is more or less open ended, whereas mut'a or sigheh marriage is nearly always for a specific period defined in the contract.

Egypt's wretched poverty often prevents a young man from taking a bride due to the overwhelming financial obligation he shoulders with a traditional marriage. Misyar allows the young woman to remain in her parents' home, freeing her husband from the obligation of renting an apartment, and clothing and feeding her. Generally the hope is the couple will eventually be able to afford housing and living expenses so they can move in together permanently. Though married, the woman remains in her parent's home, supported by her father. The couple is allowed to be alone together perhaps two or three times a week, depending on circumstances (and often upon how much the husband has paid his bride's father for the privilege). Such a marriage is a financial boon to a poor woman or girl's family, and elevates her status in society, even if she is a man's polygamous second or third wife.

The practice in Persian Gulf countries in recent years, however, has deviated from misyar's original intent. Rich Kuwaiti and Saudi men sometimes arrange a misyar marriage while on vacation, freeing them to have sexual relations with another woman, or variety of women, without committing the sin of adultery. Generally Islam punishes adultery or fornication severely.

Wealthy Gulf Arabs, while on vacation in Beirut, Cairo, or Amman, often seek out middlemen who specialize in arranging these "marriages," for a price of course. Some even secure misyar marriages online. Girls' pictures are displayed, or the middleman brings a sampling in the flesh, and the men pick the one(s) they desire. The girls' fathers generally receive gifts and cash depending upon how beautiful their daughter is; and especially if several men are vying for her, the price is often pushed quite high. For a family in poverty, such offers are seldom refused, especially since their daughter always has the chance of convincing her temporary husband to make the relationship permanent.

Obviously hard to distinguish from simple prostitution, sigheh, mut'a or misyar marriages are legal in much of the Middle East in one form or another. The length of the contract can be from one hour to 99 years or more. A Muslim man may contract with and pay for as many sigheh wives at the same time as he desires or can afford. The arrangement is designed to "meet the natural, normal sexual drives of the male," while at the same time providing financial support and cultural protection and sanction for usually poorer or lower-class women.

Amazingly practical for the Middle East, though many argue these customs are highly hypocritical since adultery and fornication are capital crimes under Islamic law and often punishable by stoning or beheading. To outsiders, such practice is often viewed, however, as Arab and Muslim cultural practicality, or hypocrisy, sweeping aside age-old Islamic restrictions. In the Middle East, it seems, there are always ways around every barrier.

Most Muslims generally attribute the practice of temporary marriage to Shi'ite Islam as found in Iran and Lebanon. Actually the Prophet Muhammad advocated the practice for Islamic soldiers away from their wives for long periods on campaign. The following is from the sacred Hadith of the Prophet, as narrated by "Abdullah," an often cited contemporary:

"We used to participate in the holy battles led by Allah's Apostle and we had nothing (no wives) with us. So we said, 'Shall we get ourselves castrated?' He (Muhammad) forbade us that and then allowed us to marry women with a temporary contract and recited to us: 'O ye who believe! Make not unlawful the good things which Allah has made lawful for you, but commit no transgression.'" [69]

As well, the Qur'an appears to condone such practices (see Sura 4:24), under specifically proscribed circumstances. Several sources contemporary with Muhammad claimed that the practice of the temporary wife was often associated with the Hajj, or Pilgrimage to Mecca, when a man was separated from his wife and home for long periods. Women were brought to Mecca by merchants as Sigheh or Mut'a wives to service the thousands of men arriving for the weeks-long pilgrimage, though such hedonistic pursuits were frowned upon by the majority of believers.

Sigheh or misyar are not lawful for non-Muslim men. Only within the bounds of Allah's True Path can a man be sanctioned for such "religious" practice, though a Muslim man may take a Christian or Jewish woman as a sigheh wife. Any children resulting from the temporary union belong to the male and are considered Muslim. When the contract runs out and the marriage is dissolved, the woman must be put in quarantine for 45 days to ensure that she is not pregnant before being allowed to re-marry.

Ancient (or even modern) life in the Arabian Peninsula cannot be compared to the modern American reality. And of course customs change with the passing years. Even between the many variant Mid East cultures there are vast differences. Still, when Sunni Muslims today criticize—and many do—their Shi'ite cousins over such practices, in reality they are not so far removed from their "barbaric brethren." With the growing popularity in Sunni lands of misyar marriage, which is hard to distinguish from the normal sigheh or mut'a variety of the Shi'ite, any fair observer at the very least must raise an eyebrow. Considering Islam's often lethal condemnation of adultery, and the harsh punishments known as "honor killing" for women caught in compromising circumstances, most would call "temporary marriage" the worst kind of hypocrisy.

The Middle East Explained

To many Muslims, however, the mut'a goes beyond temporary sexual gratification. Many believe the practice is poorly understood in the West. The institution, Muslims often maintain, is ordained of Allah, having eternal and spiritual ramifications beyond this world. *Hurru el-Amili* tells us that "The believer is only perfected when he has experienced a mut'a." His other writings indicate that "whoever has performed at least four mut'as has secured a place in Heaven."[70]

In conclusion, (trying awfully hard not to be cynical), it appears with enough cash, those promised *70 virgins* may in fact be obtained this side of heaven's gates.

Follow-up: Why do Arabs, and Muslims, dread compromise so strongly?

"When I am weak, how can I compromise? When I am strong, why should I compromise?" What is often referred to as "tribal logic" has driven Middle East politics, economics, and war for untold millennium.

It is impossible to separate the male ego, or the "conquering male," from the historical and modern Middle East ethos. Take for example the triumph of General *Abd al-Malik*. The general took control of the Armies of Islam in A.D. 685, barely 50 years after the death of Muhammad the Prophet. Abd al-Malik's principal commander, *Hajjaj*, an Umayyad (of the tribe Banu Umaya of Mecca), was one of the most ruthless and capable military leaders of all time. Hajjaj captured Arabia and took Mecca, even bombarding and damaging the sacred *Ka'bah* or Sanctuary in the process. He smashed and scattered the *Kharijite* rebels in Arabia and consolidated Islamic rule. Later, before attacking the city of *Kufah* in Iraq, Hajjaj entered the main mosque in disguise and mounted the pulpit. Tearing the veil from his face, he boldly shouted to the rebels, his enemies, within: "I see heads ripe for cutting! People of Iraq, I will not let myself be crushed before you like a soft fig. The commander of the believers, my leader, Abd al-Malik has drawn arrows from his quiver and tested the wood, and has found that I am the hardest. And so by Allah, I will strip you as men strip the bark from trees. I will beat you as stray camels are beaten!"

Testosterone flowed and Iraq capitulated, presumably after sufficient heads were lopped and blood spilled on the sandy soil. General Hajjaj was obviously a man's man, not to be frustrated in his "Godly quest." Together Abd al-Malik and General Hajjaj went to Jerusalem and built the famous Dome of the Rock on top of what was once the Temple Mount of Solomon. That beautiful structure stands today on the spot where Muhammad claimed his glorious Night Ride to the Seven Heavens to witness God (Allah) seated on his throne. Islam, though in its infancy at the time, proclaimed to the Christians and Jews of Jerusalem, as well as in far off Byzantium, the center of Christianity, that they were here to stay. The Men of Islam were men to be respected and, if necessary, feared. True men, they showed by their actions, were men who never compromised.

But since the Middle Ages, the age of Islam's greatness, it's been downhill all the way for the Children of the Prophet. Why? Muslims everywhere ask that question every day. Islamic leaders, especially terrorist leaders, continue to capitalize on the question, in effect promising an "Islamic solution" (called *al-hal*), which Allah will "soon" provide, once the satanic West, lead by the Americans, is brought to its knees.

Struggling in ignorance, poverty, and with pitiful economic productivity, and caught in an environment essentially void of freedom, unwilling to compromise and slow to change, Arab and Muslim leaders continue to blame their problems on America. They deflect the anger of their people and redirect it towards the United States, and to a lesser extent, Israel, all the while receiving *billions* of dollars in U.S. aid and oil purchases. Arab hypocrisy, it seems, knows no bounds. A great scholar on the Middle East once commented:

"Authorities on the (Middle) East have often observed that the Arab, and to a lesser extent the Jewish, character is remarkable for its two faces: On the one side, the Semite (which includes these 'eternal cousins,' Arabs and Jews) is thoroughly proud and noble, the soul of honor, the impeccable family man, the true friend, faithful to the death; and on the other, the low and cunning tramp, the sly assassin, dangerous companion and predictable rogue."[71]

The true and only workable solution, *al-hal*, is for Middle

Easterners to shoulder the responsibility, and the blame, for their unique problems. Arab and Iranian leaders must accept that leadership requires personal sacrifice, service, and most importantly, *compromise*. The corruption and pocket-lining and nepotism of the past—the sad legacy of the Middle East—must be eliminated. True leadership means long-hours of selfless service, which is why in a free society, men and women seldom seek out leadership because of the toll and sacrifice such responsibility demands. Unfortunately, few such leaders are found in the Middle East at this time.

The Arabs, Iranians, Turks, Afghans, and Pakistanis all desperately need such statesmen and women *right now*, modern versions of Lincoln, Jefferson, and Washington, or...Muhammad and Saladin. Many believe that Anwar Sadat of Egypt was such a leader. Sadly, in the dictatorial, fanatical Middle East, such leaders seldom survive long enough to have an impact for good. This is precisely why freedom and security are so critical. New, younger blood needs to be nurtured, to take the reins and move ahead with fresh, new ideas. Most importantly, old leaders must be brought to account, to stand for their crimes, and they must know in advance that they will be.

Follow-up: Why do Muslims and Middle Easterners seem to use God so unabashedly?

Initially, you may not recognize the God of the Middle East. Look again, for it is impossible to separate the Middle East from Deity—Allah, Yahweh, Jehovah, Jesus Christ, or the Holy Spirit, take your pick. Dostoyevsky, writing in *The Brothers Karamazov*, seemed to understand the Middle Easterner as well as anyone, stating "If God does not exist, everything is permissible."

To Muslims, God is meant to be used, although they would not view their actions as "using God." God is a reality, as is the wind, the sun, and the earth, all tangible things and all part of everyday life. While you may find atheists in Arab countries, or in Persian Iran, rarely will you find anyone who will admit it. God and the Middle East are inseparable. God fills the lives of Muslims, Jews, and Christians; also Arabs, Israelis, Iranians, Armenians, Assyrians, Chaldeans, and Druze; whether they want God or not, he is there.

God is a constant, a force best not rejected, at least not outwardly.

Society lives or dies based upon restraints, upon protective bulwarks. God is the ultimate restraint, the perfect bulwark. *Sharia* (or Islamic Law) is the formula given mankind by God's Prophet, or more accurately, by the leaders who followed in Muhammad's path. Not unlike the Mosaic Law, mankind ignores Islamic Law at its peril, or so we are told. All that separates the radical fundamentalist from the average "Abdul" is the radical's desire to help God along a bit.

Muslim leaders can cite examples from the Holy Qur'an to lend Heavenly justification for their often harsh actions:

"Ye believers, obey God, the Prophet, and your rulers."

And from the sayings of the Prophet, quoted by an Islamic source in the Gulf:

"A just ruler is better than rain and camels; and an unjust ruler is better than a lasting anarchy."

"Rulers are God's tools in performing his work."

"An unjust ruler is better than no ruler existing at all."

"Authority is from God. It must be obeyed."

"The ruler is the shadow of God on earth. Obeying him is necessary so that the nation will not dissolve."

"People must obey rulers; give your rulers their rights, and then ask God for your own rights."

The God of the Land of Abraham is not only versatile, but well used…and abused. He is also a jealous God, a God with limited patience, if history is an accurate indicator. And many believe the human race has selfishly trod too long on His good graces.

Follow-up: Why do demonstrations in the Middle East seem so obviously and blatantly "canned?"

Because they are. TV programs worldwide are filled with political demonstrations these days, a testimony not only to the wonderful liberties spreading throughout the globe, but also the incredible amount of free time people are blessed with. And talk about a cornucopia of choices? Every conceivable cause, movement, and crusade imaginable from "free-range farming" to the "evils of globalism." Even the historically conservative Middle East is getting into the act.

But if you are a Middle Eastern dictator, be not troubled over the possibility of losing your job. That won't happen, at least not from the demonstrators. Huge, made-for-TV gatherings are anything but regime threatening, purely a pressure-release valve. True, some opposition groups occasionally use such gatherings to criticize their governments, but rarely does anything come of it in Muslim countries. People return home, back to struggling to put food on the table, and keeping track of their teenagers.

In fact, more often than not, these demonstrations are orchestrated by, or with the cooperation of, the government. How better to identify potential troublemakers than by letting them rush to the front of a line of malcontents? There they are, for the world to see, on camera. Later, the secret police or security service will pay them a visit and, *al-la-kazzam*, magically they are transformed into tame and obedient citizens once again.

More so these days, however, Middle Eastern leaders frequently side with their demonstrators, *if* the demonstrations are anti-America. This is an excellent method of co-opting any potential opposition to a dictatorial regime: get them angry at the United States and allow the malcontents to publicly vent their frustration. This is exactly what Egypt, Pakistan, and Indonesia have done for years, with President Hosni Mubarak and Vice President Hamzah Haz leading the verbal venom against the Americans more often than not. Amazingly, Hamzah Haz of Indonesia has even referred to President George W. Bush as the "King of Terrorists!"

True, it smacks of ingratitude and hypocrisy, since most of these protesting nations receive millions (in the case of Egypt, *billions*) of dollars in U.S. aid, programs, and security protection. Leaders of these countries are walking a tightrope between local opinion and potential U.S. backlash. Most are gamblers, assuming that the United States has big shoulders and won't pay too much attention to the criticism. But how refreshing it would be to find at least *one* Muslim leader who would willingly stand up for the sacrifice in American lives offered by the red, white and blue to bring the world freedom. Of course, at the least, simple gratitude for the *billions* of dollars in U.S. aid would be appreciated.

While many commentators claim the current U.S. occupation

of Iraq is successfully bringing together both Islamic radicals and Arab nationalists in opposition to America's goals in the region, such assessment is off the mark. To be sure, Pan-Arab causes, or the promotion of Arab nationalist objectives, always bring Arab blood to the boiling point and demonstrators out of the woodwork, but such "show of Arab solidarity" is almost always façade.

In fact, *nothing* has ever successfully united Arabs, at least not since the days of Muhammad. While Islam succeeded in organizing an army and political movement following the conquest of Arabia 1,400 years ago, the real Islamic expansion and military victories beyond Arabia came with Persian, Turkish, Berber, or Kurdish leadership, all *non*-Arabs. In the heavens above, Muhammad must be exceedingly frustrated and ashamed.

Throughout history, native Arab suspicion and tribalism have undermined any chance for pan-Arab unity. We need look no further than Egypt's Gamal Nasser, Syria's Hafez al-Assad, or Iraq's Saddam Hussein; all classic examples of the purely self-serving. In a sentence, nothing of value will result from Arab demonstrations for the TV screen. Mideast dictators are far too vigilant and savvy to allow organized opposition groups to be operational for long, even if their sole focus is to attack the United States. Such movements can just as quickly turn on the local ruler and his cohorts.

Herein lies the challenge for America: Since these radical, hate-driven groups are unable to seriously organize under their government's watchful eye, they are often forced out of their home countries. Beyond Arab borders, usually in the free West, or inside rogue regimes such as the former Afghanistan, or in Somalia, the Sudan, or Iran, they receive Islamic funding and training. Their target? Principally the United States and Israel. Such is the life-cycle of al-Qaeda, and others.

This is precisely our situation today. Much anti-Americanism is defused on the Arab street through canned demonstrations, but more is turned inward, to fester in unfulfilled blood oaths against us, in the rage of young, desperate men. In effect this rage is nurtured by Mid East and Islamic dictators. Not unlike a pressure cooker, relief (for a time) coming with such attacks as September 11th, or when the deadly cancer-cell is routed and destroyed by our military and intelligence operatives.

In the end, however, it's a race against time. The pressure builds. Still, don't be swayed by the demonstrators' seemingly venomous shouts and oaths for the TV cameras. Remember what you are, in reality, seeing, and then turn off the set.

QUESTION 13

- WHAT CAN KNOWLEDGEABLE ARAB SOURCES TEACH US ABOUT ARAB CULTURE, ABOUT MIDDLE EAST WAYS?

OBSERVATIONS OF AN UPPER-CLASS ARAB BUSINESSMAN

"Middle Eastern customers are very difficult to please. They assume company owners are thieves who devise crafty ways to rob them of their money. If you are in the sophisticated equipment business, then you face the tough problem of a customer who will learn with great difficulty (or not at all) to use the precious goods for which he paid dearly. To hide his ignorance, which means loss of 'honor' or face, your customer will always claim that the machine is not working properly, thus creating the perfect excuse for not paying the balance on the debt.

"If you are an Arab salesman or manager, your Arab customers will not trust you, thinking that if you were raised in the Mideast then it is not possible for you to be knowledgeable in Western ways, hence they never take what you say seriously. They prefer to do business with blonde, blue-eyed Westerners. This is especially true in the Gulf, because the region most recently emerged from British colonial rule when the locals were brainwashed into believing only Westerners could grasp technology.

"Mistrust of others is one of the most vicious diseases of the Arab business community (and of Arabs in general). That is why so many Western firms which employ Arab managers often fail miserably, particularly in the Persian Gulf region. Bring in a Westerner, even a total idiot from the slums of Soho Street in London, and he will receive the red carpet treatment from local Arab companies."[72]

COMMENT: Colonialism has taken its toll on the Arab mind and heart, leading to several glaring contradictions. Most revealing are the views held by the upper-class Arab entrepreneur and businessman.

He is continually frustrated with the mindset of his average Arab customer towards his prime competitor, the European or American. Centuries of exploitive European colonial leaders, traders, and officials have jaded the poor fellow and confused his thinking. The Arab entrepreneur not only wrestles with his doubts in dealing with modern technologies and gut-wrenching changes all around him, but his response has been to become more suspicious of outsiders. In the Arab world, Americans and Europeans are afforded unearned status simply by being Westerners, yet at the same time are resented and sometimes feared for their knowledge, wealth, and power.

OBSERVATIONS OF AN UPPER-CLASS ARAB OF MILITARY BACKGROUND:

"The Arab is either at your feet, or at your throat. To control him, he must not be paid too much…or too little. If he is starving he will resent you and attempt to get his revenge. He will beg, borrow, or steal, doing whatever possible to take advantage of you, but always when you are not looking. On the other hand, if the Arab is overpaid, he will become fat and lazy and lose his respect for you. When overpaid, he considers you a fool, or weak and soft, deserving of being cheated. In weakness you lack honor and deserve your losses. An overpaid Arab will become uncooperative, stubborn and arrogant, spending his time eating, sleeping, boasting, and chasing women. His cooperation, and his value, generally recedes as his pay increases.

"It is a fine line. To control an Arab he must be paid "just enough," enough to keep him hungry, but never starving. Give him a little hope, but never fulfill his needs and wants completely. He must remain lean but fully aware of which hand provides for him and what that controlling hand requires in return. And punishment must be swift and certain. Always remain vigilant, however, and forever suspicious of his activities."[73]

COMMENT: While this assessment is useful in understanding the general Arab mindset, perhaps more valuable are the insights into the thoughts of this upper class elite Arab male from a military background. Over the centuries Arab military and political leadership have grown increasingly *less* effective precisely due to this mentality.

Born of Arab culture, yet nurtured in colonization or subservience by foreign officials, original thinking and initiative have never been encouraged or nurtured. In fact, such traits are avoided. The average Arab or typical military conscript has nothing to gain by personal or professional sacrifice or risk-taking. Lacking a consistent, built-in system of incentive or reward, Arabs grow up in an environment that encourages, no *mandates*, the most tenacious, self-preserving response possible. Look out for number one, or die. More to the point these attitudes demonstrate just how corrupt the Arab ruling classes have developed over a millennium of occupation by foreign powers—Middle Eastern and European. The upper echelons of society view the lowly Arab worker or conscript as a worthless beggar and thief, "either at your feet, or at your throat."

OBSERVATIONS OF AN EDUCATED ARAB-AMERICAN:

"Arabs spend a great deal of time discussing a wide variety of topics and matters, though nothing much of substance is usually accomplished. Much time is wasted in these 'bull sessions.'

"Arabs are only superficially confrontational. Ninety-nine percent of the time if challenged, they will back down. Arabs avoid serious personal conflicts, though they thrive on 'lively discussion.' Though often loud, generally this is not an indication of an aggressive personality. In fact, Arabs can be quite differential and non-aggressive.

"To avoid confrontations, Arabs often turn to intermediaries to negotiate a particularly tough point or challenge. This is done to allow one or both parties to 'save face,' to preserve their honor, and keep personal egos out of the deal. Facing a particularly difficult person, Arabs will typically attempt to go around the obstacle using the influence of a powerful friend, associate, or family member. Just about everything of substance in the Arab world is accomplished this way."[74]

COMMENT: Though these Arab social gatherings may be described as "bull sessions," they are also important forms of entertainment, but more so social "connecting," a valuable aspect of any culture. Arab society, and Middle East society in general, is highly verbal. How a man expresses himself is most important. For a woman, her personal, protective bulwark—the female support network around her—is critical to her well-being. Though little appears to be accomplished by the talkative Arab, important relationship bonds are being nurtured and strengthened, relationships the Arab will fall back on or retreat to in difficult times.

The intermediary in the Middle East is one of the most important yet little understood aspect of these cultures. The United States could better expand its efforts by cultivating useful and worthy Mideast intermediaries, and itself becoming a better intermediary when called upon.

Follow-up: Why does it seem that Arabs and many Muslims seem to carry huge cultural inferiority burdens in their minds and hearts?

Arabs, whether Christian or Muslim, have a serious problem: Dealing with reality. Between a bewildering hodge-podge of far-fetched and recycled conspiracy theories, and a boatload of cultural and historical baggage, the Arabs try to explain away a world of failures which have haunted their history.

Even today, with all that America has done in Iraq, Arabs rationalize that until the Americans give them, the Arabs, the honor and justice in the world "they deserve," that until they receive their just respect, America will continue to be attacked by their "Warriors of the Faith," and there never can be peace in the world.

For example, when I press my Egyptian friends as to why they are so against America and Israel, and in such apparent solidarity with the Palestinians, the confusion only multiplies. When I ask: "Why do you, my friend, support a people you do not know and you say you do not even like very much?" The response always is: "Yes, the Palestinians are untrustworthy. They will sell their own sisters for few dollars. They are like animals, with poor morals; they can never be trusted."

"Okay," I respond. "Then—help me out here—why do you support them so vehemently?"

"Because they are *Muslims*," is the reply from my Egyptian friend. "Because they are *Arabs*, and because they have gotten no justice in their lives. The Israelis kill them shamefully."

"Okay," I say, "but you just said they are essentially 'low-lifes.'"

"Yes, but they are Arabs being brought down and shamed; they are given no justice. This must be corrected, or there can never be peace."

"Why?" I say. "You just said they would sell their own sisters for nothing. They sound unsavory, unworthy of your loyalty. If the Israelis drive them out of Palestine, what is that to you?"

"That's just it, my American friend. The Israelis are worse; brutish criminals. They are murderers. The Arabs are brutalized and the Americans don't care about us. It says as much about *you* as it does the Israelis, doesn't it? Do you not care because they are Arabs? If this is so, then how can we, other Arab peoples, trust you? And if it happens to one group of Arabs, how soon will it be before others are also killed or shamed and brutalized in this manner? When does the shame end against *our people*?"

Fascinating, I thought. Now the Palestinians are "our people." "It seems," I respond, "you are supporting a people who are an extension of yourself. But more so, the honor of your race, the Arab race, seems to be at stake. Are you envisioning that once again, one day, the Arab race as a whole will rise to power and prominence in the world as they once were? Is the defeat of the Palestinians stifling that revival you envision? Is it reflecting on your powerlessness? Your hopelessness?"

No response. And being speechless for an Arab is a shockingly rare event.

I continue (obviously this is a *very* good friend). "Speaking honestly, my friend, today the Arabs are a hopeless people. They have no power, and little or no self-determination. Paraphrasing the Israeli politician Abba Eban, the Arabs 'never lose the opportunity to lose an opportunity.' Their lives are controlled by dictators and warlords. Tiny Israel, a nation of only a few Jews, has defeated the combined Arab armies time and again. Could it be that Israeli "depredations" against the Palestinians, a people you've said you don't even like, is really an attack on your ego, on your honor as an Arab?"

"No, no!" My Arab friend protests. "You must understand. The Jews crucified Esa' (Jesus). They control everything in the world, even the mighty American government. They are self-centered, watching out only for themselves. Leave them anywhere in the world and soon they will ruin everything, and steal away everything of value. They can't even run their own country without American assistance. As a people, the Jews are poison."

And so it goes, round and round. After talking with many different Arabs from a variety of national and cultural backgrounds, I am convinced that effectively no Arab support exists for the Palestinians based upon their Palestinian ethnicity. But there is major support for any Arab, anywhere, being "shamed" and defeated by the Jews, or by "crusading Christians." Arabs are by nature an elitist, even racist, people. Many call it merely an "historical and cultural bias." I call it what it is. Arabs also view the Americans, primarily due to the incredible amount of brain-washing they are subjected to by their media and in the mosques, as the modern equivalent of the crusading, empire building, European powers. This is tragic, for the Americans and the Europeans are a universe apart in their basic motivation, and firmness of dedication.

All said, Arabs suffer today from one mega-sized inferiority complex, exacerbated by an indigenous tyrannical political environment that stifles any kind of domestic political protest or dissent. (Dissent against America is okay, however).

The challenge for the United States in Iraq, however, would be somewhat lessened if America could be seen by the Arab world as actively working for Arab justice in Palestine. Then Arabs could get back to hating just the Jews, a much easier object for their anger than us normally lovable Americans.

Follow-up: What are some little known cultural realities I should be aware of?

THE LAND OF SMOKE AND MIRRORS

The language barrier aside, Arabs may appear difficult to understand, unpredictable, even illogical at times to the American observer. In reality, they are some of the most predictable and consistent peoples on earth, their motivations clear as glass, their long-sought desire for security born of history and culture.

Middle Easterners generally fear most the loss of personal and family (which is the same thing) *honor* and will go to almost any lengths to preserve it. Shame avoidance is an industry, and a Middle East institution. The most successful Americans working in Arab countries learn quickly to use this cultural reality to their advantage. Conversely, there is no greater threat to your success than forgetting the power of the honor-shame dynamic.

The next most important reality is perhaps easier to identify and control: It is not *what* you know, but *who* you know that counts. For any man or woman planning a career in these nations, this should be Rule Number 1. Middle East cities are built of many thousands of "village-neighborhoods" and within these neighborhoods everyone knows everyone else; probably related, too. In such a unique historical mosaic, men and women spend their lives cultivating family and tribal networks where nepotism determines who succeeds and who fails. Sadly success or failure is set in stone even before a child has the chance to prove himself. In Arabic, such prejudicial power is called "*wasta*." Without it you are nothing; more so, you are on the road to extinction.

However, with your quiver packed with honor, arrows launched by the cultural weapon of *wasta*, Abdullah, or John Doe American, can indeed slay mighty beasts and move impossible mountains. Detailed descriptions of both the "honor/shame dynamic" and the powerful wielding of wasta "for fun and profit" can be found in almost any bookstore or library, (and in previous works by the author).

The most successful American businessmen and women, as well as effective diplomats and educators, learn quickly to relax, to be friendly (but not overly so), and to be patient in establishing long-term, quiet, personal relationships, built on trust, with the *right* people. Quickly lower yourself into the cultural stream, and with oars in hand, go with the flow. Those Americans who fail in this region are almost always those who are "appalled" at how Arabs do things, how they drive cars, how they live their lives. Foolishly Americans sometimes attempt (always in vain) to change the status quo. Arab culture has been set in stone at least since Cain bludgeoned Abel to a brotherly pulp. Good luck making Arabs into Americans any time soon!

In that context, you cannot overstate the importance of patience in the Arab, Turkish, and Iranian Middle East. Addicted to your day planner? Shred it. And throw away your watch with it. While the Arab streets and bumper-car traffic are meat-grinders and most certainly the greatest physical hazard you will face, you will rarely hear of an Arab dying of hypertension or chronic ulcers. The Land of Smoke and Mirrors is also the Land Where Time Stands Still. If you insist on rushing it, you will fail.

Let's talk sex. While sexual activities are rarely discussed in mixed company, or in any public venue for that matter, Middle Easterners, both men and women, spend an inordinate amount of time *thinking* about, and *planning* for, their next sexual rendezvous or encounter. Much goes on beneath the surface, out of the public eye. If it's not seen or exposed, honor can still be preserved. Those many dusty, and often kinky, stories of the *harem* were highly undersold. Clandestine illicit affairs, primarily carried out by the male population for reasons covered in these pages, are commonplace, perhaps as much or more as in "satanic" America or Europe. Surprising to many Americans, most sexual activity is not strictly taboo in the Islamic World, *except* when it invades the light of day, threatening the family, the village community. In the neighborhood village *open* and graphic sexual displays or relations become the worst of plagues, the most abhorrent acts, punishable by extreme measures, especially for the women involved. But behind closed doors, shielded from Allah's eyes, the more humanistic, animal needs are satisfied on an ongoing basis.

Islam and Arab history contain far too many examples emphasizing the enjoyment of sex "for pleasure's sake," even accounts contained within the sacred Hadith of the Prophet. Christianity, on the other hand, places stronger taboos on such illicit activities, even branding unlawful sexual *thoughts* a sin, worthy of removing one's own offending eye to save the soul, if necessary. At the extreme are the comments by St. Paul, admonishing the believers to "touch not the opposite sex." In essence, Paul preached that if a man could not control himself, then perhaps it was best he marry, though total abstinence, even celibacy, would be the better, more righteous life.

Muslims have never been subjected to such unworkable, illogical, even punishing standards. So when you see a land with women shrouded from head to toe, and men and women at arms length, physically segregated in public and in the mosques, remember that in the Land of Smoke and Mirrors perception and reality seldom co-mingle. Honor is driven entirely by perception, by what is seen out in the open. To simply verify this, ask any American or European woman who has been cornered by an Arab or Iranian male, alone and hidden from the light of day.

Finally, the Middle East is *pure sensory overload.* Every sight, sound, and smell is designed to overwhelm and generally does. At once the Middle East bludgeons the mind and the senses, as do the many media images from this land. It is hardly a restful place, but that is why I love it so and why I've returned time and again. The Middle East is alive, and when you step from the plane, the fire is once more rekindled.

Stand facing mighty *al-Azhar* in the mega-city of Cairo; emerge the first time from the snaking rock passage spiriting you into Jordan's mysterious Petra; dive beneath the crystalline, color-drenched waterworld of the Red Sea. Stand midst any major Middle Eastern metropolis and witness the frenetic rush to nowhere.

Whether on the edge of chaotic *Midan Tahrir* in the heart of downtown Cairo, or seated atop peaceful Mount Nebo, every feeling, every thought, every sense is continually under assault. To most Americans, the pummeling is abrasive, numbing. To others— the fortunate ones—it heals, and it enlightens. I am convinced, however, that nearly all American visitors sense a primeval religious connection. Whether Christian, Jew, or Muslim, from some dark and distant age this was our spiritual home.

The Mount of Olives in Jerusalem is such a place too, and a place racing to a date with destiny, a destiny countless prophets have foretold for thousands of years. By any measure, this is an extraordinary land that men have praised God for, and shed blood to possess, since the foundations of the world. But until oil was discovered in the 19th and 20th centuries, this was a desolate, deprived, worthless land. Sometimes, however, things that appear the most worthless, are the more indispensable. The struggle to master and control this pivotal land continues with a passion; though if you saw a photo of Jerusalem's Temple Mount today you'd probably say, "Oh, what a peaceful sight."

Looks can be deceiving in the Land of Smoke and Mirrors.

SHI-SHA': THE GRAND ILLUSION

And speaking of smoke, "hubbly-bubbly," the water pipe, is an old custom which probably makes it a tradition, of sorts. A tradition for men; women not allowed.

The *shi-sha'* smoke shops are found everywhere, usually offered in tandem with tea and some light, traditional snacks like *tammaya* cakes and soda pop. The front doorway is open onto the street, beckoning the men enter, sawdust scattered on the floor, nothing fancy.

Within the "Pasha" sits stoically behind his counter and the required *sanduq*, the cash box or register, always under the Pasha's watchful eye. The cook and chief oil boiler is at the back lazily going about his business. Several boys (likely sons of the Pasha) hustle the greasy crystalline glasses of tea to the petite, battered and stained tables around which the male customers crowd.

Chatter is steady in such places, except for the "silent ones" who have chosen the ultimate in male expression: so-called *hubbly-bubbly*. Now, when looking at one of these bulky smoking contraptions one might think: "You know, with a little ingenuity this could be downsized, perhaps even made portable so every man could have one at home, there with the comforts of favorite wife, favorite chair, and TV close at hand."

Yet, if you nurture such a foolish thought right away you've missed the point. The glorious water pipe, you see, is the outward, *visual* expression to the world that "I am a man. I am my own Vizier, or Prince, seated here with other warriors like myself, allowing lesser men to scurry about waiting on me, and those pathetic people rushing by as slaves to their work outside the open door. Here I sit masterfully perched, puffing thoughtfully on my pipe and blowing smoke in the face of the world.

The hubbly-bubbly shop has always been for "manly men." A gathering of "he-bulls;" there the pipers, carefully, almost religiously, place the especially prepared glowing embers from the fire-tray onto the pipe's burn pedestal. Then, sucking on the long flexible stem, the embers glow to life pulling the gray smoke in a thick, billowing mass through the lower glass water reservoir, which then rises up through the liquid as a steady stream of rich bubbles, into the yard-long tube, the end and nozzle firmly planted in the male's pursed lips.

With a regal look of satisfaction, the pipers inhale the acrid smoke, and then (the exciting part) the smoke streams from both nostrils in thick, rope-like quantities, a steady stream of power rushing from the heart of the male-beast.

I gaze about me as several men grunt their pleasure, then stop smoking long enough to offer a short pontification in lofty fashion, then return, in bovine form, to blowing streams of manhood from their flaring nostrils.

While these special tea shops certainly do move a lot of tea, and the *tammaya* (falafel) cakes are always popular, the real action and true purpose comes from the pipes. The reason women cannot be found even in the kitchen (beyond the fact they would be disgusted by the place) is because this is a "guy thing." A Middle Eastern "Augusta National" club where men escape the hen-pecking and doldrums of life to sit unmolested for an hour or two, the Grand Pasha on his throne, the he-bull full of fire, not to be trifled with. This is the Illusion men everywhere have sought since the first time they saw a Sumerian god-king seated magnificently on his throne. And we all need our Grand Illusions from time to time.

QUESTION 14

- WHY DO MIDDLE EASTERN SOCIETIES TREAT WOMEN AS THE PERSONAL PROPERTY OF MEN?

> **"But for Eve, wives would never betray their husbands."**
> **From the Sacred Hadith of the Prophet Muhammad, Volume 4, Book 55, No. 547**
> **Recorded by Sahih al-Bukhari, Muslim theologian**

THE TEMPTRESS MYTH AND THE LILITH TRADITION

The Middle Eastern male's view of women was once a universal, worldwide view. Women were the property of men, period. They were born into the world as inferiors, the "weaker sex," lacking the size and physical strength of males and lacking the male member. In fact, they were considered by most ancient cultures as "males who did not develop properly in the womb"; nature's "second choice."

By today's scientific and cultural standards obviously such thinking is ridiculous, illogical, and woefully ignorant. Yet, we are on the road to fooling ourselves if we begin by denying our roots. We must squarely face our past if we ever hope to rise above it.

Historically, women were considered a threat to family and tribal stability and honor, based upon their supposed natural, inborn sensual proclivities, and their desire to "seduce" otherwise "upstanding men" and divert them from "certain and predestine greatness in the world." The Temptress Myth is as old as the legends of mankind, from Eve in the Garden of Eden, to Enkidu's succumbing to the Harlot in Gilgamesh, to Helen of Troy, and Cleopatra's seduction and destruction of Mark Anthony. Interestingly, "The Excuse" sheds more light on the psychological make-up of *men* than anything else.

Yet prior to Eve, Enkidu, Helen, or Cleopatra was Lilith. In Jewish rabbinical tradition, before Father Adam met Mother Eve, God gave Adam the woman Lilith to be his companion. Lilith, however, was a shrewish woman, a nag who demanded much from her husband.

Adam, she believed, was not aggressive, dynamic, nor fun-loving and adventurous enough; rather he was quiet, serious and rather dull. She wanted to re-make Adam. True, she was most beautiful, dark and mysterious and Adam loved her very much, but over time it was obvious that Lilith was not right for him. So, God decided to replace the shrewish Lilith with the equally beautiful Eve, who deferred to her husband, listened to his council, and played the quiet, supportive wifely role.

Lilith was outraged at God, so God banished her to Edom (the land the Greeks and Romans called *Idumea*) which has been identified as the land east of the Jordan River. (Edom is really representative of any land occupied by wilderness, wild beasts, and the heathen; in essence, unbelieving tribes and nations.) There in the wilderness Lilith's resentment and desire for revenge cankered and turned her into the "Night Hag," as cited in the Revised Standard Version of the Bible, "There shall the Night Hag alight."[75] The Hebrew word used in this passage is translated as "Lilith," an ancient name synonymous with a Babylonian monster of the night, likely originating from ancient Babylonian mythology. Later Jewish rabbis personified this night hag legend and gave her the name or title of Lilith.

In Jewish tradition Lilith became a demon of the night that conspired with the Serpent (Satan) to ensure the fall of Adam and Eve and their expulsion from the Garden of Eden. Lilith, it is said, is especially dangerous to young children, causing their deaths or stealing them away in the night, presumably due to her rage at her own childlessness, the curse given her by God for her rebellion. In any case, Lilith has for thousands of years remained the personification of the evil and seductive nature of women and why they must always be controlled and ruled over by their husbands and fathers.

The archaic and nearly universal view of women as chattel, as the property of males, is primarily the result of many millenniums of warfare, death and often extinction, of entire tribal families, villages, and even cities. The predatory, survival-of-the-fittest nature of males has required that women, for their own security, and the security of their children, remain sequestered within the bulwark of family and tribe. They were not considered capable by the males to fight battles or to range out great distances to hunt or raid other tribes, so women had practically no options for personal survival or personal material gain other than being wholly dependent on the male(s) in her life. In other words, they had little to offer the males beyond sexual pleasure, as domestic servants, or as "son-factories" to produce more warriors to enhance the tribe's security and wealth.

Therefore, a woman was taught at an early age, usually by her mother or older sister, to link with as powerful and potent a male as possible. To ensure this, a family would often betroth a girl even before puberty to ensure that she would be protected. If her husband-to-be was a powerful and respected man, no one would touch or harass her. Her goal, or her parents' goal, was to find a man who would give her sons, provide physically for her needs, and protect her from enemy raiders who would kidnap her and add her to the "female-wealth" of an enemy tribe as a concubine or slave. Such a captured "wife" was personal property and would be poorly fed and an abused servant of the captor's other wives, beaten and usually worked to death.

Due to the hopeless, chattel nature of women under such brutal systems, a woman seldom had little to offer a man beyond sex and servitude. Women, in order to survive, would frequently accuse other women of the tribe of being a seductress by nature. Even the traditional and prevailing Christian, Jewish, and Muslim story of Adam and Eve paints Eve alone as being morally defective, as having seduced Adam away from God.

Other cultures have similar legends and myths demonstrating the "weak moral fiber of women," the very ancient belief of women's "natural sensualness," and "inherent spiritual wickedness." Women, most cultures contend, must be protected and controlled because of women's natural tendency towards seduction, first and foremost. "Evidence" cited by men is the exorbitant amount of time girls and women spend dreaming of romance and love instead of wealth and conquest.

The historical reality, however, reveals that since the beginning of time women have had to be continually "available," ideally every minute, for the right man when he decided to show interest. Such culturally and biologically-dictated availability has made women hopelessly vulnerable to spurious accusations and dangerous condemnations, particularly by the religious establishment, in every culture, creed, and faith.

In reality, women had no choice but to shoulder this role. It is what biology, and tribal structure, has forced on them simply to survive. Traditional societies revolved around family life. Families were created and then nurtured principally by the women as a survival mechanism for themselves and their children. Of course men benefited equally. Traditional families have been the heart and soul of society, in essence the workable cultural glue that has bound tribes together for thousands of generations. "Eve's sacrifice," the ultimate personal gift, was to offer her life, her body, her spirit, *everything*, to ensure that the Family of Adam did not perish from the earth. In this quest women have been most successful. In this quest, however, their tenacity has been too often ignored, even belittled.

According to the Muslim theologian and scholar, Sahih al-Bukhari, in the Hadith, the Prophet Muhammad said the following about women: "Treat women carefully, for a woman is created from a rib, and the most curved portion of the rib is its upper portion, so, if you should try to straighten it, it will break, but if you leave it as it is, it will remain crooked. So treat women carefully."[76]

Judeo-Christian tradition says that Woman was created from the rib of man. Actually, the ancient Semitic word used was probably a form of *janib*, which can also be translated as the *side* of man. Isn't it possible that God intended for Woman to be created to stand at the *side* of Man, as partner and equal?

Leaders of the Christian, Jewish, and Islamic religions have done Eve—and by extension *all* women—a terrible, even criminal, disservice. Woman should not be condemned for her nature, but praised for her sacrifice. She is a tenacious survivor and under the burden she has born for countless generations, should be credited with this amazing success: the expansion and growth and prosperity of humankind into every region and climate on earth, creating a myriad of cultures, languages, and ethnicities.

Woman is a quiet hero, but a truly worthy one, and the heart and soul of mankind.

SLAVERY, BONDAGE, MAIDS AND CONCUBINES

Rosie sat in the corner of the maid agency in downtown Kuwait City. She was black and blue on her arms, arms she had raised to protect her face from the beatings. Only partially successful, the bruises about the right side of her face and right eye told a tragic tale. I gazed on her a moment and she immediately diverted her eyes. She slumped, lowering her head. She seemed to want to disappear.

But that was not possible, at least not in Kuwait. For the maid agency held her passport, or at least they said they knew where it was—probably still with Rosie's abusive Arab employer. In reality, she was a prisoner, unable to flee, or unable to work, without the required permission, physically broken down, beaten, horribly abused. This was not what the Philippine recruiter had promised when she had signed up and left her home in Manila two years previous. According to the maid agency, Rosie had debts she must "work off first before she could go home," money they said she "owed," for travel to Kuwait, her meals and board. It was soon obvious to her she could work many years for these slave bosses and put hardly a dent in what they said she owed them. Kuwait was now her debtor's prison.

Life had been tough in the Philippines, as well. But, it turned out for Rosie that the Persian Gulf was worse. Beaten and raped, she believed there was no way out but the "permanent solution." Stubbornly refusing to work and put up with the beatings any longer—which I truly admired her for, knowing the thrashing she must have endured for her courage—her Arab employer had driven her to the maid agency and dumped Rosie off, demanding another girl in her place.

The one thing the agency did not want was unemployed, non-producing women, especially troublemakers with lots of spunk. I had heard about Rosie from an embassy officer's maid who knew of her situation. I had arrived at the agency office to see if I could work out a deal for her. The building was rotting stucco over block, sandy façade with a crumbling block skeleton protruding at the edges. Within the steel door, a dank, cigarette smoke cave greeted me, with several yellow-toothed, raven men seated around a sagging formica table. A *qafiya*-clad Sudani served tea to the men, most appearing to be Egyptian, though one seated at the center of the table was Kuwaiti, dressed in the national uniform, the stark white *qamiis* reaching to the floor. He was gaunt and his hooked nose and narrow face seemed ashen in the shadows. Smoke swirled about his head. He did not speak, but suddenly arose and left the room. An Egyptian underling considered me a moment, then spoke: "Welcome. You are British? ...American?" He did not smile.

"*Wi-alaykum salaam*," I returned his greeting. He motioned for me to sit and a glass of sweet, gritty tea was dropped in front of me on the table.

After the usual small talk, I got to the point, asking about the maid called Rosie.

"We have many Rosies, friend," he came back. "We hire only the best, from the Philippines, from Sri Lanka, from India. I have several new, young ones coming this week. How many can we get for you?"

I pointed to the woman seated on the floor, by the door leading to the back of the offices. "Her."

The Egyptian manager thought a moment, certainly wondering if this situation could cause him any more trouble. Finally he seemed to brighten a bit, nodding. "Yes. But how do you know her?" He was noticeably more suspicious.

"I know a friend of hers."

He forced a smile. "Then you know she is a troublemaker."

"May I talk to her?"

He stroked his bushy mustache, his head wobbling a bit. "*Tayib*... okay. Go to her." He motioned towards her with the back of his hand, as if he was writing her, and me, off.

I knelt by her, studying her face. In the dim light I could see she was in pain. "Rosie, your friend Evelyn—you remember her?"

She was still looking away, then slowly turned to face me. She seemed to study my eyes. "Of course," she whispered.

"Evelyn tells me you speak English and that you are an excellent maid, that you are great with kids and that you work hard and don't complain...much." I smiled.

Noticeably, she brightened and nodded.

"Do you understand my words? I want to offer you a job, if you want one."

"Yes," she said. "Yes, yes." She sat up taller taking a deep breath.

"Good. I have three young daughters. If my wife likes you, and you get along with the girls, we will see how things go. So you want the job?"

She pulled herself to her feet as if she wanted me to get a better look at her. "I work hard and *never* take any time off…for you and your family."

"No, Rosie, you'll get time off each week. Where is your stuff?" I asked.

She pointed to two plastic sacks next to her against the wall.

"That's it? Okay. Wait here."

Returning to the Egyptian, suddenly "his Rosie" was special, in fact she was the most valuable maid the agency owned. She supposedly owed the Arab she had worked for 200 Kuwaiti *dinars* (about $740.) for some dubious reason. The manager was fuzzy on details. But the 200 dinars had to be paid in cash to release her. I knew I was being shaken down.

Finally, after finishing a bottle of Pepsi, and discussing the city of Cairo, specifically Giza where the manager had come from several years earlier, we "refined" the price to a more manageable 100 dinars (about $370.). It was more than I wanted to pay up front, though I felt guilty enough negotiating for this petite Filapina girl like so much human flesh on the auction block. The Egyptian kept commenting on her "other abilities and charms," always with a wink and a nod. It was something out of Medieval Europe, or the Deep South prior to the Civil War, I guessed, or perhaps 1001 Arabian Nights. And it was disgusting to me, but truly a fascinating look into the past.

So, I paid the manager the cash (of course, easier to pocket), and we signed the papers; Rosie was mine. The agency manager would arrange to pick up Rosie's passport from her former employer and I would retrieve it from him the following morning (I held back half the cash as incentive). As we walked from the office, a noticeable sigh of relief escaped her lips. She later told me that had she spent the night there, she would likely have been raped by one of the men in the offices. Most of the girls, she said, were abused by the men responsible for transporting them to Kuwait to work in the first place.

As we drove to our home to meet my wife and daughters, Rosie was all smiles. She kept telling me over and over again "thank you, sir, thank you." I remember being most uncomfortable with the "sir" handle, especially coming from a woman not much younger than I was at the time.

She was immediately accepted by my wife and our three daughters. Right away Rosie was one of the family. We paid her well and treated her better and through her eyes learned a whole lot about the women expatriate workers of the Gulf. Rosie, it seemed, had Philippino friends and "cousins" all over Kuwait City. The world of the poor, foreign worker is an amazing world, one hard to fathom in our surreal American prosperity and almost limitless freedom. And while in fairness, the large majority of Arab employers of female Asian maids treat them well enough, a sizable minority do not. In the highly stratified and prejudice Middle East, women, especially *Asian* women, who are also Christians, sit pretty close to the bottom, somewhere between a prostitute and the family car.

Follow-up: Why do *non*-Muslim women fare so poorly in the Muslim countries of the Middle East?

The problem of battered and abused women is endemic in the Middle East, as it is in many parts of the world. As discussed, the Arab world continues to view women, particularly *non*-Islamic women, as less equal or less worthy and always less virtuous. Traditionally they were property to be bought and sold, used and abused. Today their worst abuse, however, often comes at the hands of the women of the households where they work.

On countless occasions I've talked with Philippine maids working in Arab homes hearing incredible stories of abuse and cruelty. One young filipina, not yet 21 years old, told of being repeatedly raped by her male employer and then alternately beaten by the man's wife for allowing her husband to sleep with her. The Philippine maid was forced to work 18 to 20 hours per day by the Arab wife, seven days a week, without a bed to sleep on, only an old blanket to curl up on in the corner of the kitchen. Finally in desperation, the maid jumped from a window of the villa and fled to the Philippine embassy, a broken ankle the price of her freedom.

Adding insult to injury, the girl's employer would not return her passport until she paid him what amounted to hundreds of dollars in supposed "debts" she owed. (Arab employers generally hold a worker's passport just to prevent such "escapes.")[77] She was practically penniless. Without her passport, and with her name on a watch-list at the airport, it was impossible for her to leave the country and return home. The Philippine embassy, in their usual timidity, did not want to violate Kuwaiti law by issuing her another passport under a false name. The Philippines is so badly dependent upon Kuwait, and other Gulf nations, to employ their workers, that they seem to be unwilling to take any meaningful action, though they would usually try to sort things out. So, the girl was stuck. In poverty, left alone with no one willing to help. Many such young women end up back on the streets, often in the sex trade.

Sometimes these unfortunate runaways would be picked up by the police. In several reported incidents I heard about, officers raped these girls, then took them to the station and held them for some time in a private cell where they would be repeatedly assaulted. Sometimes the Filipina girl would simply disappear. No one seemed to care. I heard many such reports and always tried to forget the horrors these petite, powerless young women had likely faced.

Truly most Arab employers in the Persian Gulf region are not so blatantly inhumane; yet too many are and remain so today. It is difficult for Americans to understand such harsh cruelty, especially in a land of almost endless oil wealth and prosperity. With so much to go around, why can't Arabs afford to be a bit more generous to their help? Such exploitation can be defined as slavery, if slavery is forced labor under inhumane conditions with little or no compensation. These conditions are found not only in the Gulf, but all across the Arab world, as well as much of Asia and Africa. Non-payment of wages, rape, abuse, neglect, attempted suicide, and conditions of slavery, all have generally been given only superficial attention by local governments and by the international media. Why do human bondage, abuse and torture still remain in our 21st century world, where one race or creed continues to view others as inferior or "less worthy?"

In the case of Muslim nations, men continue to view women as less equal, and foreign, non-Islamic women, well below that. Facing such incredible cultural prejudices, no wonder these maids, who arrive from the most economically disadvantaged regions of the world, are considered unworthy of respect or humane treatment. They are no better than farm animals in the minds of many.

To work or live in the Middle East is a unique challenge, whether you are Philippine, Indian, Polish, or American. Each race, sex, and religion faces different hurdles, dangers, and opportunities. But one thing is certain: traditions which place people in strata, in classes of more or less "worthy," are a curse that is stifling the region. Until Arabs are liberated from such false traditions, they will continue to be damned or held back, like the rushing river so desperate to reach the free and open sea. Until education, technology, and the universal spread of truth finally sweeps Muslim lands in force, the captives will never be liberated and these nations will continue to flounder in their medieval prejudices.

QUESTION 15

- WHY DOES ISLAMIC CULTURE OFTEN TEACH THAT MEN MUST CHOOSE BETWEEN THE TEMPTATION OF WOMEN AND THE RIGHTEOUSNESS OF GOD?

This is an important concept. One vital choice a Muslim man makes in his life is the choice between the temptation of women and the righteousness of God. Man comes to earth to learn to make choices. The test comes from the many temptations. One of the greatest potentially destructive choices dangled before every Muslim man is women. The ultimate tempter.

Islamic culture and Islamic Law attempt to remove some temptation by controlling the availability of women in society, by requiring them to cover their bodies, and to keep them safely within the confines of the home, or in earlier ages, the harem.

However, women must leave the home at times, to shop, to visit family or friends, or to take children to school. In order to guard against possible fondling or groping on public transportation, the woman must cover herself from head to toe. This tells the world she is not an "easy woman," nor is she "available." Yet more accurately, the required veiling of women allows men to roam freely and unencumbered, while the woman is shackled and shrouded for the "good of society."

Many Muslim women, however, do not view veiling as shackling, but rather as providing them greater freedom. But whenever society dictates to certain individuals what they can and cannot wear, the culture, *any* culture, and its dominant religion, become that much more totalitarian. This is always manifested in fewer economic and political freedoms and opportunities. The veiled woman sacrifices something, whether Muslim women will recognize it or not. As well, if men are "tempted" by the exposed flesh and soft, flowing hair of a woman, shouldn't the tempted male be required to wear blinders, or a chastity belt, for his own good, and the good of the community?

The Sexual Revolution and the women's liberation movement both threaten the Islamic community in ways never before encountered since the time of Muhammad. At the heart of Islamic culture is the necessity of keeping the power of women contained and protected within the family and village structure. Unleashing such a power, many Islamic scholars believe, will destroy the Islamic community, or change it beyond recognition in a very short time. The latter is probably true.

In Islamic tradition, it is dangerous for a man to be truly in love with his wife. Unleashing such unbridled passion could lead the male to neglect or abandon God. Therefore, in society the roles of women and men are strictly segregated. Distance is maintained. Marriages are usually arranged, often between a much older man and a young wife, further distancing them. Men concern themselves with religion and work, women with family and homemaking. Men and women do not pray together, worship is segregated. Family time is seldom with both father and mother present. The practice of polygamy further distances the relationship; the more wives a man marries, presumably the relationships become increasingly distant and superficial.

A man can divorce his wife simply by stating "I divorce thee" three times to her face and to witnesses. In this way their relationship is even less important than a business relationship. The woman, however, does not have such freedom. It is very difficult, if not impossible, for a woman to divorce her husband in Islam if the husband will not agree. Islamic traditions are designed to limit or control the power of the woman and to enhance that of the man in the male-female relationship. It is also designed to limit the emotional bonds between husband and wife. Again, God is a jealous god. Any worldly temptation or earthly possession that distracts man from the worship of God must be controlled.

When in public, the women and girls wear the *hijab*, the traditional headscarf designed at a minimum to cover her hair, considered a highly sensual part of a woman. In an insightful article carried in the Jordan Times newspaper, several University of Jordan students reported that: "Wearing the hijab is the only choice left to me if I want to complete my university studies, to get a driver's license, or go to visit my friends. I am under pressure from my parents, from my brothers, and even from my future (arranged marriage) husband's family."

In order to avoid family clashes, or social criticism, many young women knuckle under and put it on. Another young woman, a third-year art student, stated: "My parents forced me to wear the hijab when I entered university because my cousin studies at the university too, and they pointed out it would be a bad idea for our relatives (from which her future husband would likely be chosen, the normal union in Mideast countries) in the village to see me without the hijab. But I take it off whenever I leave the university."[78]

Many young women view the hijab as a vital factor Jordanian men look for when they think of marriage. "Because there is a lot of moral corruption in our society, men look for a 'decent' girl when they want to get married. And hijab, considered as a sign of 'good manners' and decent behavior; men prefer veiled women," another university student added.

Dr. Mohsin Abdul Hamid, an Islamic academic and author of the book "Hijab in the Holy Book and Sunna," (a popular book during the 1990s in the Arab world, written in Arabic) wrote that one of the reasons for hijab is to "maintain the men's 'psychological sanity'" and (to) preserve "sound social relations."[79]

A common notion in the Muslim world is that men have a most difficult time keeping their passions under control and that a scantily clad woman on display is not the kind of temptation men should be expected to handle. Dr. Hamid goes on: "Hijab is...a kind of protection and a necessity that Muslim women must comply with particularly in the present state of the 'Muslim nation' where Arab society is in dire need of religion and the moral principles Islam calls for."

Countering this view is Rana Husseini, another university student: "I don't believe in wearing the hijab. What we really need is at least to stop slandering one another, to treat each other kindly and to be committed to Islam's morals as much as we can. I think this is really much more important than wearing the hijab."[80]

In practice, Islam is designed to ensure that women, and men, remain in their proscribed places before God. This, as the many great Islamic teachers over the centuries have stated, is for the good of mankind and the detriment of the Devil, or *Shaytan*, in Arabic.

God must be defended every day or the gates of Hell may rupture wide-apart.

Since the beginning, the sexual power women have over men has been a source of awe and fear. Many Qur'anic and some Biblical stories, particularly the story of Adam and Eve and their expulsion from the Garden, emphasizes the moral weakness and corrupting nature of women. The fear is that one day women might escape their Godly-mandated bonds and ruin society by turning men away from God's Law and sending all mankind to Hell. In recent years, as American culture—the culture of Madonna, Britney Spears, and Bay Watch—has assaulted the Islamic World, fundamentalists have erupted in anger, even fear. Part of the backlash has been Islamic terror.

In America, women travel freely and without their fathers' or husbands' permission, staying in hotels where unmarried men and women share the same hotel rooms. Women usually work outside the home with married men. They often show signs of public affection (like holding a man's hand) out on the street where everyone, even children, can see! (Heaven forbid!) They mix socially with men they are not married to, in public and in private. All these things anger many Muslims.

In American culture, romantic love is even *encouraged* and marriages are seldom, if ever, arranged by family matchmakers; and the marriages are usually between a man and women who are about the same age. Strong emotional bonds are encouraged between husbands and wives, and children are ideally to be raised by *both* father and mother. Women vote in elections, run for office, and stand on a legal par with men; they can drive cars, fly jets, and head up powerful corporations.

Women are often seen in scanty bathing suits and in movies seem to enjoy going to bed with just about any man they meet. Obviously, Western social ways or proclivities frighten the Muslim world, not that such illicit activities happen, but that they happen *in public*. They represent an overwhelmingly seductive road to cultural and religious change. And such change in the Middle East is to be feared and resisted at all cost, say the radicals.

So here we find ourselves. One underlying factor of Mideast-born terrorism, a factor seldom, if ever, discussed, has the future freedom, or continued enslavement, of women at its heart.[81]

America, and the Muslim world, must make some hard choices. But no question in the end: People—including women—will be free. No political system on earth has yet enslaved the human spirit forever. Sooner or later the slaves rise against their masters. And in the end, we hope, the suffering and sacrifice will be worth it.

In conclusion, let us quote a great American thinker, Ralph Peters:

"The transition from women as property to women as full participants in society has been the greatest revolution in human history. Its reverberations will be felt for centuries. Repressive cultures are horrified by it because it calls into question their most fundamental biological, sociological, and religious ideas. However, the oppression of women anywhere is not only a human rights violation, it's a suicide pact with the future."[82]

QUESTION 16

- WHY ARE MIDDLE EASTERN WOMEN AND GIRLS KILLED FOR THE HONOR OF THEIR MEN?

> *O ye who believe! Stand out firmly for justice as a witness to Allah, even against yourselves, or your parents, or your kin, and whether it be (against) rich or poor. For Allah can best protect both. Follow not the lusts (of your hearts) lest ye swerve and if ye distort (justice) or decline to do justice, verily, Allah is well acquainted with all that ye do.*
> --*The Holy Qur'an, al-Nisa' 4:135*

HONOR KILLINGS OF WOMEN AND GIRLS, REVISITED

In a previous work by the author[83], the tragic topic of honor killing was explored, incidents witnessed while the author was stationed in the Hashemite Kingdom of Jordan. Much more, however, needs illuminating on this amazing and insightful cultural issue.

Honor killing in Middle Eastern society is usually defined as the murder of a woman or girl for real, or perceived, immoral or rebellious behavior bringing shame to a tribe or family. Such behavior may include marital infidelity or adultery, even if only perceived, including being caught alone with a man, fornication, and "allowing" herself to be raped. It can also occur when demanding a divorce from her husband, refusing an arranged marriage, flirting with a man, even online, and failing to perform "wifely duties." This is usually broadly defined.

A man who fails to protect the women in his family circle from "sinful acts" is considered weak and shame-filled, unable to fulfill his God-given responsibility. When a woman is violated with "worldly sins," she shames those called to protect her from herself. The family, particularly the males, are responsible for keep the Jezebel hiding in every woman from bursting free. As well, the father is shamed for not raising up his daughter, or instructing his wife, to be a "good woman." To effectively execute this charge, the senior male must have total control over his women and girls. Such control over family members is not negotiable. Such patriarchal vigilance, of course, is as old as mankind.

While the religion of Islam technically does not sanction honor killings today, the vital cultural tradition of "honor preservation" overwhelms any religious resistance. To make matters worse, most Muslim governments, particularly in the Middle East, North Africa, and South Asian areas, refuse to seriously prosecute such killings, which are considered internal family affairs.

Article 340 of the Jordanian Penal Code, as well as Article 98, provide that men accused of honor killings are not prosecuted for murder but instead for "crimes of honor," which carry light sentences, usually three months to a year. The penalty for murder, by comparison, is nearly always death. Recently there was a worldwide campaign to do away with Article 340, but the proposal was defeated by the Jordanian Parliament. Members claimed that abolishing Article 340 would amount to "legislating obscenity" and that the campaign to do away with Article 340 "was an attempt by the West (America) to infiltrate Jordanian society and demoralize (to corrupt and make sinful) women."

The killing continues. Women are murdered and maimed daily by the men they should be most able to trust. Incredibly, in many cases, the killers are being assisted by mothers and aunts. Many such deaths are reported officially as suicides or accidental deaths. They are seldom, if ever, investigated, unless the elders of the family request an investigation, which rarely, if ever, happens.

The honor-killer is usually a father, an older brother, stepbrother, or cousin, though sometimes he is the woman's husband. The common choice to take the life of a "wayward" daughter is a teenage half-brother. Middle Eastern judges, police and courts are usually more lenient with a teenage male, far more than they would be with an older uncle, for example. The judge understands how important a strong young son will be to the family over a lifetime. Sons are security, income, protection, and pride, all rolled into one. Sons are money in the bank in Middle East culture; Social Security,

Arab-style. As the boy matures, he will shoulder most of the financial burden of the family and provide shelter and income for the parents in old age. It's the bottom line, pure and simple: Middle East society places greater monetary value on the life of a son over that of a daughter every time.

Middle Eastern tradition requires all girls and young women to be taught the strict meaning of, and how to avoid, *eib*, or "shame." They are also keenly educated on the importance of *sharaf*, or "honor." A girl's life revolves around remembering her most important life mission: to protect her virginity at all cost, until the family arranges a proper marriage.

For boys, on the other hand, the topic of virginity is not emphasized. Young men are taught to have *gharra*, or *ghayrat*,[84] which means to be penetrating, aggressive, to seduce (women), to be passionate, but more accurately, sexually potent or virile. A man lacking such qualities is shameful. He is, in effect, not a man. (Sales of Viagra™ in the Middle East are more than brisk.)

The United Nations Population Fund estimates that perhaps 5,000 women and girls are murdered by the males in their families each year. These honor killings occur in nearly all parts of the world, but are associated almost exclusively with Muslim culture. Many more women than that are maimed. This is why some women are veiled: to hide scars and disfiguring done to them by angry husbands or fathers. Women have noses cut off or split with a knife or razor, ears hacked away, or their faces slashed. Sometimes they are splashed with acid. Such punishment, their husbands will say, comes from their failing to obey orders or for perceived flirting with another man. Such punishment is "deserved," so women must learn their place in the world, which amounts to little more than the personal property of the men in her life. Failure to conform, many Muslims believe, may lead to the collapse of traditional Islamic society. Religious teachings from the Qur'an, the perpetrators claim, backs them up:

"As to those women on whose part ye fear disloyalty and ill-conduct, admonish them, refuse to share their beds, beat them..."[85]

In the Hashemite Kingdom of Jordan, *Hoda*, 40 years old, was released from prison after a three-year sentence for having sexual relations with her step-son. Upon returning to her parent's home, she was shot to death by her father who cited the necessity of restoring the family honor.

Also in Jordan, a young woman, accused of having sexual relations with a Palestinian, was tied to a chair by her brother, who then gave her a glass of water and read to her from the Qur'an. Then he calmly stepped behind her and slit her throat with a kitchen knife. Her flowing blood, he was heard to say, cleansing the family's shame, returning their lost honor.

24 year-old Kajal Khidr was taken by members of her husband's family in Northern Iraq. Accused of committing sexual offenses, she was tortured and permanently scarred and mutilated, her nose partially cut off. Since she was pregnant, the family told her she would be killed once the child was born.

After spending time in a local hospital, she fled to the city of Sulaymaniya in the north of Iraq and later to Syria. There human rights workers resettled her and her child in a third country where she now lives. Her husband's male relatives, accused of torturing and mutilating Kajal, were arrested but then released. The courts argued that the men had acted to protect family honor. No charges were filed. The men are free today.[86]

On April 6, 1999, while visiting her lawyer's office, Samia Sarwar, age 29, was killed by her own mother. She had fled her husband's home, who she claimed was beating her, and sought out a human rights lawyer, Hina Jillani, in an attempt to obtain a divorce. While seated in her attorney's office in a Pakistani city, Samia's mother appeared at the door and entered with a large bearded man next to her. The lawyer, Hina Jillani, demanded that the unknown man leave immediately. To this, the mother responded: "I cannot walk. He's my helper." As the mother sat across from her daughter, the man suddenly pulled out a handgun and shot Samia in the temple. She died instantly.[87]

Dozens of other recent examples could be cited. Most, however, are never formally or officially reported. These are highly secretive family tragedies. There are few if any incentives for people within these tribal groups to come forward. Most believe that outsiders would not understand anyway. Obviously true, though just because something appears inexplicable does not lesson the heartbreak or limit its barbarity. That such often occurs in rural villages among the uneducated does not excuse such actions, nor pardon government officials who allow such brutality.

Though men and women in America would be appalled by such actions, many say it is not America's responsibility to end it. The leaders of Muslim nations can no longer excuse these so-called "honor killings." They must stop them. But currently the only form of protection most of these nations offer a woman or girl is imprisonment in a hostile local or national jail or penitentiary! Most women would rather die than spend their lives in such "protective custody" in such squalid and dangerous places.

True, these are old and proud cultures; and yes, they do things differently than we do. However, who but the most heartless among us, or the most blind, would view that as an excuse? Who among us can turn our back on the taking of innocent human life? By so doing we are little better than those tribal butchers of innocent women and girls. And lacking honor by our inaction—as any Arab would surely tell us—the sooner *we* fall, the sooner *we* are buried in the world, the better.

Such barbaric cultural practices must be ended *now*. The point remains, in spite of the whining, the complaining, and typical hand-wringing in the United Nations, in Europe, in Asia, and in Muslim countries, the world looks to *America* to end this ongoing tragedy. As is always the case, and in spite of official statements of opposition to the U.S., the world expects the Americans to make the sacrifice, in lives and treasure, to bring change to these despotic regimes and end the brutal killings of Muslim women and girls. Among the many already cited, this is but *one* more reason why democracy must succeed in Iraq, why America must succeed.

Question 17

- WHY IS THIS WAR AGAINST TERRORISM ALSO A "WAR FOR AMERICAN VALUES," FOR DEMOCRACY, FOR FREE AND OPEN MARKETS?

America is at war, though many struggle to understand why because the nature of warfare has changed so radically. It should be obvious to even the casual observer by now that at its heart the war in Iraq was a part of a global, multi-faceted strategy and not solely to control weapons of mass destruction, nor to address any single issue. This latest strategic installment, following the Cold War and Desert Storm in 1991, is to ensure worldwide freedom, and most critically open, stable markets, with the United States in the leadership role. At its heart, this is a war to ensure that American values remain pre-eminent.

Do not be fooled by the foreign, and sadly even some American, media outlets questioning America's reasons for going to war. Certainly the United States truly wants peace, freedom, and prosperity for the people of Iraq and the world. This is not, as many have claimed, a "war for empire" or a "war for oil." Secure, open international markets are essential to America's continued leadership and security. The business of America is *business,* guaranteeing freedom, prosperity and opportunity for the greatest numbers of people. However, convincing the world, and winning the support of the American Left, will prove a far greater challenge than actually beating the hapless Iraqis, or even the terrorists, on the battlefield.

Day by day, the protesters marshal their disparate forces, though the so-called "peace lobby" is missing the point entirely. At its heart America's cause is *not* solely about vanquishing a troublesome tyrant and his weaponry; nor about defeating the terrorist horde. Nor is it about guaranteeing U.S. access to cheap and abundant fuel. While all of the above are important, the American military occupation of the Persian Gulf region is key to U.S. leadership, peace, and worldwide stability; in a word, global *hegemony* for American values, free markets, and U.S. strategic dominion in a dangerous world.

The Gulf, dripping in sweet crude, is an absolutely irreplaceable energy storehouse and principal export supplier for China and Europe. Our goal was never simply to oust Saddam Hussein. Our objective, evolving over the past decade, through at least three different administrations, was to establish a pro-U.S. government in Iraq, a friendly regime and future ally—in OPEC, and within the heart of a most dangerous and hostile territory—backed by the full power of the United States.

The war on terror was never solely the result of an al-Qaeda sucker punch on September 11th, 2001, though that was the catalyst setting America in motion. This is part of a well-orchestrated and skillfully executed plan: *Mastering the global strategic power of oil.* Absolute hegemony over strategic resources and real estate is the bulwark of security. Remember, it is not the *price* of oil, or even the often outrageous profits. It is the *power* of oil, the strategic muscle—military, political, and economic—bestowed on the nation with its hand firmly on the spigot. A modern army's lifeblood is oil. A modern economy is dead-on-arrival when the oil stops, and no nation is addicted more severely to the "black gold" of the Gulf than the sometimes hostile nations of Europe and the enigmatic Peoples Republic of China.

It was never sufficient to simply oust Saddam or we would have done so back in 1991. At best such an accomplishment would have been a band-aid, a temporary fix, anyway, due to the almost universal infection of the weapons of mass destruction (WMD) Pandora's Box, and widespread Middle East nurturing of deadly Islamic terrorist factions. If not Iraq, then Iran, Pakistan, Saudi Arabia, Syria, or...? The objective all along was to establish a pro-U.S. government in Iraq, backed by the overwhelming power of our military, combined with our always persuasive, absorbing economic might. A *pro*-U.S. Iraqi regime? Modern miracles happen all around us. Why not between the Tigris and Euphrates?

With a cooperative, democratic Iraq, the U.S. can then turn its sights on the Islamic Republic of Iran, or one of several other threatening, brutal dictatorships. Pressing them to end support for terrorism, we will close their terrorist training camps and cut off funding, loosening the bands of despotism in the process and help them join the world of peaceful, prosperous nations. In the process, critical funding for Palestinian terrorist factions will dry up. With nowhere to turn, such factions and rogue nations will be much easier to pacify. In a more secure environment, Israel will likely be willing to dismantle Jewish West Bank/Gaza settlements and begin to cooperate with the so-called "Road Map to Peace."

This is the heart and soul of the Bush peace plan. "Peace through strength," rather than "peace through consensus," or the historically disastrous peace through never ending negotiation. For a decade and more we've tried that bankrupt approach. In many ways, 9/11 was the result. The terror-mongers will never go away peaceably through appeasement or negotiation. There's just too much at stake.

In reality, the United States would rather lop-off Florida and set her adrift into the Caribbean than give up military control over the Persian Gulf region. Quite literally the Gulf is that critical to U.S. national security and economic prosperity into the 21st century. Any president allowing the retreat of the United States from this vital region would severely compromise U.S. security. More so, you could mark America's decline in the world and the beginning of chaos and war from that point forward.

Nothing hates a power vacuum more than the oil-rich, strategically situated, Persian Gulf. Therefore, we will "negotiate" from a position of strength and never abandon our responsibilities to the region. We are there to stay. And without a doubt this is *precisely* what Middle East dictators fear. Any other approach on our part will fail, which means increasingly devastating terrorism and more innocent American dead.

The so-called "peace lobby" is dangerously naïve, if not damaging to America. Pulling a "Jane Fonda," Democratic congressmen, as well as Sean Penn and others, have sponsored their own hopelessly foolish pilgrimages to Baghdad in years past. Such efforts, perhaps well-meaning, gave Saddam cheap propaganda victories and encouraged greater Iraqi resistance, costing many hundreds of lives that could have been spared with a determined, rock-solid American front.

Mr. Penn, can't you read between the lines here? War was a done deal the moment 9/11 occurred and the towers fell and our

Pentagon was left in ruins. And with American forces already deployed to the region before your "sojourn" took place, such pacifist meddling could not possibly help make our troops' job any easier, or any less hazardous. Though every American should be free to pursue the path they deem necessary or prudent, such irresponsible actions must be accounted for. Yet we seldom see such costly and damaging interference prosecuted in our courts, and *never* when it is perform by our celebrities. Why is that? Where much is given, much is expected. And everyone should be held accountable for their individual actions.

The Left's political dogma of "peace at any price," their new-age mantra, sets America up for future acts of terror, international blackmail (like an iceberg, most of which we never see), and horribly costly future wars to be fought by our children *on our own soil*. We have already explored in detail how Middle Easterners view the use of power and the projection of strength and weakness. Their ways are not our ways.

The time has come to halt the national hand wringing and feet dragging by some of our leaders. God help us if we don't get the job done at this critical juncture. If we hesitate, our enemies will view this as weakness, an opening to exploit, and rush even faster to acquire horrible weaponry. If we vacillate, the probable nuclear war we leave our children to fight, at home and abroad, will cost millions of lives and conceivably bankrupt our nation, ravaging and denuding major parts of the world. Having seen these terror groups from the inside, I know their goals and objectives. God help us, *we must win this war.*

Certainly there are risks. The world we entered on the morning of September 11th 2001 is not for the timid; but no other nation on earth can shoulder the task. It is time to act, America; but more so it is time to lead!

Follow-up: What are the differences in leadership style between Bill Clinton and George W. Bush and how does this relate to advocating American values and waging the War on Terror?

President William Jefferson Clinton loved to talk; one of the truly best talkers we've seen in the White House in many years. Many Americans, and even more foreigners, loved this president. Truly he was exceptional at connecting with people on a personal level. Hardly a day would go by that he wouldn't talk about his many good intentions—plans for this program, and that goal and objective, as if verbal intention, in itself, was enough. Often the media would defend him saying, "Oh, yes, he means so well. He truly cares! The Republican Congress just keeps getting in his way!" This is what we heard from much of the media for eight long years.

President George W. Bush, however, is a very different type of President. He gets tongue-tied and confused at times. Too often he doesn't have much to say, his sentences short, pithy. Certainly if you wanted President Bush to act and respond as President Clinton did during his eight year reign you've been too often disappointed. More importantly, however, you'd be making a grave mistake in judgment. Obviously, Osama bin Laden, Saddam Hussein, and the Taliban, too, have made that same mistake.

Like President Clinton, Arabs love to talk. And as a people I believe they are the world's best. Everything must be discussed, worn out, thoroughly dissected; intentions weighed, honor and shame considered, everything to the minutest detail. Rarely, however, does anything concrete actually get done. We've already discussed their dismal regional and national productivity figures backing up this statement.

Yes, when it comes to talk, President George W. Bush comes up short. Simply, he is not the "Great Communicator;" but that's okay. For he measures his success in deeds, and I suspect, measures his failures in good intentions, unfulfilled. If you question such a statement, read President Bush's report to Congress on September 20, 2001, the so-called "Bush Doctrine" on terrorism. Then read between the lines. President Bush is deadly serious here, you can sense it in his stance; you see it in his eyes. It is essential that the world get in step with this president, or they will be marginalized and left behind.

Obviously United Nations' leadership is struggling with America's path already succeeding in the Middle East. Many in the world community are far from thrilled to see America establish a pro-U.S. government in Iraq and spread democracy throughout the region. Such a successful effort will only enhance America's power and influence with the most important oil-rich states. China especially is troubled over U.S. control of so much of their energy lifeline.

Those who believe that the Bush Administration is obsessed solely with Iraq and Saddam Hussein, for whatever reason, have missed the point. Truly they should read his words in the September 20th statement cited above. This is *not* exclusively about Iraq and never has been.

The President's report to Congress commits to accomplishing a whole lot, especially creating jobs and opportunities all over the world. America is in a strong position now to demand certain concessions from other nations in exchange for security and prosperity. At enormous cost, America protects the Europeans and the Asians against rogues; it funds a long list of development projects and grants and invests hard-earned American dollars all over the world. Most of all, the U.S. provides a costly security umbrella, which in turn allows other nations to invest safely in infrastructure, education, and in feeding and employing their own people. America does the job. We rarely complain, even in the face of unjust criticism and physical attack.

In our highly stratified—which means *unequal* or *prejudice*—world, most people understand such thinking, *if* you talk to them alone, one-on-one. Truly, they admire American freedom, and they admire Americans, in spite of the steady drumbeat of media propaganda to the contrary. Though American liberals and leftists, as well as a handful of foreign radicals, will stir up the masses against perceived American "inequities," the average world citizen has other priorities. Each knows where his or her bread is buttered and thanks primarily to corrupt tyrants and strongmen, the masses are exceedingly hungry. America offers hope.

The Bush Doctrine calls for a "war of ideas" to make terrorism as unacceptable in the world as slavery, piracy, and genocide. This is important, for in too many lands, slavery, piracy, and genocide are still widely practiced by the local Saddams and Osamas. Reading between the lines, the Bush Doctrine, and the "war on terror," encompasses so much more. This fact alone has tyrants running scared. Bush's approach is truly wide-ranging and ultimately effective. Then why do our media people have such a hard time "getting it?" Perhaps they don't want to.

President Bush will be known by history as the leader who "put words into *actions*." Violent and bloody attacks against the innocent, such as those killed in New York's Twin Towers, and against Israeli or Bali discos or tourist hotels, are being dealt with by overwhelming force, on multiple fronts, much we don't see.

The Bush Doctrine also promotes human rights and the spread of democratic, free-market ideals, both sticky issues among the despotic elite. In spite of lip service, or "slick words and good intentions," no one before President Bush has openly, seriously championed the idea in the Middle East. George Bush also insists on reforming foreign aid, which the U.S. now sends to many lands in a number of different forms with minimal accounting. Iraq, with Saddam now a bad memory, will be the first great test of the Bush Doctrine. Others will follow.

Opposition to our striking Iraq, *especially* from our so-called "allies," will not go unnoticed. Germany and France continue to enjoy a little "whine," all the while kowtowing to and groveling before Saddam right up to U.S. occupation and victory. You'd think France and Germany would be smarter than that, that they would have gotten on board right up front. Now they are marginalized, outmaneuvered by "Bush Junior," and left to crouch, sulking over a few gnarled bones. Expectedly, they lament.

Russia continues to be bought off. (There is a huge fire sale going on in Russia right now, two-for-one, bring your own bag.) Though surrounded by the greatest treasure-trove of natural resources in the world, Russia remains baffled by Economics 101, playing the blame-game and still looking for someone else to solve their problems.

Middle East countries should learn a lesson from the Russian failure. Without the rule of law and lacking honest, capable leaders, sound banking practices, and safe and secure private property, freedom and democracy, as well as a sound market economy, will remain beyond their grasp.[88] Obviously a workable formula for freedom and prosperity is not rocket science, but practical world application takes hard work and sacrifice. Russia is a perfect example we can all learn from: the tragic spawn of liberalism and socialism run amok, leaving the Russians a host of very bad habits to overcome.

The Peoples' Republic of China can be expected to follow a prudent, quiet, conservative course, as they always have, methodically pursuing their military upgrading, weapons sales to Iran, and a steady economic expansion worldwide. Just too much to risk with so much of their oil coming by tanker from the U.S.-occupied Middle East and passing through such U.S.-controlled bottlenecks as the Straits of Hormuz and Malacca. Oil is liquid prosperity for the Peoples' Republic. They have much to lose by rocking the supertanker.

Truly we have entered a brave, new world. Everything is different now. Clearly Osama bin Laden's gravest mistake was thinking that the World of William Jefferson Clinton and the World of George W. Bush were one and the same. The next worst mistake made by Muslim nations, and by the Europeans as well, is that they failed to listen when President Bush stated "you are either with us, or against us." The President intended this statement to be absolutely clear and non-negotiable. Such is not a statement of "intentions," but *actions*, actions already in high-gear. More importantly, in the coming years, America and the world must learn to *listen*. A strong, effective, decisive leader—the kind we need in today's world—should only have to tell us once.

QUESTION 18

- WILL SUCH MEN AS OSAMA BIN LADEN ALWAYS PLAGUE US, THREATENING GLOBAL PEACE AND FREEDOM?

Osama bin Laden is immortal; he will never die. If not him, then the next Osama, or Saddam, or Abu Musab al-Zarqawi. Mankind's history, in many ways, is the history of bin Laden.

The periodic cassette recordings, supposedly of old Bin Laden's voice, demonstrate graphically just how fascinating is this era in which we live. Technology, it seems, can keep even the effectively "dead" alive, perpetually inspiring the radicals, those Mujahadin "warriors of the faith," on into the eternities. More importantly, Osama bin Laden will continue harassing the "Great Satan" with jabs and abuse and colorful threats of holy vengeance poured down on our "cowardly heads" forever. Technology has assured it. Amazing the God-like power of technology.

In fact, Islam, married to today's technology, has the power to do us one better. In the Middle Ages, when several raucous Muslim holy men stirred up other Muslims a bit too much and got themselves killed for their meddling, their loyal followers refused to accept their deaths, proclaiming instead that Allah had "taken these holy fellows unto Himself," affectionately hiding them away, to be brought back at some future time. The *imam*, or Muslim teacher or cleric, was "too good," and his worldly mission yet unfulfilled, to be allowed to suffer death at the hands of the scrofulous and ungodly. In other words, Allah would relieve the holy man of the burden of being unappreciated, hiding him away until some future time when he would be brought back triumphantly to finish his mission and unite the true believers against the satanic ones. This concept of the "Hidden Imam" one day returning is *very* Middle Eastern in its cultural mindset. A messianic tradition is at the heart of the Middle East.

For some reason, al-Qaeda has not deemed it worthy to produce a photo of their Immaculate Leader holding a recent copy of the

Kabul Times or the *Pakistani Gazette*. Still, as though speaking from amid the crystalline fountains and shade palms of *janna* (heaven), for what it's worth Osama pauses to push his virgin allotment aside long enough to send another message of hope to the troops in the form of a scratchy Memorex.

The Muslim faithful, yesterday and today, struggle with the idea that God would allow the "purest and most righteous" to be "chastised unto death." Such happenings tend to demonstrate the possible (pardon me) "impotence of God." No, sir! Such impiety is simply *not* acceptable to the fundamentalist. Allah would never fail to protect his messenger or holy warrior, how could he? Such a shameful act must never be attributed to God, they say. As well, such a "brave hero" as Sheikh Osama bin Laden would never hide away as a coward while his followers fought and died for him. Such an act is below cowardice; such is shameful in the extreme. God must have certainly willed his disappearance.

Therefore, the best solution for all concerned is the ancient, tried and true one: *The Hidden Imam*. At this point in time a certificate of death grows increasingly unlikely. Certainly no true believer wants a confirmation, with some Mujahadin turn-coat accepting his cool $50 million dollar check from the gloating Americans as they slap the cuffs on Old bin Laden. More so, they must never see the body of bin Laden shamefully displayed to the world as a "trophy" of the Americans (again demonstrating Allah's weakness). But as a "Hidden Imam," OBL becomes infinitely more powerful: the-martyr-who-isn't, removed from the shame of defeat; the holy one who will one day, in God's due time, "return in power and glory."

From the onset it has likely been the radical's plan and hope, if facing defeat, that God's Warrior would simply "disappear," which he has conveniently done very well, thank you. Even for the Americans, Osama's vanishing act has its advantages.

Perhaps in the real world Osama was incinerated at Tora Bora or buried alive by a Bunker Buster. Maybe he died, sick and wounded, curled up alone in some dank grotto. More likely he's still alive, huddling under a bed in a flea-infested safehouse in Pakistan, or perhaps returning in drag to his tribal homeland in the craggy mountains of Yemen. Perhaps the always treacherous Ayatollahs are providing safe haven in Iran, or he lounges supinely in a spider hole somewhere, Saddam-style, a dusty rock for his pillow. It really doesn't matter just as long as he is *never* seen again in the flesh. A living Osama is the kind of enemy you do not want on your hands: letting his ACLU lawyers milk America's legal system, all the while enflaming the zealots for blood vengeance, for a "thousand years of martyrs," and in the process us hardworking Americans footing the bill. Heaven forbid!

But as a *Hidden* Imam, he can periodically check-in, seemingly from the heavens above, to deliver further insults and venomous threats, to tweak the noses of the mighty Americans and further console his troops over their growing losses and dwindling resources. While we would rather not hear from him at all, with the wonders of modern technology the Hidden Imam will undoubtedly continue his irregular ramblings. And we can handle it, just as long as OBL doesn't return to deliver those scratchy cassette tapes in person.

SADDAM BIN LADEN, OSAMA BIN HUSSEIN

The young Osama bin Laden was much more spry. During the 1980s he arrived in Kuwait. I was there and at a distance we watched him work his magic.

Moving among the wealthy and stumping in the mosques of the Gulf, Osama raised money for his "jihad" in Afghanistan against the Soviet occupation. In those days the United States backed the Mujahadin fighters who caused the Soviets such trouble in the craggy mountains and valleys of the "Top of the World," as Afghanistan was called. Osama was a fighter. And he was an idealist. But above all that, he was also an opportunist.

A younger Osama, bankrolled with lots of Gulf cash, would hop a plane for Beirut, to the "Paris of the Middle East." We've seen a young OBL out "clubbin'," a barmaid on each arm, partying away the weekend in style. Then, dragging himself back onto a plane, he'd wing home for some serious recuperation and repentance. It was obvious he was hard on himself, but just as obvious he had an admirable zest for life, and he loved the ladies.

Unfortunately for him, his was not the image a "pious" young zealot, a "warrior of God" should project. Soon his cronies in the "battle against evil" became worried, pulling him aside an Islamic intervention in the works. "Osama," they told him discreetly, "you've got to straighten up. You're giving the cause a bad name and you'll never rise to prominence if you keep up this pace."

Apparently, Osama got the message. At least he got noticeably more discreet with his lifestyle. But it seemed so unfair, I mean, if the holy warrior in Heaven deserved *70* virgins, then the earthly variety dedicating his life in Allah's service ought to deserve at least three or four!

The many trivial "bennies" aside, terrorism is big business, always has been. And it *is* a business, commanding its own brand of perks and lucrative extras, including plenty of cash, fancy cars, plush hotels, and all the women a manly-man can handle. Such are the rewards of *jihad*, the "blessings of a virile God," bestowed upon the dedicated life of the Ultimate Holy Warrior.

Thus, the bottom line is always the bottom line. "Osama bin Hussein" or "Saddam bin Laden" it doesn't matter. It never does. Remove one and another is right behind, salivating for the chance to take his bloody, murderous, self-aggrandizing place. That's why freedom is so very hard to preserve, requiring continual vigilance and sacrifice, and why we will always do battle with the despotic, the opportunistic, the "evil doers" among us. Freedom, so goes the cliché, is never free and, thanks to "Saddam bin Laden," never will be.

DELUSIONS OF BAGHDAD BOB

Osama bin Laden (OBL) and that charming Iraqi "Baghdad Bob" (the smarmy, smirking, Iraqi government spokesman we watched on the television the final days of the Iraq war) had much in common in life. Both dealt in propaganda and almost laughable lies, and both were delusional regarding their chosen enemy.

Right from the start of Osama bin Laden's "sacred jihad" against America, he failed to understand America was not the Soviet Union, the enemy he claims to have driven from the mountains of Afghanistan back in 1988. Nor was America in 2001 the same America Bin Laden attacked when he blew up our embassies in Africa during the 1990s. Like Admiral Yamamoto, the Japanese

Imperial leader who, following Japan's attack on Pearl Harbor in 1941, threw cold water on Japanese victory celebrations, stating: "I fear all we have done is to awaken a sleeping giant, and fill him with a terrible resolve."

Bin Laden never understood America, though he spoke as if he were an expert. Though well versed in *Islamic* history, such knowledge is but a tiny piece of the puzzle, a relatively worthless piece to be sure when dealing with the dangers and challenges of our modern world. If he had been savvy, OBL would have known ahead of time that his 9/11 attack would be his demise. But like Baghdad Bob, he had long since fled the real world.

Had bin Laden done his homework, he would have discovered what happens when Americans are attacked, especially on their own soil, so close to home. A deeply bred doggedness, born of freedom, combined with a unique Patriot's heritage, makes America an absolutely unbeatable enemy. Forget the incredible physical resources at the fingertips of the Home of the Brave. In his delusion, bin Laden actually thought the Americans would respond like the Soviets did in Afghanistan in the 1980s and soon flee the dangers for safer shores. Osama is the poster boy for the foolishness of acting brazenly on a little knowledge.

The reality that all OBL's everywhere must learn: If President George W. Bush had been unwilling to lead the charge against the terrorists, Americans would have tossed him out and replaced him with someone who would. This is the strength and beauty of the republican form of government; this is democracy in action. Freedom, the power offered men and women by their representative government, a freedom ultimately granted by God, *always* prevails over kings, warlords, and tyrants. From the moment those jets slammed into the World Trade Center, into the Pentagon, and onto a lonely Pennsylvania field, both Osama bin Laden *and* Baghdad Bob were finished.

QUESTION 19

- WHAT ARE SOME IMPORTANT TRENDS TO WATCH IN THE WAR ON TERROR, TRENDS NOT GENERALLY IDENTIFIED?

SOUTHWEST AND CENTRAL ASIA: A NEW CRADLE OF TERROR?

There exists a growing instability in Southwest Asia and the former Soviet Islamic Republics of Central Asia. To make matters worse, this instability is being given little attention by the United States Government due primarily to responsibilities elsewhere, especially in Iraq and Afghanistan.

To meet larger strategic equities, the U.S. is leapfrogging the situation for the moment, deferring a course of action. One day soon, however, America will have to shift its attention, and its resources, back in this direction. In Afghanistan, the building and modernization process has been slow and often disorganized, with nations sometimes failing to meet aid and development commitments. Economic success is vital in order to defuse support for radical Islamic groups competing for power and influence against the forces of freedom and democracy. The leaders of Pakistan, Afghanistan, Uzbekistan, Turkmenistan, Kazakhstan, and the several other "stans," appear to be compounding many of their own problems due to their native corruption, nepotism, and inept leadership. Of course, we should expect that.

Among national leaders in the Southwest Asian region, only Afghanistan's Hamid Karzai can lay claim to legitimate popular election. All other nations are headed by the usual gathering of long-standing powerbrokers, warlords, and dictators, men who have plagued the region for centuries. Rumblings for democracy abound—particularly among the youth—while growing economic frustrations compound throughout the region among the masses of mostly unemployed young. These inept leaders too often deflect internal criticism onto the shoulders of the Americans and other interlopers or outsiders. Many women are turning in desperation to prostitution just to survive and support their families.

Perhaps the greatest immediate concern is Pakistan, a nation with widespread grass-root's support for a variety of terrorist and radical Muslim factions such as the Hizb al-Tahrir, the "Liberation party." Yet, the U.S. government appears to be unwilling to pressure President Musharraf any further to do something about it just as long as he provides the American military with access to military bases. America needs Musharraf in the war against al-Qaeda and remnants of the Taliban next door in Afghanistan.

As well, Jammu and Kashmir, the disputed territory between Pakistan and India, remains a powder keg. Several of these Asian Muslim republics smolder over border, and other, disputes. Fundamentalist Muslims continue to advocate for an "Islamic solution," the establishment of an Islamic Republic, joining each of these nations into one mega-union, or a modern "Islamic Caliphate," as established thirteen hundred years ago by the followers of Muhammad.

Should any one of these dozen or so Central Asian nations, run by mostly warlords, collapse into unfettered lawlessness, another opportunity for a terrorist safe haven could emerge like we saw in Afghanistan under the Taliban. Should this happen, America could be back to square one in the war on terror.

Experts appear to agree that sooner or later the United States will be forced to spend billions of dollars propping-up these shaky governments and anemic economies. Perhaps a type of Marshall Plan will be required for the region, one with teeth, forcing clannish warlords to tighten belts, limit corruption, and cease the perpetual feuding which is their way of life.

It seems that in spite of the rich deposits of oil found in the region, particularly in Kazakhstan, Central Asia is a highly speculative venture. No guarantees. Worse, time is short. Fed by a new generation of poor and frustrated youth, the next al-Qaeda-like jihad against America could be germinating right now within one, or more, of these Muslim nations. While we already have the military resources in the region, as yet our well-developed, strong-arm methods may not be necessary. Investment, economic development, and education, however, are. We must spot the growing dangers and head them off, supporting democratically capable leaders who stand a chance of turning Central Asia around.

CENTRAL AND SOUTHWEST ASIA: A GROWING BATTLEGROUND BETWEEN AMERICA AND RADICAL ISLAM

Central Asia is made up of many nations, mostly former republics of the now defunct Soviet Union, their names mostly unknown to Americans. They contain, however, some ancient and fascinating peoples and cultures.

Hundreds of millions of Muslims populate this region, which includes the countries of Afghanistan, Pakistan, Iran, Azerbaijan, Uzbekistan, Kyrgyzstan, Baluchistan, Tajikistan, Turkmenistan, Kazakhstan, Chechniya, Tatarstan, Bashkortistan, and others. Here the birth rate is among the highest in the world.

As well, Islam has resurged since the collapse of the Soviet Union in the early 1990s. These people appear poised between two philosophies or world views, struggling to determine which path is right for them. Their choice is a critical one, between so-called "Middle Eastern-style Islam," and a more Westernized, educated, moderate form of the faith.

Al-Qaeda and Osama bin Laden are the best (or worst) examples of the Middle East-version of Islam, as were the Taliban in Afghanistan. Such are fundamentalist, totalitarian, even fascist, built on an angry foundation of terror, war, and subjugation to Allah and his earthly messengers. The terror-succoring Wahhabi sect, originating in Saudi Arabia, is another example of the fanatical wing. To be sure, such Islam is *not* true Islam in the eyes of many believers. Still, this Middle East variety is with us and since September 11th has our complete attention. As well, the legacy of the Taliban remains in parts of Afghanistan and Central Asia. Radical Islam anywhere is a noxious weed, not easily eradicated.

On the other hand, the Western-version of the faith is more democratic, moderate, and driven by liberal values of tolerance and cooperation. It allows others to live and worship in peace and expects the same freedom in return. It preaches open-mindedness, democracy, and a certain acceptance of secular values, both in culture and in the government. Obviously such willingness to accept compromise and co-existence is a good sign. There are challenges, however.

With the collapse of the Soviet Union, these Central Asian nations have experienced an upsurge of Islamic fervor. Thousands of mosques have been constructed, remodeled and reopened, many with money from Saudi Arabia and Iran, both nations competing fiercely for influence throughout the region. There has never been a "separation of church and state" in radical Islam.

Much of the money, however, comes with strings, or flaxen cords, anchored firmly to the radicals' views being spread beyond the Middle East. Islam, both Iranian and Saudi Arabian-style, is highly activist, hate-filled, and ultimately totalitarian. Saudi and Iranian cash are bribes, basically, designed to win converts to the "Holy War."

Many in Central Asia, facing the building "Islam vs. the United States" whirlwind, do not want to be caught in the middle. The U.S. war on terror has them nervous. Yet they understand they must ultimately choose, and that choice will determine their level of security and prosperity for years to come.

In the end, of course, it will be the *people*, not the dictators, nor the Americans, who decide their path, though most agree it will be America's success or failure in Afghanistan, Iraq, and also in Pakistan, which will be the pivotal factor in their choice. Should we lose Afghanistan to the radicals once again, we may lose Pakistan, and then the entire region. Our greatest nightmare, as outlined, is yet another safe haven breeding ground for the armies of Islamic terror.

We must win this war.

BOUGHT AND PAID FOR: GENERAL PERVEZ MUSHARRAF

Pakistan has a problem: General Pervez Musharraf. The good general and president has spent much of his career developing and nurturing useful, yet dangerously radical, terrorist factions to execute a clandestine war on India, which has a much superior military than Pakistan's. (Yet another example of how weakness breeds terror.) With the operational distance such terrorists provide, General Musharraf has pursued his political and military goals relatively unscathed.

Neither new nor original, war by proxy riddles the pages of history. Tragically, such clandestine wars are too often waged on non-combatants, so-called "soft-targets," by a rag-tag horde of the worst kind of mercenary.

General Musharraf continued this policy in Afghanistan in the 1990s by protecting, propping up, and supplying the Taliban. As far as Musharraf is concerned, such "religious" mercenaries, like all mercenaries, have two advantages: One, they provide excellent political deniability and operational cover; and, two, they are expendable.

Then came 9/11. Suddenly lots of American soldiers, spies, and most importantly, *dollars*, the very best of hard currencies, arrived in Pakistan to begin the war on terror. There is much at stake here for America; but more so for Musharraf and for Pakistan. The Americans are eager to clean out terrorist hotbeds and build strategically critical oil and gas pipelines crisscrossing the region. The U.S. presence not only protects American interests, but further props up President Musharraf's regime, as long as he cooperates.

But Musharraf is in a quandary. His applecart is toppled for all the world to see. With his well-documented support for Islamic radicals, including Osama bin Laden and the Taliban, General Musharraf finds himself caught in a trap of his own spinning. What to do with all those terrorist fighters who were once on Musharraf's payroll? How to make them go away quietly, without a whimper? If not, then how to control them? With America breathing down his neck, what's a terror-mongering dictator to do?

But that's not the extent of the Good General's dilemma. The entire Pakistani missile and nuclear weapons program should have a stamp on it: *"Made In China."* Pakistan's intermediate-range *Ghauri* ballistic missile, hand-crafted by the clever Chinese, is even named after a 12th Century Muslim warrior and conqueror of Northern

India. General Musharraf seems to delight in rubbing India's nose in it, which has drawn disgusted looks from his new American "partners," who are uneasy finding so many Chinese hanging out in Pakistan these days. But without Chinese assistance, the technology of mounting a nuclear warhead on a missile would be beyond Pakistan's ability. On almost every front, General Musharraf feels the pressure.

The General is a typical Muslim despot. He murders or expels his enemies, and buys off the rest, his new-found "friends." But now the Americans are squeezing him on one side, and the Indians on the other, with his struggling people grumbling at his feet. His life these days must be a living hell. Like so many dictators, Musharraf is trying to play "God-on-earth." Yet his future depends mostly upon his ability to cooperate with the United States, and he knows it. His future will probably be determined by how valuable he is meeting America's regional and global objectives, and his success in the war on terror.

And certainly there have been successes. Musharraf is making some kind of effort against al-Qaeda and the Taliban. But with him positioned squarely "between a rock and a hard place," he knows he's in trouble. The Bush Administration has exploited that vulnerability with skill and patience. The General has sold his soul to the highest bidder, the one with the cash. Bought and paid for, he waits restlessly, unsure of his future. It's going to take time, however; and for the good general's sake we hope he can handle the stress.

DID TIMOTHY MCVEIGH UNKNOWINGLY SET AMERICA UP FOR 9/11?

On April 19, 1995, the Oklahoma City Federal Building was bombed by 27-year-old Timothy McVeigh, killing 169 Americans, including children. At least in part, that attack may have set us up for September 11th 2001.

McVeigh's deadly action shifted some of our focus off Mid East-born terrorism at a critical juncture, distracting our domestic intelligence and investigative agencies at the moment al-Qaeda was ramping up its operations to attack America. Our intelligence and law enforcement agencies should have intercepted al-Qaeda. Osama bin Laden and his zealous lap-dogs were not that good. But we didn't, and at least in part I believe we have Timothy McVeigh to thank, which is ironic because McVeigh always considered himself such a "fine patriot."

Not only did we redirect some intelligence resources that, in hindsight, should have focused exclusively on radical Islamic groups, McVeigh caused us to shift focus to domestic, so-called right-wing militias, a favorite target of the U.S. Administration during the 1990s. The Oklahoma City bombing was such a devastating attack on America it became a kind of smoke-screen for Islamic terrorists scheming both inside and outside the United States. Thank you, Mr. McVeigh.

Enough said, except for the obvious and frightening follow-on: *What future vulnerability do we now face because of the manner and nature of the 9/11 attacks? How has 9/11 made us more vulnerable, the way the Oklahoma bombing did at that time?* These are questions our leaders are asking, or should be. They should be consulting the finest experts in the world. For just as al-Qaeda took us by surprise then, the next attack will be just as sudden and unexpected. Sadly, once more we could be blindsided.

If we do not recognize and counter every possibility in advance, a future surprise attack is inevitable. In other words, if we focus only on the most recent attack and view that as the primary threat, we will always be vulnerable.

THE GIFT

Regimes everywhere, from Russia to Israel, and China to Algeria, were handed a powerful gift on 9/11 by Osama bin Laden. Due to this incredibly deadly attack, which nearly brought the United States to its knees, many nations have determined to wrap their internal security policy, no matter how brutal, in the banner of the "fight against terror."

On August 26, 2002, President Bush gave China exactly what it wanted: the U.S. added the *Uighur Independence Group* (UIG), a Muslim separatist faction fighting the Chinese government in Western China, to its list of terrorist organizations. For years China had tried to brand these separatists or insurgents as "terrorists," but Washington had refused to go along, pressuring the Chinese to back off their attacks against the UIG. 9/11 changed all that. The Chinese were thrilled.

While Osama bin Laden is a source of inspiration to the world's revolutionaries and troublemakers, as well he has given every tyrant in the world the political ammunition to eliminate internal dissent by force. Every dictatorial regime, to one degree or another, worries about appearing too despotic and brutal when oppressing domestic troublemakers, reformers, minorities, even women's groups. But now Osama bin Laden has, perhaps more than any other single man, made life miserable, even deadly, for the world's subversives—Muslim, Christian, Sikh, whomever. It is open season on dissent and protest, with the world's tyrants taking full advantage. You can bet, however, that Old bin Laden has not lost a wink of sleep over it.

QUESTION 20

- WHAT ARE THE IMPORTANT, LITTLE-KNOWN LESSONS WE HAVE LEARNED THE HARD WAY?

> *The most dangerous Middle East policy the United States can have is to stir up Islamic hatred without, at the same time, instilling a deep-seated respect for the courage and determination of the American people in the mind and heart of every Muslim. America's Soldiers, Sailors, Airmen, and Marines are doing just that, at the same time, inexplicably, their sacrifice is being trampled by Hollywood and the American Left, effectively weakening America in the world. Who on the Left can explain and justify such actions in time of war?*
>
> --Richard P. Robison
> *The U.S. War in Iraq, One Year Later*
> Presented at the University of Phoenix,
> **March 19, 2004**

LESSON #1: ISRAEL CAN BE BEATEN. CAN AMERICA?

After a generation-long attempt to stop terrorist attacks on Northern Israel coming from South Lebanon, the Israeli army finally gave up and withdrew its forces from Lebanese soil on May 24, 2000. Too many casualties, too little success, at least in the minds of people back home. The Israelis even gave their long and deadly foray into Lebanon a name: *Operation Morning Twilight*.

Somehow, however, the name "Morning Twilight" lacks the warrior-effect, even testosterone, of the American "Shock and Awe," used in Iraq in the spring of 2003. Actually, the outcome of Israel's Morning Twilight says it all. After two decades, the

Israeli population, which is far more patient with its military and with combat losses than most Americans, had finally had enough. They capitulated. Calling it "Israel's Vietnam," the government in Jerusalem acquiesced and pulled out of Lebanon almost overnight. The hasty retreat that spring morning brought uncomfortable images to my mind of another spring, April 1975, and the American retreat from Saigon.

Why is Israel's experience in Lebanon so important for America today? Due to Israel's hasty flight after so many years of inflicting consistently heavy casualties on their Hezbollah enemy, Arab and Iranian leaders, as well as their many terrorist minions worldwide, have re-assessed their view of the Israeli enemy. For years Israeli resolve appeared as rock-solid and steadfast as Jerusalem's Wailing Wall. To their enemies, Israel was viewed as iron-willed, undefeated and undefeatable. But now, due to their sudden withdrawal from Lebanon in 2000, which Muslims everywhere considered a genuine Israeli defeat, all bets are off. Israel, it seems, can be beaten.

America has embarked on a grand military adventure in Iraq, occupying not only the nation of Iraq, but major areas of the Persian Gulf as well. The U.S. Fifth Fleet effectively controls all important waters and many ports on the Gulf and in the adjacent Arabian Sea. The Muslim world, and especially Iran, is watching, as well as leaders and despots as far away as China and North Korea. We are being carefully scrutinized for weakness, assessed for cracks in our armor of political and military resolve. If we falter, if we lose heart and grow weak-kneed, the enemy will rejoice. At that moment they will know. America, too, can be beaten.

Effortlessly we rolled over Iraq, in fact "shooting a sparrow with a cannon." In most instances, the Iraqis threw down their weapons and blended back into society. Head to head, in a stand up fight, Arabs lack the will. In reality, Arabs are usually talkers, not fighters. And in spite of U.S. media reporting, most Iraqis prefer Americans, even on their worst day, to Saddam Hussein and his plundering cronies and hired killers. Such leaders are just not worth dying for.

But people from the Mideast to Asia—especially our long-standing enemies—are now wondering: Will America stay the course if things really get tough? After 22 years in Lebanon, an

The Middle East Explained

eternity in today's sound-byte world, Israel finally gave up and limped home. In the domestic arena of public opinion, the U.S. is far more vulnerable politically than Israel. We are the very reluctant leaders of the free world. While most Americans struggle to grasp exactly what we are trying to accomplish in Iraq, these two critical challenges—global leadership and success in Iraq—are linked. For U.S. objectives to succeed, Americans *must* understand what is at stake. And as it nearly always is, victory is up to us, not to France or Germany, NATO or the United Nations. History tells us that at the critical juncture, the U.S. *always* goes it alone. American lives are on the line; once more we are paying the ultimate price for world peace and freedom.

President Bush has guts. No honest, objective person can doubt his courage. The president is confident we can get in successfully, with minimal pain, and accomplish most of our goals in a reasonable time. He's betting that our superb military will eventually accomplish the task before most Americans begin demanding our withdrawal. President Bush has mistakenly determined to keep official explanations simple, even shallow, hoping that America's goals can be wrapped solely in the flag of fighting terror. This is insulting to Americans who understand that the war encompasses so much more. This is the principal area where his thinking fails. Americans must know the whole truth; they have a right to know.

No doubt about it, our military will maul any enemy we face straight up on the field of battle. Iraq, under the brutality, corruption, and nepotism of Saddam Hussein and his family, was hopelessly, fatally weak and impotent. Of course, President Bush's greatest challenge is not in Iraq, but here on the home front. Americans need to understand up-front the extent of the sacrifice required of them in Iraq. At this point, they do not. At this point they are in the dark.

First, we must secure the Gulf, its oil and its strategic location, and then degrade and eliminate the many terrorist factions harbored by other nations in the region. We must ensure the continued strength of the U.S. dollar, the bulwark of the global financial system. We must cut off outside funding and support for the several deadly Palestinian terror factions within Israel, Gaza, and the West Bank and bring peace between Arab and Jew. We must slow the spread of WMD throughout the Middle East and Southwest Asia. We must make the world safe and free.

In the process, unseen challenges will arise, and Americans will die, as many have already. This is an ugly, drawn-out war; and it is far from over and as real as any we have ever fought. Truly these are depressing thoughts. Americans are not militarists and war-like by nature. Ernest Hemmingway said: "Never think that war, no matter how necessary, nor how justified, is not a crime. Ask the infantry and ask the dead." War is criminal.

Perhaps more frightening, wars often set in motion unpredictable side-effects and unseen outcomes. A glaring example is the lesson we will teach our enemies by our actions, or our inactions, lessons the enemy learns when we've had enough, turn our troubles over to the U.N., and high tail-it. The moment America determines to take this road is the moment history will mark our decline in the world, and the moment tyrants begin their militarist and WMD expansion on multiple fronts, in nearly every land.

Several Middle East experts have opined recently that Israel's wave of deadly suicide bombings were encouraged, even set in motion, by the aforementioned Israeli retreat from Lebanon. In appearing weak and vulnerable before the Muslim enemy, Israel paid in blood with the lives of their young and innocent. Unseen outcomes.

By making war on Iraq, what lessons have we taught our enemies? First of all, we've got their attention; but as Thomas L. Friedmann has said repeatedly regarding Iraq, in so many words: "You break it, you bought it."[89] No turning back short of complete victory. Once we remove our swords from their scabbards we are wholly committed and our options rapidly melt away. Once our soldiers move into battle anything but absolute and total support, from our politicians, from our media, from our academics, from every American, will be viewed by a host of enemies as chinks in our armor. Protesters here at home today do little beyond encouraging our terrorist enemies to fight on with greater resolve, to kill more Americans, and ultimately *to take the war to American cities*. (Such visible opposition, such protest, by any American during time of war is hard to comprehend or certainly to justify. Simply, it is foolishness on a monumental scale.)

The lessons of Lebanon are real, enlightening yet troubling, and vitally important, not only to Israel, but especially to America. Only a fool fails to learn from history. The war on terror cannot be won at the table of negotiation or appeasement. The world has gotten too dangerous for that, the enemy too fanatic.

Unfortunately, tyrants and terrorists the world over understand this far better than do we. Israel made a mistake; one that has cost untold numbers of innocent lives since May of 2000. Israel can be beaten, their enemies now know it. The Jewish State is in grave danger, the threat multiplying with the numbers of horrible weapons their enemies are now acquiring. Time is not on their side.

For America, the choices we make in the coming months will determine if we can avoid the same fate. I am gravely concerned many Americans are not even focusing on the challenge. Interest seems to be waning. Yet, these are some of the most important decisions made by the United States since World War II. God help us if we, through our fear or ignorance, choose poorly.

LESSON #2: BROUGHT TO OUR KNEES BY THE ROADKILL OF HISTORY

On September 11th 2001, the greatest nation on earth was brought to its knees by a dirty band of extremists hiding out in far-off caves, likely etching their plans of attack in the dust of a cavern floor or scratching them on chalky walls. Amazing. And even more amazing was that within weeks this same nation, now on bended knee, moved a huge army halfway around the world to pulverize and shred those same caves with space-age weaponry and soldiers who operate day and night, under all conditions with machine-like efficiency and discipline.

Many of the nations and factions currently opposing the might of the United States, and those which harbor these wretched terrorists, are in fact the "roadkill of history," to quote former U.S. National Security Advisor, Condaleeza Rice. Apparently she means that these are nations controlled by warlords, dictators, and religious fanatics who could never lead in a prosperous, modern world. They are men who prey on the weak and the innocent, who live by their own rules and fear anything resembling freedom, openness, and accountability. The roadkill of history is just that. No one wants them, no one respects them, everyone hates them. They are the off-scourings, the wretched oppressors, those destined for history's dustbin. They may have successfully sucker-punched us, once. If they do it again, we will deserve it.

LESSON #3: THE GREATEST MEDIA DISASTER IN HISTORY?

According to a well-placed Arab official for an international airline, the greatest potential failure facing the U.S. is America's inability to effectively influence the foreign press regarding U.S. intentions in the Middle East and our war on terror. In the Middle East region, this has been a public relations disaster, perhaps the worst in American history.

Due to a flood of mostly Arab press reports, the Muslim world views Iraq vs. the U.S. as the United States vs. Islam. This inequity is hard to imagine when considering the mammoth worldwide media resources of the United States. Even *Radio Sawa*, the pro-U.S. Arab radio station set up by the State Department to broadcast the American perspective to the Middle East, is considered a joke by most in the region. For some unexplained reason, the U.S. seems unable to field a global program on the same level and quality as the BBC, the British Broadcasting Corporation.[90] Why is this?

We must create an effective educational program, built on conveying clear, concise facts, in Arabic and Farsi (Iranian), as well as other languages. Programs must be delivered competently, with the right amount of passion. Simple statements by President Bush denying any negative charges against America "do not cut it," this Arab official stated. Such defenses must be delivered by leaders who are known, respected, but mostly *trusted* in the region, such as Jimmy Carter or Muhammad Ali, and others. To date, neither former President Carter, nor Muhammad Ali, have been willing, or able, to assist in this mission.

In the end this war on terror, and the war against despots like

Saddam, will not be won solely on the battlefield, but perhaps more so in the media. The hearts and minds of a billion-plus Muslims spanning the globe must be enlightened and won to the side of peace through a variety of competent media programs and outlets, including popular American movies and music. Frankly, we are losing the media war in a major way, the most important global quest we face. In the end, I am certain, the camera will eclipse the gun and bomb as the deciding factor in victory or failure against terror. A miracle worker of film and radio needs to step forward, now more than ever.

LESSON #4: MAKING WAR ON GOD

President Bush says this is not a war against Islam, yet most of the world's 1.25 *billion* Muslims believe it is.

I stood in front of the Islamic center known as *al-Azhar* in the heart of Cairo, Egypt as Friday noon prayers were about to begin. The sun warmed my face as I removed my shoes with respect before entering the ancient mosque. I felt the grit under my feet, working its way up between my toes as I passed through the massive stone archway. The faithful crowded the entrance with grim faces, turning as one towards *Qiblah*, the undeviating direction to Mecca. This is al-Azhar, the premier center of Islamic learning and power in all the world.

Times are hard in Egypt. Perhaps a good barometer is the falling Egyptian pound, the indigenous currency, trading well over 5 L.E. to 1 U.S. dollar. (When I was studying here in the 1980s, the pound and the dollar were nearly equal: 1-to-1.) People are hurting, and they are turning to Islam for answers. More so, they are looking for someone to blame.

The Volkswagen-sized speakers snapped to attention with the flip of an invisible switch and a raspy, nasal voice rolled out over dusty, rabbit-run alleyways and twisting lanes. Unlike in parts of the Gulf, here earning a living can't afford to stop for Allah. Everywhere, impossible crowds and endless "bumper cars" jammed into every impossibly narrow space, all rushing by with grim, jaded faces. Every kind of vehicle, from every land, filled nearly every square inch of pavement. Truly Cairo's clogged thoroughfares are a modern world wonder, with the prolific Egyptians jockeying and posturing for advantage. Too many people, not enough earth. Yet somehow the system here functions, a testimony to the ability of the Egyptians, if necessary, to muddle through.

The message, shouted from every mosque throughout the city, and especially from mosques with muscle, like al-Azhar, is "the Americans thirst for war." Americans are "naturally bloodthirsty creatures," and will not be satiated until Saddam's Iraq is theirs. The message is everywhere—in the countless little neighborhood mosques, in the stores, on TV, radio, from cabbies, in the schools, everywhere. "Bush seeks revenge. This war was not merely against Saddam, but against every Muslim everywhere; which means against God's innocent people, and by extension, against God himself! To fail to resist is shameful!"

Muslims, like Christians, have always been taught that only Satan makes war on God. Every Muslim, young and old, understands where such logic ends and who's to blame. The problem America faces has never been in defeating the Mideast tyrant on the battlefield. Saddam went down with the first punch. The greater challenge by far is penetrating a billion and more hearts and minds from Marrakech to Bangladesh, to convince them we are not the enemy, that we are not the "Great Satan." God help us if we do it wrong; because…

Only Satan makes war on God.

LESSON #5: THE OVERWHELMING FORCE OF GLOBALISM

Both extreme right and leftwing groups, in Europe and in America, increasingly fear the force of globalization, which at its heart means the free movement of labor, goods, and information worldwide. For several years now we have witnessed the world awash in the flow of products, services, and most of all, intelligence. We are literally swimming in a river of goods, services, and information, rushing and swirling in every imaginable direction.

Predictably the world's citizens are demanding that same freedom of movement for themselves, as individuals. Travelers abound, causing a backlash against immigrants and the rise of rightwing groups who oppose them, particularly in Europe. These same forces, ideological cousins, will soon sweep America. We cannot avoid it. Our border issues, the issue of illegal immigration, will dominate future elections and political campaigns. Violence will follow on the heels of these challenges if we do not begin addressing them immediately.

Increasingly promoted by many rightwing groups, and some far left ones as well, is the anti-Israeli hysteria sweeping Europe. Certain European political factions even support recent terrorist attacks against the Jewish State and against the United States. Europe is a steadily mushrooming incubator of anti-Americanism and anti-Semitism, beginning on both the left and the right, and now seeping into the center. For so long Europe fled the specter of looming fascism, and then communism, relying on America for their very existence and survival. European memories are short, it seems. A new generation is rising which does not remember America's sacrifice in their behalf, nor do they care.

As well, the European establishment, the so-called "moderates," has long-since lost its backbone, criticizing America when politically expedient. In reality they fear the seductive spread of the extreme right's political agenda through broad segments of their society. At the same time they are unable to chart a secure, yet productive course of their own. The Europeans are dangerously floundering.

But like the spread of global information and technology, goods and services, *people* are going to be nearly impossible to stop. They will arrive by the millions, their children and elderly parents in tow, just as long as opportunities abound and jobs go unfilled. They will come, from every land and from every race, creed, and nationality. And any nation foolish enough to dam the stream will also damn its own future prosperity and freedom.

Globalism is an unstoppable reality. What Europe and America need is a coherent, sensible, rewarding system of immigration where political maneuvering is eliminated and where people are rewarded with citizenship *only* after demonstrating a willingness and ability to contribute to society. The current system is broken. The danger comes from political and cultural activists—right or leftwing—who use this hotbed issue to further their own extremist causes.

LESSON #6: CYBERWAR IS COMING

Information systems warfare is coming in the United States, where a handful of skilled PC commandos could inflict greater damage on America than any nation or traditional terrorist enemy could.

How will this happen? Their weapons could be so-called logic bombs, and of course increasingly dangerous computer viruses. Such devices travel at the speed of light, the electron becoming the perfect smart bomb, the e-weapon of mass destruction. Imagine the chaos if U.S. phone systems were suddenly overloaded and shut down, or our banking institutions simultaneously attacked, erasing or transferring account records on a massive scale? Attacks on our computers linking electrical power grids, or computers operating nuclear power plants, dams, port facilities or air traffic control systems, would go far beyond mere inconvenience.

Imagine if the ensuing chaos were simultaneously coordinated with massive terror strikes in a variety of key locations. The cost in lives and treasure could be catastrophic. It could take years to recover. Obviously we are vulnerable, and our government is scrambling to get ready. So far we have dodged the bullet, but with the rapid spread and availability of hacking software, we are in a race against time, perhaps one we cannot win.

Cyberwarriors have the advantage of striking when and where *they* decide, and they can do this from the safety of a foreign land. Government planners refer to this possible future event as an "electronic Pearl Harbor" which will, at the least, paralyze America for a time. In the recent past we have had about a quarter of a million hacker attacks against the U.S. Department of Defense computers *per year*. We must realize that the day of global integration is upon us. We are on the cusp of a world so incredibly inter-dependent that our greatest enemies could be the enemy within.

An old Arab proverb says: "Better a thousand enemies without the house, than one within."

QUESTION 21

- IN THE WAKE OF THE IRAQ WAR, WHY ARE BRUCE WILLIS AND PAULA ABDUL HANGING OUT ON MUHAMMAD STREET?

TWO GLIMPSES INTO THE MIND AND HEART:

THE SURVIVOR

I am standing on a hill overlooking Amman, Jordan. This ancient city is located on the edge of the Great Syrian Desert and situated squarely between Iraq and Israel. I try to imagine a more precarious piece of real estate. Rushing by me are crowds of jostling Arabs. Confronting me in silence are the 2,000 year old Greco-Roman ruins, pocked and battered, yet mostly intact. Considering the pollution assaulting the stone, the ruins are incredibly preserved— columns and facades, the amphitheatre and what remains of shops and stores, yet not so much different from the "modern" ones just down the road. These inspiring ruins, however, are seemingly ignored by the impatient Arabs rushing by. Too busy fighting day-to-day struggles.

In important ways, however, the city *has* changed, especially over the past 10 years. These are hard times; war has made it so. Every Jordanian knows war, the most recent just ended next door in Iraq. A war between great armies. It had happened before, in 1991; I was there. Desert Storm pitted lightning technology and strategic brilliance against medieval, in-grown incompetence and outrages hubris on the part of the "Maximum Leader," Saddam Hussein al-Tikriti. Thanks primarily to their self-serving dictator, many Iraqis met their Maker in 1991. Many hundreds of thousands more have died over the past decade at Saddam's always brutal hand.

The killing continues.

Peaceful Jordan used to be a simple place, filled with kind, simple people. Change, however, is now roaring at them like a runaway scud. More devastating, the information, technology, and commerce of the West washes over them with impunity, taking no prisoners, piercing their hearts, and leaving them culturally numb and battered.

I try to gaze into the eyes of the Jordanians as they pass. In fact, most are not ethnically Jordanian at all but Palestinian, driven out of their ancestral home, Israel (or Palestine), over the past half-century. Studying their faces, I try hard to connect. I smile and they seem to want to smile back, but something has hold of them. They avert their eyes and hurriedly rush on by. Something is coming, you can feel it in the steady wind blowing off the east desert. Change with a capital "C." Many fear this relentless unknown.

Endemic insecurity and perpetual fear takes its toll. It guts a culture, buying off and co-opting these ancient, formerly stable systems and family or tribal-based institutions. It corrupts; then it rots. History tells us that people will nearly always sell their souls, and their freedom, for the promise of security, despite brave words shouted at Allah's sky by soon-to-be martyrs. In reality, normal people are never martyrs or terrorists. They have families, wives, children, too many responsibilities to the living to flirt with death. Too much to lose.

Everywhere I look the old respectful bulwark of tradition is now being discarded like so much trash. This day I saw *two* different Arab men as Steven Seagal wanabes, sporting six inch ponytails no less! It is 'Eid al-Fitr, the four-day feast marking the end of the Holy Month of Ramadan. This evening people are everywhere—families, packs of young men, some holding hands, which is completely normal among Arab males—brothers, cousins, life-long friends.

But then I see couples, and women in skin-tight jeans, standing up close to young men, flirting, sometimes touching, and right here in the public eye! With all the neon around there is no cover of darkness, no harem-sanctuary. Allah forbid! What has happened to rob Jordan of her purity, her innocence?

I am in awe of the myriad of new malls, stores and shops with American names, and the newest innovation: "internet cafes," all wide-open to the streets. Unrestricted internet access…for a price. Mini-malls, gaudy, and lurching out to snatch you from the brisk, hazy night. Brilliant, florescent neon everywhere blinds me. How does Jordan, a country which imports virtually all its energy, afford the light bill?

Looking up, I can't believe it. It's *Bruce Willis*, sporting "Police"-brand sunglasses, surveying his realm atop a huge glowing billboard over Muhammad al-Sajjad Street, arrogant, virile, commanding attention. That lit billboard could just as easily be on the Strip in Las Vegas. What was once fiercely rejected is now being willingly embraced, more so *absorbed*.

American cultural penetration continues on schedule, despite the oaths and threats shouted from the minarets by the Islamic fundamentalists. Like holding back the sea, Muslim traditionalists are fighting a battle they cannot win. In victory, however, does Hollywood, does America, understand its God-like power over the children of men? Does it comprehend its responsibility? In the minds of millions of young Arab men, Bruce Willis *is* the new-age Arab material-guy, sporting all the necessary accoutrements. Sales of Police-brand sunglasses (or knock-offs, thereof) are more than brisk, they are rabid, not to mention the absurdity of Bruce Willis towering over a street named "Muhammad."

Overshadowing even Bruce, however, was the menacing and manipulating Saddam Hussein. In the past Iraqi intelligence officers, spies, and assassins have roamed Jordan freely, using the millions of Iraqi refugees and entrepreneurs as camouflage, as "cover for action." Today, however, unlike in 1991, pro-Saddam posters and banners are gone with the wind.

In years passed Saddam neutralized Jordanian opposition to his maneuverings through a brilliant combination of verbal and monetary support for the Palestinian cause (remember, the majority of Jordan's population are ethic Palestinian), coupled with critical oil shipments to Jordan, and much lucrative trade across their mutual borders. Since Gulf War I, however, the United States has skillfully countered Saddam's influence with *hundreds of millions* of dollars in pay-offs (sometimes called "foreign aid") from always generous American taxpayers. Millions of crisp new $100 dollar bills to fund the American-influenced commercialization process, some say "buying" the political cooperation of Jordan's rulers.

However, "aid" is, and always has been, a double-edged sword. In the process of passing out bucks—and here's the hook—the U.S.

"encouraged" Jordan to avoid this time the isolation which followed Gulf War 1991, when Jordan was mercilessly swept into diplomatic and economic oblivion as punishment for loyalty to Saddam. This time they got the message. This time, under New King, son of Old King, Jordan got in step.

Now Saddam is gone and America is *the* powerbroker in the Middle East. September 11th has impacted so much more than most could ever have imagined. Thoroughly fascinated by the changes before me, I venture inside the International Safeway Mall near 7th Ring Road in West Amman. Modern malls have long since arrived in the Middle East, with lots of designer labels everywhere; the latest jeans for women and men, with fashionably worn and dirtied legs and posteriors, at a premium of course, though too much like the garb of street beggars for my taste. (I'm long-since "hopeless," my daughters tell me, a product of the practical '50s and '60s. Functionally archaic, I guess.)

Everywhere I look young women are wearing these jeans so I price them, do the math with the exchange rate, and…whoa! I thought Jordanians were saddled with broad-based, endemic, under-employment, debt, and creeping poverty? Out of work, odd-job guy or gal paying a premium for the latest in street-people fashion? More so, Jordanians have always prided themselves in wearing only the finest, neatest and cleanest when they venture out in the public eye. Honor is *everything*. Culturally, they should have absolutely no interest in such grunge-wear. Am I missing something here?

I enter a music and video shop and there on the wall, big as life, is a practically nude poster of Paula Abdul. While she looks pretty good, she is completely out of place here. Just up the street a short distance is a mosque; another in the opposite direction a stone's throw away. Even more incredible, right next to Paula's bronzed, voluptuous form is Eminem, no less, likewise partially clad and big as life. I stand in amazement amid the latest American CDs and cassettes, many knock-offs to be sure, but well done knock-offs, and at a fraction of the cost. At least the fashionably dressed Jordanian won't pay much for her tunes.

I slip up to the counter and speak a little Arabic to two 20-something males managing the store. They both smile at each other

The Middle East Explained

and answer back in perfect English, better than mine.

Sheepishly, I beg the question. "Gentlemen, with all the fanatics running around these days, don't you worry that some religious-type with no sense of humor is going to come in here with a gun or bomb and do you harm?" I point at the offending posters.

Again they glance at each other, grinning. "No, not really. It's no big deal, not anymore. Times have changed."

I'm already shaking my head. "This isn't possible, friend. I mean, I lived in Jordan before Gulf War I, and it *was* a big deal back then. You'd get in trouble for that!"

"Yeah, man, it's great, huh? Everything's changed," he came back, strutting a bit. Finally, I'm getting the message.

Then the other fellow, sensing my frustration, offers a slight qualifier. "Well, there were a few minor complaints from some of those Mullahs (religious teachers or leaders)," and he points subtly in the direction of the nearby mosque. "But mostly about Eminem, some things he said, I guess, I don't know. Politics; it's no big deal. We don't care about those things, anyway."

Now I am *exceedingly* confused, "No big deal? These Mullahs halfway around the world here in Jordan *know what Eminem says*? And no protests at all about that naked female poster?"

They laugh. "Yeah, they know. And, yeah, we get a lot of guys who just come in to stare at her, sometimes for half-an-hour. What guy doesn't like Paula Abdul? Anyway, she has a Muslim name."

I stagger from the shop to catch my breath. They have even adopted a near naked Paula, based upon her name?! Commandeering a cab, the driver races with me towards the heart of the city, though I was in no hurry to get there. Pedal-to-the-metal all the way, per usual in the Middle East.

After the usual and expected introductions, the cabbie, Muhammad (of course), seems to warm to me. A talkative fellow, and in keeping with his name, claims a long-time religiosity. In his early 50s, and with 10 kids to feed, besides grandchildren, he often works 16 hour-days, seven days a week. Muhammad seems reflective of his place in the world.

"You know," he says in Arabic, "God help us, the cursed Iraqis are everywhere these days. The war, you know. They were forced here because Saddam is a butcher. He robbed his people, then drove them into Jordan for us to care for."

I glance sideways at Muhammad, though I never like taking my eyes off the suicidal traffic here. Casually he fishes an unfiltered Turkish cigarette from a wrinkly pack and lights the acrid thing, holding the steering wheel with his knee and cracking the window. Without a flinch he nearly swaps mirrors with an oncoming Mercedes.

"Friend," I say with an audible 'gulp,' "I thought that over the years Jordanians generally admired the Maximum Leader."

Lazily he returns my glance, clicking his tongue in the negative. "Please, do not call him that. We do not like Saddam anymore. Look at that billboard." He points with his cigarette as we pass a huge sign along the roadway written in Arabic, *"Ordaan Owelaan."*

"You know what that means, friend? 'Jordan First.' It means 'Never again,' not like the last war, anyway. In *this* war, we are watching out for *number one*, God willing. *This* time (2003) Saddam, the Butcher, is on his own. Last time (1991 Gulf War) everyone—the British, the Egyptians, the Saudis, even the cursed Syrians—got something out of it. Not Jordan. We got nothing but starving refugees. This time, God willing, we are on the side of the victors. Saddam deserves his fate, you know. We do not mourn him or his family." He points at the sky with his hands, then slaps the steering wheel. "We have nothing left here, friend," he mutters in pain, then just as suddenly, steels his jaw against the world. Once burned, the Jordanian has an eternal memory. He offers me a cigarette which I decline. Politely he asks if I would mind his smoke, though he has already smoked a couple of cigarettes. Apparently I had just entered the "realm of the friend" after discreetly discussing such—for the Middle Easterner, anyway—dicey politics. This is how trust is built.

"*Ta-faddal*, friend, go ahead," I came back. He lights up and settles back.

"The king is wise," Muhammad continues. "He is young but he knows his people and they will back him. We loved his father. But because we are a good people, Jordan is always being used. But not *this* time." The pride of a man who believes he is in-charge shone from his face.

The Middle East Explained

We coast past the American Embassy compound in the *Abdoun* section of Amman, sprawling and impregnable, seemingly lying close to the ground, trying to keep its head down. Police and soldiers, along with military vehicles are everywhere. "We cannot stop here, someone will shoot us," Muhammad insists, way too serious for my tastes. It is raining and visibility is bad. The soldiers seem on edge, assault rifles protrude everywhere. The roof of the embassy bristles with antennae and multiple satellite dishes, all in the open, not even attempting to camouflage the spy contraptions anymore. The whole area around the compound is lit by floodlights, streaking like lightning in the pouring sheets of rain. The robust fence, razor-wire, and concrete blast walls and a platoon of armed men stand as monoliths to Fortress America. This is what diplomacy has become. This is what *America* has become.

"Muhammad, why does everyone want to kill us?" I ask, which makes him smile, his expression then mutating to weary cynicism. I press him.

"I don't know," he replies curtly, but in a way which says he truly does. I nod my own understanding, born of the seemingly impossible changes I see everywhere. I try to imagine such gut-wrenching change if it were to occur in the United States almost overnight. Comprehension, again, settles over me like a shroud. Sadly, a truthful answer is hardly what anyone wants, or expects, anymore.

"Jordan has changed over the past decade," I say, cutting at the squirming silence. "It is no longer the Jordan I knew."

"Yes," he says softly, in resignation. "And it will never be the same again. After the first gulf war the Iraqis and many more Palestinian workers from the Gulf flooded our cities and towns. We were overrun with refugees, you can see them on the streets selling their used clothing, their shoes, chewing gum, cigarettes, their children, anything. Jordan is awash in the displaced and the unwanted. And now with 'Bush, Son of Bush' returning to our land with a great army, what will this war do to Jordan? How will it change us? God knows. But *this* time we will watch out for ourselves. Yes, Jordan First. If not, friend, we will not survive the war, or the peace."

Jordan First. The prudent path, the path well trodden, the path of the Middle East survivor. In the historic change now sweeping this land, every Middle East nation should take note, keeping their eyes on the wise and always pragmatic Jordanians.

SKY PEOPLE

Some people never complain, though they have every right to.

Recently I stood at the window, peering from the tenth floor suite of the Ambassador Hotel, trying to shake off the numbing effects of jet lag. Downtown Cairo, Egypt, and a yellow dawn spread like a disease, like all dawns in this archaic mega-town, filthy amber dust from the endless desert pressed in to choke off the works of man. I am certain the living desert would like nothing better than to kill and cover this mammoth city of humans. Nowhere on earth is the contrast so stark, the contrast between the city of man and the eternal, empty wilderness of sand. You can literally stand with one foot on the lush green which hugs the Nile Valley, the other foot on virgin desert, extending out a thousand miles and more.

The rush, the madness of crowds. Cairo is the perfect example of man's seemingly hopeless quest for survival. But in Cairo's madness, slowly it becomes clear that without people bustling about in their daily, individual, hopeless pursuits, life, the world, the universe, everything, would quickly become meaningless. Though life is vain, it is essential we live it. More so, conquer, subdue, and endure. The people of Cairo struggle as mightily in this quest as any.

Below me, behind the hotel, are dust-covered concrete and block structures as far as the eye could see, crumbling, tired buildings, with cracked, scaling, dying facades. Living within are millions of souls—families, moms, dads, and countless children, lower and middle class Cairenes, struggling to life with the surging eastern sun.

Composed of countless "village neighborhoods," the City is endless, but more so, timeless, where family loyalty is the essence of life, where conformity is the bulwark of security and the first requirement of tribal honor.

Hugging the Eternal River for life, the living city, one of the world's largest and oldest, moans and sputters, people gritting teeth against another day, another dollar (or Egyptian Pound). Here the

The Middle East Explained

ancient and modern rise up, side-by-side, though I can't always tell which is which. The tools and the toys have changed, but never the people, not in the things that matter. But the most fascinating aspect of this great human effort must be the Sky People.

Below me, amid the rubble strewn rooftops of every apartment building and structure, I spot movement, people emerging, resurrected, sporting their timeless *galabiyas* and brightly colored full-length dresses. These are the Sky People, those dirt-poor citizens lucky enough to find a postage-stamp plot of ground atop the canyons of the living city.

Every rooftop in the Arab World is flat as pita, nothing more than a slab of concrete. And crowning every rooftop is every conceivable type of garbage and refuse, piled as high as another story and more. Cairo, like all of the world's mega-cities, places the highest premium on space. Landfills are hardly ever conveniently located, or even available. As a result every rooftop becomes its own miniature landfill: excess building materials, left-over plumbing and masonry from past remodeling projects, auto parts (no one can explain to me how a full auto body or engine block finds its way 5, 10, or 15 stories up!), and mountains of battered furniture. I see at least one kitchen sink; but wood—dimension lumber—in this desert landscape appears to be the most valuable commodity of all. I watch as the Sky People eagerly pluck every last piece of usable wood from the heaps of trash, cleaning and stacking the offering for future use.

Cairo is hot most of the year, a prevailing dust-breeze laced with lethal pollutants ever present. Unfortunately for the Sky People, ten stories up the pollution does not diminish. It seldom rains, so rooftop junk is soon coated nicely with a sticky grit, giving everything a graying, mummified appearance. Amid this jumble of roof-trash, amid the heaped squalor, is one of the truly amazing testimonies to the tenacity of human beings: *families*. Husbands, wives, grandmas and pa's, and many dirty, barefoot and tattered tykes, living together atop the world, gazing down day after day, year upon year, on the most crowded and noisy place on earth, entire lives lived on perhaps a 1,000 square feet of concrete, most of it shared with trash.

Some call them Roof People. The fathers or grandfathers are often *boabs* or doormen, maintenance men or "keepers," for the buildings they live on in exchange for their "space." All week long, when my opportunities allowed, I would watch bits and pieces of the daily lives of half-a-dozen such families within my view.

Before dawn the women were up, preparing food, gathering and breaking up scraps and splinters of paper and wood-trash with which to cook. Hailing other women on adjacent roofs, separated by deep, deadly canyons with twenty (or so) foot chasms separating the buildings, the women would catch up on the news and share quick stories. None would spend long chatting across the concrete canyons, though things (perhaps gifts or cooking ingredients?), were sometimes tossed over.

Shortly after dawn I spotted several toddlers and young children amid the piles which had been pushed and stacked against the sharp corners, an attempt to provide some kind of "yard." Toddlers, not yet toilet trained, went about naked from the waist down. It was warm enough and diapers appeared beyond budgets.

One young boy mounted a small bike, pedaled around his roof-yard, the 3-foot high perimeter wall all that kept the little guy from oblivion. The sun rose and the heat of the winter sun's rays seemed to stimulate even more activity. Each family had constructed some type of hovel mostly from available trash—refrigerator-box walls, old doors nailed and lashed together overhead as a makeshift roof, sometimes even incorporating the building's sturdy, angling satellite dish into the design. Again, the contrasts. Several hovels I saw had been painted, though with multiple colors that didn't come close to matching. Leftover paint, leftover homes, but for a people of extraordinary ingenuity.

A young child screamed in pain and an older sibling rushed to the rescue, the young one having a discrepancy with a mangy looking roof-cat. Every rooftop seemed to have at least one feline. As the sun swelled with intensity, the children appeared seemingly from nowhere, hopping and jumping and laughing, climbing the heaps and the myriad of antennas, even balancing atop the life-saving short-walls like mountain goat-kids, fearless of the heights, playing with glee within inches of a grisly death. The boy with the patchwork bike raced about his roof, a sort of BMX track amid the trash. He skidded close to the roof edge with abandon and I held my breath.

The Middle East Explained

His mother was working nearby hanging wet laundry. She casually said something in his direction and he parked it.

One young father exited a hovel with an armful of the most hopeless stack of splintered scrap wood and dropped it next to a short bench. Plopping down, he then began sorting and eyeballing each stick, holding up the various pieces to see how they'd fit his plan. His wife seemed to be making comments, offering "helpful suggestions" from the side the entire time, which he appeared to ignore. With a short saw in hand he finally wore a piece of wood in two and then casually started at another. I came back to the window later and he'd just about finished what appeared to be shelving. His wife was now sweeping the floor of their little piece of the heavens, three children playing at their feet, one standing dutifully by his handyman-father with an eager, tiny, willing hand.

Next roof, different family. The young parents not only had several children, but also grandma. I could see they had more usable space, as well. Theirs wasn't as clean and organized, though that may be due to the mini-barnyard in the "front yard." I had already heard the rooster prior to the dawn. Eight or ten chickens scratched and clucked about. A stringy cat sprawled on the hovel leaning precariously against the roof's edge, which was not painted, at least not recently, built from scraps of plywood and what may have been crates. The wife barked at someone inside. Little work seemed to get done on this "farm." However, the place had lights and at night, what appeared a TV glowed within. None of the hovels in my view appeared to have much more than tattered cloth for windows, no effect in stopping the hungry mosquitoes that visited the rooftops in swarms each night.

Directly below my room-with-a-view and to my right, was another roof, housing at least two families. At noon, with the sun directly overhead and my visibility the best, I gazed about the city. Straining through the smog, I could see perhaps a half-mile is all, but could not see a single roof that wasn't inhabited. In this city of *18 million-plus* Egyptians, the defining, limiting factor seemed to come down to space—real estate—most of it vertical. Laundry flapped everywhere—from wires stretched across rooftops, from antennas and dish supports, from plumbing vent stacks, as well as many windows on down the face of every building, like flags on the 4th of July.

Perhaps the most fascinating aspect was the individuality of these Sky People. Some took a real interest in improving their little world, decorating, painting, and a daily sweeping and cleaning was never neglected. One place even had a row of plants, in pots of course, ringing the perimeter of the roof, and what appeared as vegetable grow-boxes secured to the roof edge. Just hauling up all that topsoil would have been daunting. Amazingly some had even made their world relatively pleasant, I thought. Others, for reasons I can only guess, seem happy with squalor, with trash left in its natural state, as God intended.

Though the Middle East has a multitude of failings, most of them man-caused, at least the Arab elites and rulers seldom politicize and try to capitalize on the squalid lives of their poor. More often, they ignore them, or let the desert do their work and cover them with sand. Perhaps there are too many, and in such large numbers the starving are dangerous. These rulers are too busy looking over their shoulders at the lean, hungry eyes staring down from the sky. I believe they are whistling in a grave yard, terrified of what happens when the Sky People, when all the poor and struggling masses, finally come of age.

In the wake of war, as America takes the courageous road of encouraging, perhaps forcing, democracy upon the region, the Sky People are watching, and they are taking notes. Dictators everywhere sense their world is being turned upside down. As I have talked with these struggling Arabs and visited their rooftop "mansions," I sense that the future for their children will be very different. They know that without education and without escaping their sky-bound prison, their children's future will be bleak. But technology and information, but mostly education, are shattering the chains shackling them to their cardboard hovels. American ideals of freedom, a new world of educated choices, is what will free the Sky People if they are willing to venture forth, and if they have the courage to embrace the change that is sweeping towards them.

Hardly a day passes that I don't think of these tenacious rooftop men and women, these families, and they make me smile. For I know that such individualist spirit, the human will to live, will carry these survivors to a victory of freedom and prosperity. Amid the war and terror, oppressed by corruption and the ignorance of generations, one constant emerges crystal clear: the burning desire to improve the lives of their children, the one force, the hope, which will inevitably unshackle them.

Against such an overwhelming force—the force of individual freedom—the tyrant and the terror-monger cannot prevail. Freedom is the destiny of the Sky People, and for all peoples everywhere. A new generation of Arab, Jew, Iranian, and Turk has arrived, a very real "product" of modern technology and intelligence, modern medicine, modern values: a new generation of promise, a generation more in common with the rest of the modern world than their parents.

Rooftop trash…or prince's palace? Today I see fewer and fewer differences between the two. Technology and information, and the freedom such "miracles" are bringing, equalizes both prince and pauper, and it will do so in our lifetime. The future belongs to the Sky People, a generation of hope, and the heart of the Middle East.

QUESTION 22

- WHAT IS THE END GAME? HOW DO WE FINISH TERRORISM ONCE AND FOR ALL?

> *The heights by great men reached and kept were not attained by sudden flight, but they while their companions slept, were toiling upward in the night.*
> *--Henry Wadsworth Longfellow*

ENDING MID-EAST MYOPIA

After roughly two decades, Israeli troops pulled out of Lebanon on May 24, 2000. They left behind a celebrating Shi'ite Hezbollah, reveling in the streets, guns blazing, now in full control of South Lebanon. However, looking closer, peering behind the superficial celebration, it is clear: all is not well in Hezbollah Land. With the Israeli enemy no longer close at hand, the Hezbollah terrorist organization now faced a new type of danger, the danger of losing legitimacy. The potential of losing financial backing from their Shi'ite brethren in the Islamic Republic of Iran seemed to cut their celebrating short. Hezbollah, the "Party of God," was faced with by far the worst calamity any terrorist army can suffer: *operational irrelevance.*

In order to retain its lucrative Iranian support, Hezbollah must deliver, it must continue to carry the war to its Israeli enemy. There are no free lunches in the terror business, and it *is* a business. Hezbollah must dig up, or create, the opportunities to hit the enemy on all fronts. And should the chance to strike America arise, you can bet the Party of God will give it serious consideration, *if* it is financially profitable, and *if* they think they can get away with it.

Although the Israelis have retreated south to the "safety" of their northern border, this tiny nation is anything but secure from the several Palestinian terror factions (which also receive Iranian and Syrian support). Many Israelis feel desperate; the threat has not abated in the least. But most just want to forget their years battling

Hezbollah in the south of Lebanon, and worse, their hundreds of casualties.

The terrorist powers, however, cannot allow this to occur. Hezbollah will continue to hit across the northern frontier of Israel, raiding and murdering while being supplied and directed by the Iranians and others. As long as Iran, Syria, and even Lebanon continue to allow Hezbollah to train and organize, and even encourage them, the work of death will continue into the next generation and beyond.

As long as a Jewish State exists in the Holy Land, indigenous Palestinian terrorist factions such as Hamas, Islamic Jihad, and the Aqsa Brigades, cannot end the "war that never ends." Every terrorist knows that if the enemy were to suddenly vanish, so would the "eternal struggle," and immediately *irrelevance* would be the horrible specter rising before their bloody eyes, unless of course they could quickly locate another "enemy." The business of terror, like the business of organized crime, is just that, *a business,* a highly lucrative one, in essence a market response to a specific challenge. This is an enterprise of *action*, which brings the successful purveyors of the trade power, money, women—anything in fact, if they can deliver the goods for their customers. Simply, when the customers and their money finally go away, removing the incentive, the terror likewise will vanish.

The Israelis have faced the business of terror for years, and paid with many, many lives. The Palestinians have also sacrificed thousands of innocents to the cause—an eye for an eye, in the land of the blind. Myopia plagues the Middle East, bankrolled and driven by such "stalwarts" as Iran, Iraq (in the past), Libya, Algeria, Syria, Saudi Arabia, and by factions within Egypt, Lebanon, and Jordan. Worse, it is the type of myopia caught in a degenerating spiral downward. Each bloody death, each tit-for-tat, reinforces and regenerates the enterprise, the culture of retaliation and revenge. And business is good these days.

These mostly Islamic myopics are so lost in the forest that they may never find their way out on their own; they must be led (sometimes kicking and screaming). The United States has a plan to end the violence in the Middle East. The plan is built on the principle of negotiating from a position of strength, backed by the full power of the U.S. military. The initial probe began in Afghanistan against the Taliban and al-Qaeda. The flagship event to correcting the myopia and ending the killing is the war in Iraq. From there, I don't believe even the President and his cadre of international maestros knows for certain what the future will bring; however, most certainly the day of endless, neutered "negotiation" is over. The hard choices the near-sighted must now make will be forced on them by the Americans and their allies. We cannot, *we will not*, leave this war to the next generation. The world has become too lethal to allow the near-sighted to continue, business as usual.

Follow-up: Can we win this war?

Sometimes I wonder. This war, against such animals that will attack a grade school (as happened in Christian North Ossetia in 2004) and butcher hundreds of people, many of them young children, is beyond my capacity to comprehend. Yet we know that to the terrorist, there are no rules, no bounds or morals. This is a "war in the name of Allah," and as yet I don't think we comprehend what that means.

The movie *Apocalypse Now*, set during the Vietnam War, comes to mind. In that film, a U.S. Special Forces team, headed by Colonel Walter Kurtz (played by Marlon Brando), is operating behind enemy lines. They come to a village, and in an effort to help the villagers and "win the hearts and minds," they inoculate the children of the village against polio, then move off into the jungle in search of the V.C. (Viet Cong).

Soon an old man from the village comes running after them, begging them to return. The U.S. soldiers head back and find the V.C. have slipped into the village as soon as they left and took a machete and hacked off every child's arm who had been vaccinated, a pile of little arms lying in the middle of the village.

It was a powerful moment in the movie, as Colonel Kurtz tells of it, stating that at that moment he wept like a grandmother. Then as he thought about it, he marveled at the genius of it all, the absolute will and determination of the enemy to do such a horrible act. He said: "Perfect, complete, crystalline, pure." He realized the V.C.

enemy was stronger than we are, for they would kill, maim, and torture without hesitation, without weakness. In the end, Colonel Kurtz knew it was our morality and compassion that defeated us. (Look at how we squirmed at the relatively trivial, even ridiculous, activities of Abu Ghraib Prison.)

I believe that Abu Musab al-Zarqawi, the Beheader, has seen *Apocalypse Now.* He wants to imitate the actions of the Viet Cong. By brutally killing children, women, non-combatants, the terrorist creates an image in the mind of his enemy of pure, heartless dedication, a killing machine, in the name of God: perfect, detached, stopping at nothing to achieve its ends. Such an image is usually magnified in our own minds, the seedbed of nightmares. It causes us to marvel and be struck with such death-rattling fear that we are incapable of responding. We flounder, we wring our hands and hesitate.

There is nothing new here. This is the method of the of old, the Assassins (our word *assassin* comes from the above Arabic word, which also gives us the name of the drug, hashish, believed to make a man unafraid of death and pain.) The Assassins are always with us. And they have *never* been defeated through kindness, understanding, or negotiation.

WINNING THE WAR OF PERCEPTION VS. REALITY

Perceptions, what people *think,* are important. All of us operate on incomplete or erroneous information sooner or later, perhaps every day. Fortunately, most people are not faced with critical, life-threatening decisions every day and therefore can afford to be wrong regularly without doing serious damage.

In the War on Terror we cannot afford such luxury. More so, we cannot afford to keep from the world why we do what we do.

The war of ideas is a war of education. Right now in the world we, the United States of America, are losing that war.

First of all, we need to aggressively counter several lies being force-fed to the people of the Middle East, Europe, and the world. For example:

    1-Osama bin Laden claims that America is raping, pillaging and profiting by Middle East—Islamic—oil. This is blatantly false and can be easily be countered; but first we must be willing to talk about it. For some reason the Bush Administration is unwilling to touch the "O" word. Perhaps this is due to past and present ties the Bush Family, and Dick Cheney, have with the oil industry. Perhaps such connections Bush believes constitutes a no-win political situation when the discussion turns to oil. But the reality is the radicals are getting much mileage on this one. Cut them off at the knees. Release the numbers. Show just how much this war and our efforts in securing the region are costing *America* and that it is *Arab* countries and their citizens who are profiting by oil sales, *not* Americans. The Americans provide a service, only. The numbers are there. Promote the truth. Throw it back in Osama's face.

2- Bin Laden and the radicals can be greatly weakened if Saudi Arabia and the so-called "Gulfies" (Kuwait, Bahrain, Qatar, the UAE, and Oman) begin immediately an aggressive plan of liberalization, initiating democratic reforms. If the people believe they actually have a say in the governing of their country, the bin Laden's of the world quickly lose their luster, more so, their relevance.

3- Saudi Arabia must move now to end its endemic corruption. The Saudis need to set up a high-profile "Minister of Corruption" who has a free hand at cleaning things up. The average Arab sees nothing but hypocrisy, nepotism, and woeful double-standards. Again, *the key to neutralizing bin Laden and his ilk lies in Saudi Arabia.*

4- The U.S. intelligence community, particularly the CIA, must be rapidly overhauled, streamlined, and unfettered. Politically correct, bureaucratic restrictions have got to be set aside and skillfully limited. Of course, there is danger here. But unless the CIA understands once more that it is the point of the spear, and the shield,

United States security will remain in jeopardy.

5- The CIA must establish an effective Office of Media Relations that can promote to the world the many successes the U.S. has carried out to bring peace, freedom, and stability to the world. There is a culture of the hording of secrets within Agency walls that must be reformed to allow those amazing accomplishments to be widely known. This is a tough mission, but vital. In the wake of 9/11, and the WMD disaster in Iraq, the CIA's credibility is close to zero. The world must respect, even fear, the skill and ability of this organization; not laugh at it. America lives or dies on the quality of its intelligence.

6- The U.S. must expose the extensive terrorist training activities of Iran, Syria, and others, and hold their feet to the fire to force closure of these terrorist bases. With an aggressive, coordinated approach, we can drive these rogue nations back on their heels. Then, we go on the offensive. Just the threat of military attack, in most cases, will be enough to make a difference. Of course, only if the enemy knows we are serious.

THE MARRIAGE SOLUTION

Fighting terrorism must go beyond merely hunting down and killing terrorists. In all endeavors, we can and must think creatively.

For example, a story written by Bruce Hoffman in the Atlantic Monthly[91] tells how the Palestine Liberation Organization (PLO), headed by Yasir Arafat, eliminated one of the most blood-thirsty and wide-ranging terrorist groups of the 1970s, their own "Black September Organization."

Black September was made up of the most dangerous and fanatical Palestinian terrorists in the PLO. The group was actually created as a professionally-trained hit team to offer some distance between themselves and the more "legitimate" political activities of the PLO, headed at that time by Yasir Arafat.

Black September was very effective early on, assassinating Jordan's Prime Minister in the lobby of the Sheraton Hotel in Cairo, following the expulsion of the PLO from Jordan in 1970. In 1972 Black September assassinated the Israeli Olympic wrestling team in Munich, Germany. Such high profile attacks achieved the ends Arafat wanted, bringing the plight of the Palestinians to the forefront in world media.

The problem for Arafat came later in the '70s when the PLO was embraced by the United Nations and other international organizations. Suddenly the PLO realized that the monster they had created, Black September, was now a liability. What to do? Short of killing all these young, dedicated fighters, how could they stop them from continued terrorist attacks? The PLO terrorist lives for his next mission, for the blood of his enemy. This was a seemingly impossible challenge for Arafat until an aid came up with a plan. Why not marry off these young Black September fanatics?

PLO leadership then traveled throughout the Arab world to many of the scattered Palestinian communities and approached more than a hundred beautiful, young women and made each an offer difficult to refuse. Arafat himself called on each young female to marry one of these men and give the young fighter a reason to turn his back on the business of terror once-and-for-all. The PLO sold this to these young women and their parents as a "patriotic duty for Palestine." As well, each couple would receive an apartment in Beirut, with a refrigerator, stove, television, and $3,000 in cash. If they had a baby within the first year, they'd get an additional $5,000. Each young man was promised a non-violent job with the PLO in Beirut or elsewhere as additional incentive.

A "mixer," of sorts, was organized in Beirut and the hundred or so young women were flown in. The plan exceeded all expectation. Nearly every young terrorist married one of these women and soon had children. To test these terrorists-in-rehab, the PLO would periodically ask one of them to travel to Europe for some unspecified task. Each refused, fearing he might be arrested and not make it back to his wife and children. Within a few short years, the entire Black September Organization was successfully rehabilitated and disbursed. The problem went away.

Obviously al-Qaeda, or Hezbollah, will not be eliminated in such a fashion. The Black September example is probably unique in its scope and place in history, though this concept regarding the neutralization of young male fighters may still have practical application. In essence, the "Big Stick" may not, in the end, be as effective as some highly creative and probably simple solution we have not yet explored. In nearly all Muslim countries, the vast majority of the population is in the 15 to 30 year-old category, under-employed and frustrated, the perfect age and circumstance for aspiring, motivated terrorists. Lean and hungry and with a dim future in the job market, they are prime candidates for violent behavior. So, what can be done short of rounding them up and cutting their throats?

Certainly not all terrorists are the young, single, foot-soldiers willing to sacrifice their lives so freely. The more dangerous are the older, wiser officers or commanders, the powerbrokers at the top like Osama bin Laden or Dr. Ayman al-Zawahiri, who jockey and strategize to maintain their position of control at all cost. Like a dangerous snake, the head must in the end, be severed.

But below them, those young, dedicated "pawns," potentially many millions under the influence of the terror-bosses, each one must be reached, somehow. Perhaps re-focusing some of the billions of dollars used in the War on Terror to such unorthodox methods just mentioned may accomplish this vital task, and in the end prove more effective than killing and blowing things up.

Admittedly, it's a long shot.

Follow-up: What is *Hawala* banking and how is it used to financially support terrorism?

How do you move millions of dollars anywhere in the world and with no paper trail? Human ingenuity always has an answer: *hawala*, the terrorist's bank of choice, which was used to move some operational funds for the 9/11 terrorists.

How does it work? Simple, really. Hawala is built on trust. In a smoke-filled room in Dubai, in the United Arab Emirates, where banking regulations are, to say the least, "loose," Abdul sits behind a desk. He is online, in reach of a telephone. "You want money transferred to New York, London, Cairo, Jakarta, no problem!" He says with a grin as wide as his face. This is how he does it:

Abdul has contacts, many of them tribal or extended family members, in New York, London, and most major cities. They're not hard to come by; they're found in the local Arab, Pakistani, Iranian, or Turkish communities in most, if not all, major cities.

If you want to send $10,000 to New York, for example, Abdul calls his cousin, Hamid, who has a restaurant in Queens. For a relatively small commission or service fee, the transaction is made. First Abdul and Hamid establish "bonafides" by reciting a short password, which is changed frequently to protect their "net." Then Hamid, the New York operative, delivers the $10,000 dollars to its U.S. destination. Abdul in Dubai then has several ways to reimburse Hamid. He may ship $10,000 worth of Arab food products for Hamid's restaurant or other products including travel to the destination of Hamid's choice. Such benefits are transferable. Abdul may provide a combination of trade and services and/or investment in Dubai's local economy in Hamid's name, or in another regional or global investment. The *only* thing that can kill the Hawala system is betrayal or deceit. Amazingly such betrayal is relatively rare (and dangerous). Hawala traders often have investments and interests in multiple foreign cities around the world.

Another method is to *over-invoice* an import product in exchange for money transfer services. Assume that Abdul owes Hamid $10,000. Hamid may buy $10,000 worth of computer or telecommunication items and ship it to Abdul accompanied by an invoice for $20,000. Abdul pays the $20,000, which covers the $10,000 he owes Hamid. Also, there is what's called *under-invoicing*. Abdul buys $20,000 worth of goods and ships it to Hamid, invoicing him for only $10,000. Same outcome.

This business is profitable and almost impossible for local governments to regulate, to assign bank charges, and most importantly, tax. Hawala has been used for many years in money laundering operations and to cheat on import and export fees and taxes.

One definition of hawala is the transfer of money (or value) without money movement. The process typically takes one or two days while official bank transfers can take up to a week. Avoiding the banking bureaucracy, which is terribly inefficient, even unreliable in many parts of the world, is another reason. Hawala may be the only way to transfer funds abroad for a foreigner living illegally in the United States. Banks often require a social security number to execute a transfer of cash overseas, information an illegal person may be unwilling or unable to give.

Hawala traders often speculate in foreign currencies, transferring funds into currencies where a positive move will benefit the trader. Traders also speculate in the black market, profiting by natural fluctuations in currency demand or in true value, as opposed to official government rates. Hawala traders avoid overhead by trading from an existing business of sorts, such as an import/export shop, a restaurant, travel agency, and businesses such as gold and jewelry trading, rugs and carpets, auto dealing or auto repair and car rental. The hawala transaction is only limited by the creativity of the transactors. Such combinations of cash, product, service, and investment are potentially so varied as to frustrate even the most experienced and dedicated investigators.

Some typical signs of hawala activity might be in the large amount of U.S. bank account activity of a company, especially from within Mid East or South Asian ethnic communities. Often notations are written on checks—a red flag—indicating that "jewelry" was purchased in the transaction. Outgoing transactions to London, Dubai, or Switzerland are other red flags, these being major and primary hawala centers. As well, Hawala accounts are seldom seen to balance, due to the casual make-up of the business.[92]

The hawala system is an important weapon of the terrorist, particularly the radical Islamic kind, though many groups use the system for drug-trade money laundering activities, and for normal, personal transactions around the globe. International terrorism is big business and it runs on cash. Cut off the cash and most of the more lethal operations will wither. Since September 11th, the U.S. Government is pushing hard to penetrate key hawala networks and to monitor major transactions. To skirt such efforts, terrorists are shifting to smaller, less noticeable transfers. Such money movement is harder and takes more time and effort; but that's the name of the game. We turn up the heat as they get more sophisticated. The battle rages.

Follow-up: How have Middle East Muslim nations encouraged, funded, and supported terrorism?

As has been hammered on in these pages, terrorism is big business. According to a March 2003 report from the Christian Science Monitor newspaper,[93] there is solid evidence that, for years, Saddam Hussein funded Palestinian terrorism in the West Bank and in Gaza City. The report told of a man named Abu Alla who operates an office in Ramallah in order to disperse Iraqi cash payments for terrorist operations. "Abu Alla" claimed that Saddam had dispersed about $15 million to Palestinians in some way associated with terror attacks.

While Abu Alla insisted that the money was "not given as an incentive for terrorism," the recipients of the money, mostly the families of suicide bombers killed in attacks against Israelis, are nearly all very poor and in great need. The office is operated by the Iraqi Ba'ath Party, which holds special ceremonies when handing over checks to the Palestinian families. In the article, Mr. Abu Alla tried to play down the Iraqi donations stating that Saudi Arabia gives double or triple what Iraq gives. The Iraqis refuse to funnel the funds through the PLO, fearing that the PLO will skim some of those funds, or take credit for the donations. The article quoted a PLO Ambassador, stating such funds always serve the donor's interests first, to "make propaganda for themselves."

Recent reports out of Europe indicate some European leaders are concerned that the more than $100 million per year given by the European Union (EU) to the Palestinian Authority may be partially funneled into terrorist operations against Israeli civilian targets. In January 2003, the Tory leader, Iain Duncan Smith called upon the EU to investigate how their donations were being used by the Palestinians. There is evidence, he stated, that at least a portion of these donations were being siphoned off for terror attacks carried out by Hamas, Islamic Jihad, or the al-Aqsa Brigade. According to Smith's speech before a Jewish charity in London, the Palestinian Authority may have hidden the use of the funds by claiming to have more employees than they have, or by manipulating currency exchange rates.[94]

Follow-up: Do terrorists, including Osama bin Laden, build support for their goals and objectives by playing the "Palestinian card"?

Terrorism as a form of "foreign policy" scares people, especially Muslims. They have dealt with it for centuries. One could successfully argue that early Muslim extremists, called the "Assassins," invented it. And no people on earth are more wearied by it than the Palestinians.

However, finding a solution for the Palestinian-Israeli conflict, if even possible, will not persuade al-Qaeda, Hezbollah, Islamic Jihad, Hamas, etc., to lay down their arms. Worldwide Islamic terror is no longer solely about Palestinian land and rights. Actually, it never was. Sheikh Osama bin Laden only started talking about the Palestinians and citing Israeli depredations recently. Osama does not care about Palestine. Let me repeat, Osama bin Laden cares nothing about the fate of the Palestinians unless their fate can somehow be linked to his personal dreams of Islamic conquest. His goal is to drive the Americans from the Persian Gulf region; then, butcher the Saudi royals and set up an Islamic State or Caliphate in Arabia giving him full control over most or all "Muslim" oil reserves.

When originally reforming and re-fitting al-Qaeda to attack America in the mid-1990s, bin Laden seldom talked about Palestine. To most Gulf Arabs, Palestine had been a minor issue, anyway. Gulf Arabs I have known over many years don't particularly like the "Pals." They never have. However, due to Israeli retaliatory attacks against Palestinian villages in 2002 and 2003, bin Laden finally concluded that the Palestinian issue had propaganda value among the Islamic masses worldwide. This would further legitimize his broader objectives against the United States, since America is the principal ally of Israel. Osama may be slow, but eventually got in step.

Backing the Palestinians played well in the *suuks* (neighborhoods and marketplaces) and mosques of the Muslim world. It had great propaganda value. Before their successful attack on 9/11, bin Laden and al-Qaeda were viewed by most peace-loving Muslims with skepticism. Most believed the terror-mongers, those who killed in the "name of God," should not be trusted. Bin Laden had to package his war against America carefully so as to successfully "sell" it to leery fellow Muslims. Middle Easterners are a cynical lot. They have much experience dealing with terror as a form of foreign policy, and with despots claiming to "act in the name of Allah."

Worldwide Islamic terror is *not* about Palestine, at least not among this generation of Mujahadin, the sons of those who fought the Soviets in Afghanistan, the generation that gave us Osama bin Laden. True, the Palestinians are a great people, yet today they are mere pawns. In reality, the terror is driven by outsiders—trained, supplied, and most importantly, *rewarded* for their deeds. Cash is the facilitator, payoffs going to everyone including the suppliers, the recruiters, and the trainers, and finally to the dead homicide bombers' families. Lots and lots of cash funneled to a hard-pressed people. Sadly, because of the profit in it all, the terror will continue. More tragically, the Palestinians will continue to be used by other Arabs and Muslims and America will continue to support and arm Israel. Like clockwork, "in the name of Allah," the killing goes forward.

It must be obvious by now that this war is largely for regional control of key lands and resources (i.e., Persian Gulf oil), critical for global control and hegemony, helping ensure national security and financial stability. But for men like Osama bin Laden, pride and honor must be factored in as well. I have watched bin Laden since the 1980s. The man is no mystery. He has consistently sought power, wielding Islam as a weapon for his own ends. He is no different from any other tyrant of history.

If you want to quickly end Palestinian terrorism, you must brutally eliminate the Palestinian's financial support network and their source of weaponry, aggressively undercutting their inspiration to fight on. In essence, cut off the money, cutting it to the bone. This is but *one* objective in the U.S. drive into Iraq. Such successes, however, will not lead to any kind of equitable settlement for the Palestinians, nor will it end totally global Islamic-born terrorism against America.

If you want to quickly end Israeli West Bank settlement building, which stirs up Palestinian hatred and frustration, cut off all Israeli aid immediately, (this amounts to billions of dollars yearly) and threaten to sever political relations unless Israel backs down. Given Israel's current deep economic struggles, they will cooperate. They have no choice.

Of course, for political reasons in the U.S. and abroad, this will never happen. But let's at least be honest about it. Our current national policy of official disinformation and blatant denials is killing innocent people, including many Americans. And it mocks the sacrifice of those who have died. Putting an end to Middle East violence begins by being candid with ourselves. It begins to end when we attack the roots, not flaying at the branches. Those roots are found in Iraq, as well as Iran, Syria, and Saudi Arabia.

Follow-up: Will terrorism ever be defeated without the Muslim community's full cooperation?

Terrorism CANNOT be defeated without the full cooperation of the worldwide Muslim community. Islam, get off the fence! According to a recent report in London's Daily Telegraph newspaper, of the 30 current conflicts going on in the world, 28 involve Muslims or Muslim nations! Yet how is this possible from the religion which claims "peace" as a core value? Let's take a closer look.

Muslim apologists immediately answer in defense that this just shows how "strategic and vulnerable Muslim lands are today." They claim Muslims are caught in regional and global cross-fires between non-Muslim powers. And also, many Muslim lands have commodities (oil) that nations and groups fight over.

While this may be true, the greatest concern to America in the wake of 9/11 is *Muslim*-born terrorism. Terrorism is the response of a defeated, down-trodden, weak and vulnerable people. The Losers. Unable to match America straight-up on the field of battle, the Muslim enemy skulks the shadows, seeking the soft underbelly, the helpless, the weak. They wait for the perfect moment to strike, and then run for the caves.

Whether the terrorist has the right to attack in this cowardly manner can be debated. What cannot be debated is this: The great world religion of Islam has a native defect which cannot be eradicated from *outside* the House of Islam. This defect is as old as the religion itself, born in insecurity and oppression. It is the legacy of the *Hashashin* (the Assassins), the dark hand of the professional killer, the terrorist's terrorist, as well as the Mujahadin, Warriors of the Faith.

This disease called terrorism has gripped Islam today because Islam has allowed it. The religion is politically weak and lacks a strong central leadership core recognizable to all Muslims worldwide. Like Christianity, the religion is fragmented; but *unlike* Christianity, powerful terror factions have institutionalized murder in diverse corners of the globe. Islamists seem unwilling to adapt, or even prosper, in the modern world. They would rather return to some mythical former day of "Islamic grandeur." Any student of history knows that turning back the clock always leads to disaster, more so to societal suicide.

In reality, terrorism has gripped Islam because Muslims nurture it by offering safehaven and funding, and in too many cases, moral support. True, the terrorists and radicals are but a tiny minority of the faith. Most Muslims would no more fly a planeload of innocents into a building packed with even more innocents than any good Christian, Jew, Hindu, or Buddhist. At its core, Islam may indeed be a religion of peace, though many are withholding judgment for obvious reasons.

The greatest truth of history is that the mainstream or the masses seldom lead. The activists, the radicals, the revolutionaries *always* drive great events. The masses are too often merely bystanders, raising their families and too busy with their daily lives to get involved. But Muslims everywhere can no longer afford to stand idly by. The war has begun; the gale sweeps us from the East, yet in New York, the Persian Gulf, Yemen, Bali, everywhere Muslims remain silent. Bodies of the innocent are stacked like charred cordwood and Muslim leaders and a *billion* followers cower in silence. This is shameful.

I repeat: Only Muslims can stop the murder of innocents by removing the terror-mongers' hiding places, bases of operations, and most critically, funding. If Muslims and Muslim nations would do the honorable thing and collectively pick up the sword *against* terror, the terror would cease overnight. The fact that they do not is the single greatest damning evidence that Muslims are squarely on the fence, shivering in fear, or perhaps even a bit pleased, to see America bleed. Nearly every Muslim I have talked with admits as much, but privately, *never* in public. I understand their fear, as Islamic terror comes double-edged. As well, to admit it brings dishonor and shame. But lack of concrete, widespread Muslim condemnation and action against the terror is Islam's single greatest censure. The Religion of Peace should also be the Religion of Courage. But *courage* must be proven with *action* or such is merely an empty word.

Get off the fence, my brother. Support the forces of freedom and democracy. For honor's sake, for *God's* sake, take a stand and remove your shame before Allah. *Kilmat ya'rayt, ma'amaraat bayt!* (Wishful words do not build a house!)

Allah's Apostle, the Prophet Muhammad, has said, *"...for every day on which the sun rises there is a reward of a Sadaqa (charitable gift or blessing) for the one who establishes justice among people."*[95]

QUESTION 23

- DOES AMERICA HAVE A MORAL OBLIGATION, EVEN DUTY, TO LEAD THE WORLD?

I FEAR FOR AMERICA

Did we really expect the soldiers and cronies of the world's premier tinhorn dictator to battle to the last man? I know Iraqis. I've lived and worked among them for many years. They know which side their pita is buttered. They understand life under the lash after a generation of brutal Ba'ath Party rule in a land that should be the premier Mideastern nation, a land of prosperity, freedom, and diversity. Iraq has the resources, location, and people to do just that, and now has a window of opportunity. Two key questions remain: Do Iraqis have the vision? Does America have the will?

The rebuilding, or more accurately the *reshaping* of Iraq, is a monumental task. Saddam's Ba'athist regime is defunct. Good riddance. But the greatest challenge the United States is facing in bringing peace and prosperity to the Middle East lies closer to home; within the U.S. Congress, and with the Democratic Party and the American media, all appearing ready to pounce on every perceived miss-step by the Bush Administration. Do we have the courage to succeed in Iraq and the will to set partisan politics aside to accomplish the greater good? Don't hold your breath.

Listening to the almost daily attacks from fellow Americans saddens me. It seems many politicians and special interest groups are willing to sell their souls for 30 pieces of self-serving political silver. I fear for my nation that has become so self-seeking; for politicians so unwilling to surrender personal power for a time, even if it means freedom and prosperity for millions of souls. In today's political climate, I fear for America. I fear what we have become.

The greatest challenge has always been one of education, of enlightening the American people about what is going on. President Ronald Reagan was masterful at doing just that. Today, Americans are too often talked down to by the media and by government officials, or simply ignored. This is a mistake. Americans want to know. Academia, the media, and our leaders need to educate us further, to explain what is actually going on when we see on the TV, for example, a Shi'ite demonstration in Iraq chanting "America go home!" It is *not* enough just to report the demonstration and leave it at that. Pictures and verbal images can be deceiving, especially coming from the Middle East, the "land of smoke and mirrors." Demonstrations are orchestrated, they are *always* orchestrated, and for a variety of reasons, the most important generally cloaked.

For example, a local Shi'ite cleric, Abdullah,[96] sees the Americans moving with determination and ability and he gets anxious. Wealth, power, control, all are slipping through his boney fingers. So he gathers his followers, many of whom are from his extended family and related families (which make up the local, tribal-based neighborhood). From the mosque *minbar*[97] he calls upon Allah and heaven, in a loud voice, to hear and answer his plea. His message goes something like this: "Men of the Faith. Evil is among us and we must be vigilant. God in his goodness and mercy has used the Satanic Americans to destroy the Ba'ath Party plague and its murderous leader, Saddam. Evil upon evil, corruption to end corruption. Such is the mysterious, all-powerful hand of Almighty Allah. Saddam is gone. But now, we must drive one more plague from our midst. The wicked, sinful Americans have come, with their tanks and jets and weapons of war. How can we prevail?"

The whole crowd shouts together: "Islam! The faith of the Prophet, the power of the Martyr!"

The cleric, Abdullah, nods his approval, holding up his hands for order. "You are wise, my brothers. Let the Americans know of your anger, of God's anger. Tomorrow, we gather here. Tomorrow our voices will be heard. Islam is the solution!"

The rally ends wholly electrified as the cleric's aids move among the crowd to coordinate the next morning's demonstration. The media is notified, of course; the Americans must be warned so the situation will not get out of hand. Everything must be properly orchestrated or people could be killed. Abdullah does not want this. That would be messy and not help his cause. To accomplish his goals, martyrs are not always necessary.

On the morrow thousands of the faithful gather. They are

instructed carefully. Bring no weapons; do nothing to provoke the Americans. "Remember," Abdullah tells his lieutenants, "the Americans are patient; they will be careful not to injure anyone unnecessarily." When the demonstration begins, slogans are shouted, signs are raised and the men march to the appointed place where their spiritual leader rises and delivers another speech. This mullah likes to give speeches. The media is there; so is the world. Cameras roll, the commentators comment, the Shi'ites make their point, and the reporters madly scramble to get their "story." This is *not* what Americans back home want to see, they muse; some gloat as they shoot their stories off via email. Yes, truly, this is "important," this is "ominous for America."

Finally, the demonstrators shuffle back to their homes, thoroughly worn out, yet entertained by the day's festivities. Abdullah, however, does not go home. His assistants have already arranged a meeting with American military officials. Soon they sit together, tiny tea cups in hand, filled with the usual sludgy, sweet brew; translators perched close by.

"My American friends, welcome," says Abdullah, a pompous smile painting his gaunt, lined face. "Thank you for your patience with our little gathering today. And thank you for not overreacting."

The American officers nod. They know the routine.

"You see, my people are restless. Perhaps they are even a little angry," Abdullah continues. "I am trying to contain them, but you know they have been through much in their lives. And they are running out of patience."

"What can we do for you, Abdullah?" The senior American officer asks, thoroughly jaded after more than a year in Iraq.

"Yes, yes," says Abdullah, his native demeanor not wanting to cut to the chase too quickly. Such is crass, lacking honor. "Well, my American friends. There is much to do here. And I truly want to help you do it. My people need everything—better water, more electricity, jobs, housing, you can see there is still much for you Americans to do for us. Certainly these things will take time. We are a patient people—'patience is of Allah,' you know. And I realize you are busy…but I fear that without *me* to comfort and soothe my followers, they may not be easily satisfied."

"My friend, they will never be satisfied," says the American Colonel, matter-of-factly.

Abdullah thinks on this a moment, stroking his piously short beard with his cupped right hand. "Yes, well, such is the nature of man, is it not? But I am a most valuable asset to you, for I watch over my people living in these *suuks*. I can be of great help to you. But I need your assistance. I need to be included in all planning matters. And I need certain...funds, you know, to cover my many expenses in your service. Saddam took everything we had."

The Americans glance at each other. Same old tune. But the Americans are growing accustomed to this tune, though they never like it. "Of course, Abdullah, my friend. We can work together here. As a team we can rebuild these peoples' lives."

Abdullah ponders the statement a moment, then brightens. "Yes, of course, the people...we can work together for the people."

As he leaves that day, he knows whatever the Americans offer will not be enough for him. These matters often require renegotiation, several times. His mind is racing ahead to the next step to turn up the heat on the rich Americans. They are so vulnerable here in Iraq. And with vulnerability, and with the incredibly lofty nation-building objectives of these idealistic Outsiders, Abdullah should be able to squeeze much blood from these stones. Such is the way of the Middle East, the way it was done to the Persians, then to the Greeks, the Romans, the Europeans, and now finally, to the Americans. Some things never change, Abdullah muses, only the nationality of the players in their midst, those who never seem to fully grasp what is happening to them.

Abdullah smiles and hurries back to his mosque, his little entourage hustling to keep up.

Follow-up: Is America a modern Roman Empire?

To many in the Muslim World we have become the modern equivalent of the Roman Empire. Of course, even a superficial look at history would immediately discount such a claim, though some minor similarities exist.

Suppose for a moment we have raised the banner of Caesar, of the Praetorian Guard, of the centurion and his armored legions. Is this the case? Is America, as popular British historian Niall Ferguson claims, actually "empire-lite," as detailed in his book, *Colossus: The Price of America's Empire?*[98]

Consider the facts. We are unchallenged in the world. We have individual *states* in our country with higher gross production capacity than nearly every other country, or collection of countries, the world over. The U.S. dollar is the world's international currency, in oil trading, in weapons' transactions, in most global enterprises and purchases. U.S. securities are the most popular international investment safe haven. Even our terrorist enemies use our technology, our transport and communication systems, even our banking networks, to execute their killing designs, due to our incredible efficiency, profitability, and openness. Their world is so hopelessly restricted and inefficient—functionally bankrupt—they must use *ours* to attack *us*. Their religious system, the one they want the world to adopt, is effectively and functionally worthless in today's world. They testify of this truth by their daily actions and Western market choices. Do they not see the irony, but more so, their blatant hypocrisy?

Other nations recognize the overwhelming dominance of the United States. In 2001, in a quiet signing ceremony in Moscow, Chinese officials met with Russian President Vladimir Putin to sign what has become known as the "Shanghai Pact." Chinese President Jiang Zemin, in naming it such, perhaps drew a historical tie to the old Warsaw Pact. The treaty is, in its own words, designed to "work together to preserve the global strategic balance." The pact, including four former Central Asian Soviet republics, claims the right to clamp down on "terrorism, extremism, and separatism and to maintain regional security." Amazingly, for the first time in its history, China agreed to conduct joint military maneuvers with these Shanghai Pact members, which took place the Summer of 2003. According to an article in the *International Herald Tribune*, contributed by specialists at the U.S. Naval War College in Newport, R.I., China's strategy is to "help stabilize China's inland frontier...permit(ting) Beijing to adopt a more eastward-looking maritime strategy and focus its military capabilities on Taiwan."[99] This frees China to shift resources to the Southeast, putting further military pressure on

Taiwan, and ultimately challenging the United States for dominance in the Pacific.

Following the establishment of the pact, the Islamic Republic of Iran expressed interest in joining. It is conceivable that Syria, which is involved with Pact members, would also be interested in signing on. Iran, increasingly pressured by the U.S. over its blatant support of terrorism, would find better cover for its actions from Russia and China and perhaps greater leverage on the United Nation's Security Council, where Russia and China are permanent members.

Of course, assuring access to Persian Gulf and Caspian basin crude oil is at the heart of every discussion and every maneuver. China imports about half its oil from the region. The trend is strongly upward and China remains highly vulnerable. Conservative projections put China's oil import needs at 75 percent of totals or more by the year 2020. Shanghai Pact members see few viable options beyond eventual confrontation with the United States "empire" over control of key Middle East sources, hence their desire for strategic alliance. The threat from Washington, China believes, must be countered and energy bottlenecks eliminated.

An International Energy Agency (headquartered in Paris, France) report outlines the basic goals of long-term Chinese energy security: "Their basic strategies are maximum development of domestic resources, creation of strategic reserves, seeking foreign technology and investment, establishing reliable and secure oil trading channels, and making strategic investments in upstream production facilities abroad. These approaches mirror the classic moves of nations which found themselves in import-dependency in the past. In fact, China has already moved farther and faster to take advantage of inward investment in its energy industries than did Japan at an analogous stage of development."[100]

The U.S. war against Iraq, and American inroads in the Middle East, has further galvanized Shanghai Pact members; all apparently believe U.S. superiority in the world must be countered and limited. The cooperation and coordination the Shanghai Pact brings, almost all of which is highly secret, appears to be intensifying between member states. And oil security and oil profits, among other factors, are at the heart of the alliance. So, where does this lead us?[101]

The world hates, fears, and admires America all at the same time. A classic love-hate relationship. We *are* a modern Rome; and yet we are not. Perhaps Mr. Ferguson, as mentioned above, is right. We are empire-lite. Perhaps more importantly, Americans need to understand better the leadership role we have shouldered and why we must not withdraw from the world for any reason.

While history does repeat itself all too often, America is grounded in moral, spiritual, and cultural beliefs which were not prevalent in ancient Rome. America's global objectives of democracy, self-determination, peace, and stability for all peoples are unique in world history. Don't count on President Bush to be the mighty Caesar. More so, our terrorist enemy is changing, he has put on new clothes.

Before Iraq can build long-term peace and modernity, the oil wells must flow. Iraq must become the premier land of oil production, as well as democracy. What a monumental task! Iraq needs at least $6 billion in investment just to return to the pre-1991 production levels of 3.5 million barrels of oil per day. Eventually that figure should be higher.

As well, Iraq needs tens of billions of dollars of infrastructure investment to modernize industries devastated by decades of neglect, war, and international sanctions. Such capital investment simply will not happen without security and stability, plus the recognized international legality of the new, U.S.-backed Iraqi government. America must ensure that the new administration in Baghdad has broad internal and international legitimacy and support. Anything less will fail.

No one doubts the massive potential of Iraq's oil and gas industry. According to most experts, the world total of known oil reserves is somewhere over 1,000 billion barrels. Iraq has somewhere between 150 and 250 billion barrels, possibly as much as one-fourth of the world's proven total!

By comparison, Britain's much heralded North Sea reserves total only 5 billion barrels, though it does make Britain the European Union's largest oil producer. What an incredibly pathetic contrast! Iraq alone is sporting *30 times* more oil, at the least! And it's cheap oil, costing on average around $2 dollars per barrel to lift in many areas. North Sea oil costs $15 to $25 dollars per barrel just to pump the stuff from the ocean floor, an expensive and risky venture.

Iraq has so very much going for it: The bountiful Tigris and Euphrates rivers, rich farmland with two or three crops a year, a large and capable population, and of course dirt-cheap, quality oil and gas. What nation could ask for more in natural resources? Iraq should lead the world's club of energy producers and provide a world-class standard of living for its diverse population. A modern Eden could be created in the "land between the two rivers." The fact there isn't is but one further, and highly glaring, indictment of the Butcher of Baghdad and his Ba'ath Party parasites who used and abused Iraq's many bounties for so long.

While America is not, and never will be a modern Rome, the world needs the United States now more than ever, with its technology, its wealth, its leadership and democratic example. While the Middle East has suffered from poverty and oppression for centuries, it took Western, principally *American*, know-how and technology to teach the Arabs and Iranians how to use their resources. From the beginning of the Age of Oil, Middle Easterners have stood back and watched the Americans and Europeans bestow unimaginable wealth on their heads, and they thanked *Allah*, continually. That is fine. America does not seek adulation. Peace and prosperity are reward enough.

But ironically, and deservedly, at some future time it will likely be American technology that will eliminate Arab wealth overnight when another "miracle" source of energy is created by Western scientists. In that day Arab oil will become worthless and the Arab world will once again sink into obscurity. Once more Allah's children will slide back into irrelevance and hopelessness. *Now* is the time, my Arab friends, to take sound advantage of your position, not simply exploiting it at the expense of others. Establish long-term development and prosperity among your people and stop racing to line your own pockets as Saddam and his sons did. Amazingly giving, when you look at the facts, the United States is ready to help you accomplish this goal.

Educated Arab and Iranian elites already understand this, though the radical religious leaders are still largely clueless. Of course a new, major energy source is probably a long way off. Until then, the Middle East will remain the world's strategic powerhouse, and every nation will lust after the god-like power it bestows on an energy-starved world. And at the head of it all, leading the way to hopefully a better world, will be the so-called "American Empire." As we have always been taught: "Where much is given, much is expected."

QUESTION 24

- WHAT QUESTION HAVE WE FAILED TO ASK THAT PERHAPS WE SHOULD?

Mistakes have been made in this war. But advancing freedom is never a mistake.
   --William Safire, November 23, 2003

There is one further question we all must ask ourselves, a two-part question:

Am I, are we, willing to do whatever it takes to defeat terrorism and bring peace, freedom, and prosperity to the world? What can I do to further this worthy quest?

Unfortunately, as I travel our great country, speaking to various groups, I am not certain Americans are prepared for such a challenge. Of course many are; but too many seem to be floundering. Certainly any worthy goal requires hard work, often pain and suffering. In essence, we sacrifice for the greater, long-term good. While our military men and women have set the prime example, so many without hesitation offering their lives, most Americans seem confused, reluctant, even afraid.

Yet the solution is before us, *if* we have the courage and the will to stay the course. Failure is not an option here. Failure guarantees a future of increasingly devastating and deadly attacks on American soil. In response, our government could even be forced to scrap our inspired Constitution and adopt a despotic techno-totalitarianism in order to secure our land and borders. At that point Osama bin Laden and his ilk will have won and America will turn inward and cease to be a force for freedom and good in the world.

So, what must we do to end the terror and inspire and nurture freedom? What is the ultimate solution? Actually, it has five parts, and be forewarned, each requires an iron-will on the part of every

American:

1- We must force our enemy to fix his attention on one particular target or objective; an element that is important to him. We must keep his attention *riveted* on that objective. With his attention thus occupied, we must move aggressively on his flanks, and in the shadows (covertly), in the places he least expects. (We are doing this in Iraq, and in Afghanistan; fighting the battle *there*, not in America's cities. Brilliantly we have riveted the enemy's attention on our Mid East forces and operations.)

2- Through the highest quality intelligence, gathered with greater skill and tenacity, we must identify the enemy's strengths, not merely his weaknesses. We then use those strengths, as well as weaknesses, against him. Most of this dirty aspect of the war will never be seen by the public. It will require a clandestine service void of hubris, that immoral, selfish arrogance which currently plagues much of our culture. If not, we will fail.

3- When we are ready, we must surprise the enemy by hitting him hard and fast where he least expects, in the place he thought was impregnable. This takes creativity (and cultural and regional insight and knowledge) to identify the finest, most effective points of penetration. But they are there, they always are, waiting to be exploited.

4- Then we must use our own best strengths, and our vast resources and superior technology, to <u>absolutely destroy the enemy's will and ability to resist</u>. Overwhelming, total victory sends a message that dictators and terror-bosses everywhere understand. This is key: *absolute victory*. No compromises, no half-measures, no face saving outlets or partial wins. This is hard for Americans; we are a merciful people. At this stage, however, mercy only prolongs the pain and leads to more death. Political correctness or playing by "the rules" will not work in dealing with modern terror-regimes and murderous cells. The reasons at this point should be crystal clear.

5- Finally, none of the above will succeed without *unity*. Those Americans who oppose the war on terror, and thwart the war on Middle East despotism, which provides safe haven and funding for the many terrorist minions, are offering hope and inspiration to America's enemies. This is a logical, easily proven fact, reported time and again from intelligence operatives and military units on the front lines, *especially* in Iraq and Afghanistan. History will not be kind to those who give hope to our enemies and who stand in the way of our warriors' gallant efforts.[102] Americans continue to die (some in the clandestine services, unseen) because our enemies believe America is not fully united in this cause.

To win this war we must learn the lesson of Hannibal which is: *Absolute, total victory, whatever the cost.* Hannibal, the great and terrible Carthaginian general, led a heavily outnumbered force through Spain, over the Alps, and into Italy to attack Rome in 214 B.C. The story of his miraculous journey, particularly as he cut and clawed his way over the snow-covered Alps with a force of 40,000 men and 69 war elephants, is a textbook example of superior leadership and bold innovation. Hannibal was outnumbered, operating essentially without supply lines in foreign lands far from home. He is considered one of the greatest military geniuses of all time, though what little we know of him is seen only through the eyes of his enemies, the Romans.

Marching his men southward towards Rome, he flanked, then surprised the otherwise superior Roman legions and cut them down. He showed no mercy. It is obvious from his tactics that he knew his Roman enemy well. He knew that even when going down in defeat, the Romans would fight to the death. Hannibal used this knowledge to his advantage, inflicting some of the heaviest casualty figures in the history of warfare on an enemy force. The numbers are staggering. Following several key battles, *one-in-four* Roman male citizens of military age died in fighting with Hannibal's marauders.

At the Battle of Cannae in 216 B.C., Hannibal purposely exposed his weak center line, allowing the Romans to throw their best and strongest forces into breaking the middle. In other words, he gave the Romans a target to focus on, and to distract them from his true objective. When the Romans were, like a bulldog, determined to chew through Hannibal's middle, he used his own strength, his Numidian (Berber) cavalry, to hit the Romans hard on both right and left flanks. This forced the Romans in on themselves, preventing them from fighting in their preferred or desired manner, in their armored lines and columns. They were forced to do battle by Hannibal's rules, on the ground of his choosing. Within hours, thousands of Romans lay dead and dying in the August sun.

After thoroughly defeating the Roman army and totally destroying its ability to fight, Hannibal did something wholly uncharacteristic. He hesitated. He refused to immediately attack the now undefended city of Rome. He pulled back and reformed. He pondered a negotiated settlement. He allowed the Romans time to regroup.

Of course there were excuses for his hesitation. There are always excuses. But his pause then allowed the otherwise defenseless Romans to appoint a new commander, raise a new army, which then renewed the desperate campaign to drive Hannibal from their land. Such hesitation undoubtedly led to Hannibal's defeat.

Though Hannibal knew how to take a relatively small force, outnumbered and ill-equipped, and with lightning moves, conquer a great enemy; he, however, on the cusp of victory, ignored the greatest lesson of military history: Victory must be absolute, overwhelming, and final. No exceptions. Anything less and the enemy will return, with vengeance.

Again, I pose the question: Are we willing to do whatever it takes to finish Islamic-born terrorism once and for all? Do we as a nation have the collective will? Does each of us have the courage to make the ultimate sacrifice, if necessary?

Follow-up: Why is hope for the future—The Vision—always grounded in the freedom of mankind? Why is freedom always non-negotiable?

On September 1, 1989, while stationed in Amman, Jordan, I wrote the following in my journal:

"The Muslim world must eventually, in its entirety, enter the modern age in order to be tested, tried, and proven. Otherwise it will be damned by an eternal God, the same God the Muslims call 'Allah.' Short of this, Muslims (will) rob themselves of God's most important gift—*freedom*."

The human race always flounders when there is a scarcity of men and women with vision, and the dedication to a positive quest for freedom and opportunity. Such a worthy goal is grounded in education, and in throwing off the false cultural shackles of despotism so long imprisoning the world. We must help build nations free of unnecessary government and religious restrictions, which damn the soul and limit personal opportunity for growth and development. Governments and organized religions can free and empower, or just as easily bind, tax, and destroy. The essence of this vision is an unshakable commitment to freedom.

In the Muslim world today, *especially* in the Middle East, the social structure is too restrictive to allow the growth and self-betterment of men and women. Cultural and religious restrictions are everywhere, killing opportunity. In most cases people obey Islamic Law because they are forced to do so, by family, society, government, by "religious police," by terrorists, by a host of age-old cultural restrictors and enforcers. Islam is a nation of followers, but with few true leaders or statesmen in the classical sense, leaders with a positive vision. Where is the Muslim version of Abraham Lincoln? Where is Thomas Abdul Jefferson? I can't find him, though I've searched long and hard.

The upper crust of Muslim society is wholly corrupted by power and wealth. The masses are oppressed at every turn and woefully ignorant of the truth. We can draw parallels to the Europeans during the Dark Ages. While some highly educated people existed, essentially the masses were unaware of their possibilities and hopelessly limited or "damned" in their freedoms, as a river is damned from rushing to the sea, preventing it from reaching its desired goal. True, the system forced people to stay on the "straight and narrow," but at the same time prevented them from learning or progressing in almost every way. Centuries crawled by with little or no scientific, medical, or technological advancement. Conditions degenerated, with religious leaders purposely blinding and crippling their own people, keeping them shackled and in the dark.

Parallels are found in the Middle East today. Medieval-like restrictions clog all facets of society, negating opportunities; restrictions designed to secure and prosper the elites and to protect tribal and family "honor." In practice, these native restrictions merely stunt the Muslim, Christian, and Jew, both male, and *especially* female.

To shatter the shackles once and for all, it is necessary for nations to allow freedom of religion, speech, assembly, of the press, and the elimination of social discrimination in all forms. The Muslim world is comprised of a host of honest, God-fearing people. These are folks who live close to the precepts of Allah—close, supportive family units, little juvenile delinquency, few pre-marital pregnancies, practically no visible violent crime (except terrorism), little drug use, few divorces and little deviation from society's established norm. On the surface the water is undisturbed; but beneath the placid calm is a world of cultural chains, abuse, even murder, outlined extensively in the previous chapters. Certainly freedom and opportunity, in the process of empowering men and women, will undermine some traditional Islamic ideals. Change, however, is necessary; in fact, it is inevitable. Islamic culture is damming (restricting) *one-fifth* of the world's population.

Fortunately, technology, information, and intelligence are excellent dam-busters. They are unstoppable, though the lovers of power and ultimate government control, the "religious police," like Osama bin Laden, and others, have tried to turn back the clock. Such men are fools, blind to the mighty river rushing over them. All people, everywhere, will soon have their shackles smashed, left free to choose for themselves. The slaves are rising against their masters and no force in the universe can rein them back in their fury. Freedom is to die for, the sweetest of all Godly gifts, a right and privilege men and women in every land will risk all they have to achieve.

THE NUTS AND BOLTS OF WINNING HEARTS

During recent discussions with several Turkish associates, who represent one of the largest Turkish development companies, a group heavily involved in rebuilding Iraq, I was amazed at their simple, yet workable advice for America.

Truly Middle Easterners have an affinity, a certain love and respect for America they have a hard time explaining. What is frustrating them now, something they cannot fathom, is that they are not hearing much from President Bush.

Now certainly the President has much on his plate, and for

The Middle East Explained

obvious reasons he can't be wandering around chatting with the common people in Mideast lands. Still, most of these people would certainly like to hear from him.

The Turks loved President Bill Clinton. When he visited Turkey after their killer earthquake in 1999, he traveled to a badly damaged area to see the devastation firsthand. While there he picked up a baby, held the little girl and kissed her on the cheek. The baby cooed and played with his nose and President Clinton looked at the little one and laughed and the Turks went wild for him. And they've loved him ever since, my Turkish friends assure me.

Now trying to emulate William Jefferson Clinton's example would probably not work for George W. Bush. They are very different men. But the Clinton example has some application. First of all you cannot compete with the tsunami of anti-American media found in the Middle East by disengaging. It's not possible, no matter how good your local Ambassadors are, or how much *Radio Sawa* broadcasts positive vignettes of America's generosity and grandeur. Simply, *the President must engage the people*. He must make the effort to get on the ground, in the neighborhoods, in the streets, among the common folk.

Obviously such an approach carries risks; no, MAJOR risks, though those risks are nearly all physical. Other than the possibility of getting "seriously killed," politically there is little down side here. The Arabs, the Turks, the Iranians will love you, Mr. President, it's that simple. Learn a few words of greeting in Arabic and Turkish and you will build a grassroots movement of support from Marrakech to Bangladesh overnight. Worship in a leading Mosque for Friday noon prayers, visit a 2,000 year old Coptic Christian church in Egypt, and the Middle East will explode with support for you, Mr. President. Memorize a short speech in Arabic, this coupled with a strong statement of support for a free state of Palestine on the West Bank and Gaza and you will not be able to contain the flood of support from the Arab and Muslim street. Again, the greatest challenge is the security issue. Deal with it and the rest is a slam dunk, a guaranteed win for your administration and the United States.

There is no way to ultimately defeat the radicals without full engagement, on many key levels. In the Middle East the family is central. And like in much of the world, the family is under assault, both from the modern, material world, but also from the radicals, the *mullahs* and fundamentalists. Look what the radicals are saying, how they use the worst of American-Hollywood Culture against us. And Europe is even more corrupted, more rotted from within. Such obvious moral decay gives hope to the Osama bin Laden's and his ilk. They are, in fact, counting on the influence of "Shaytan" (Satan) in America and Europe to further their dreams of Islamic conquest.

The danger today is that by becoming complacent and passivist in our approach to Islamic political movements, if we sit back and just watch, the radicals could very well seize control, through a variety of means, and cause death and suffering on a massive scale. The danger is that such radical movements operate on a clandestine level, called *taqiya* in Arabic, relying on "hook or crook" to steal and hold power. Anything goes. They have even tried to gain power using democracy, meaning the ballot box, in several regions. "One man, one vote, one time." But make no mistake, in the end fascism is their goal, *never* democracy, a fascism wrapped in the pious robes of Islam.

REACHING BACK

In essence, all the good intentions amount to little if the perceptions, the images, are something very different. This is a war of ideas, of education, of images on the screen. The Arabs in particular and Muslims in general, have a problem. Their considerable historical baggage is playing into the hands of the terrorists. On 9/11, as my Arab friends explained, Arabs and many Muslims stood a little taller that day. It was as if a half-a-millennium of shame at the hand of the Christian West was, at least partially, wiped clean. Arabs, my friends assured me, felt a bit better about themselves to see America cut down a notch or two.

"Why," I asked, "should America pay such a heavy price?"

"Because America is proud in the world and does not think about other people. Maybe now they will notice us."

Notice you? 3,000 dead, and many more sacrificed to resist global terror because we "weren't paying close enough attention"? The United States has liberated more captives, righted more wrongs, and financed more development projects and *hundreds of billions* of dollars to lessen world suffering than any other nation in history! Maybe now America will notice us? What the hell kind of twisted, sadistic, just plain wrong-headed thinking is that?!

Still, that's not even the point. My Arab and Turkish friends, in their much pontificating, have told us everything we need to know to win this war. As I said up front, this is a war of education, of ideas, of reaching out with our two hands. And when done with American ingenuity and skill, the world will reach back. In essence we must drive a wedge between Muslim terrorists, and everyone else, rewarding our friends and eliminating our enemies.

THE GREAT MISUNDERSTANDING

The world has not yet been told the *real* story of America and America's success in the world. Generally most nations and regions operate on very different principles from the way or method America was built up to its greatness today. In most lands the rich are rich and powerful because they either inherited their wealth from privilege, or they stole it from the poor and downtrodden. The assumption, therefore, is that Americans are "rich" for the same reasons. Terrorists, such as Vladimir Lenin, Pol Pot, Fidel Castro, and Chairman Mao spouted these lies at every speech throughout their careers.

True, there are those in America who inherited their wealth; however, the vast majority of Americans are immigrants (or the relatively recent descendents of immigrants), most arriving with little more than the clothes on their backs, destitute, struggling. Americans used their God-given freedom and opportunity to succeed and build a prosperous life for themselves and families. *This* is the manner and method by which Americans have enriched themselves.

Until the world comes to understand this truth, that Americans are not like the elite overlords in other lands, that Americans have not risen to greatness on the backs of the poor, the purveyors of propaganda and hatred will continue to brand us unjustly. And since most people tend to believe what they want to believe, if nothing is said to counter these lies, America will continue to be labeled as "evil" in the world.

THE VISION

Iraq was formed out of the former Ottoman provinces of Mosul, Baghdad, and Basra. Each province is separate and distinct. Each has its own character, personality, culture, and nationalist and religious make-up. Creating a democratically cohesive entity out of native chaos will be tough, as we already know. Iraq may not succeed as one entity, but perhaps three: The Kurdish North, the Sunni heartland, and the Shi'ite South, held together for some years by a strong American presence. Eventually, however, Iraqis must stand on their own. More so, they must choose to stand together. They cannot be forever coerced.

Many do not want to see a viable, democratic Iraq, especially backed by the might of the United States. Such things make world dictators nervous, especially those in Iran, Syria, and Saudi Arabia. History will judge if this is imperialism. World history is nothing if not a treatise on imperialism. Even Islam, the "religion of peace," practiced blatant imperialism. Arab Muslims rolled out of Arabia in the 7th century, conquering all the way to Morocco and Spain on the west, Europe's heartland on the north, and India on the east. The Ottoman Turks, under the banner of Islam, wielded the sword clear to the gates of Vienna. Was Islamic imperial expansion a bad thing? Yes and no, though when the Muslims decided to sit back and rest comfortably on what they had conquered and achieved, that very moment singled their decline and inevitable collapse.

From this we learn two lessons: America must never rest, but more so, must never indulge in the sweet brew of imperialism. It is seductive and ultimately all-consuming. Once successful in Iraq, we must pack up and leave, or risk corrupting ourselves. The United States is wielding its power for good in the world. *Overly militarizing America and harboring such globalist objectives will galvanize the world against us.* Soon our friends will be only those whom we have bought off. Such militarization would require posting hundreds of thousands of American forces in far off lands under dangerous and difficult circumstances. We are seeing just how much such a costly commitment requires in the Middle East. Multiply that by eight or ten other theaters of operation? No, Americans are not ready for such sacrifice. We are not empire builders.

Besides, there are better paths. If enough of the world will support our effort, the Vision might take hold in every land. Leverage is a powerful concept. It says that we cannot do it alone; but by maximizing our otherwise limited resources, we can magnify our effort. This requires other nations, both leaders and followers, with the same vision. So far, few are on our side, mostly due to greed, ignorance, and the lust for power and jealously over America's vast influence in the world.

Regardless, we cannot wait for the timid and self-serving. It is always better to have faith and move forward assertively, rather than to hesitate, dragging feet in the face of progress. We have too many feet-draggers already.

We stand at a crossroads in history. Certainly the obstructionists, whether they reside in France, Russia, Washington, D.C., or Hollywood, are on the wrong side of history. The coming decade will set the stage for the rest of the century. Where will we be ten years from now? Where will *you* be? I wish I had a crystal ball, but this I know: We must not be standing in the same place we were on September 10th 2001. Thanks to a leader with vision, we have momentum and momentum is awfully difficult to create.

As President Ronald Reagan always told us: "We are the light on the hill." America, let the world know you are committed to the freeing of the world's slaves by pulling down dictators and despots everywhere. Neither the world's powerbrokers nor the terror-mongers will like it. Neither will the world's mercenaries. Vision always makes virulent enemies. We can handle it. But suddenly turning passive in our international quest, and retreating along with the weak-kneed and capitulating, will guarantee failure, even destruction of all we hold dear.

Considering America's overwhelming might, power, and influence today, anything less than total and absolute victory over despotism will be a disgrace. Anything less, I am certain, will be judged by history as criminal. Our vision of the future is a vision of hope. It is America's vision, the vision that made America what it is. Let us re-dedicate our lives to this quest and move ahead with power and faith. Only then will we be found worthy of the task; only then will our gift of freedom be acceptable to a struggling, yet hopeful, world.

ACKNOWLEDGMENTS

The Author takes full responsibility for the content, including any possible errors in word or concept. Still, from its inception, some amazing people have taken an interest in and enhanced this work.

Ragai Makar, friend and mentor over many years and an extraordinary Middle East specialist, looked me in the eye and said: "You've got to publish this book!" Since that meeting I have felt an urgency to push this project through to fruition. Ragai has seen much in his long life, his perspective an incredible well of wisdom I wish somehow the world could tap. I've known no one, at any level, who has a greater knowledge and institutional memory on the Middle East.

Thank you Jabra Ghneim for your long-cherished friendship over nearly two decades. Your intelligence and native skill in publishing, in helping to refine this work, is second to none. Even in supreme adversity, forced on you because of your loyalty to our country, you stayed true on course. I will always admire you for that.

Martha Hammond not only gets in and gets things done, in this case she took the manuscript apart and like a whirlwind forced me to focus on what was important. A longtime friend and fine editor, thank you for keeping me on track.

Thank you, Rachae Read, for editorial insights, useful comments, and a boatload of detailed corrections. Your literary talents are yet undiscovered, though this work has been blessed by them. Rachae sees the world different from most folks, her perspective enhancing the quality of anything she touches, including this book and from the very first page.

Thank you George for backing me in tough places, Nehir for your integrity and honor, Kamal for your wisdom, Abdullah for your spirit, Raju for your loyalty, Izz-i-din for your hospitality, Nermine for a rock-solid beginning, Moheb for your eternal friendship, Josephine for your kindness, and Dr. Wahid for your amazing insights and truly miraculous work in the Middle East. To each of you I dedicate this effort.

I will always appreciate the kindness and encouragement of Elder Joe Christensen and his wife Barbara, who took the time to read and comment on the manuscript in its early stages. The genuine, positive example of the Christensen family, in both the written and spoken word over much of my lifetime, has been an inspiration.

Thank you Mother and Father for roots in faith, hope, and charity, yet instilling that certain passion for freedom and acquiring knowledge, thereby shattering life's shackles; and Beverly for your powerful, yet velvet example of perseverance, courage, and pure grit.

Finally, and most importantly, thank you Robin, my amazing and beautiful companion of nearly three decades. You've shared this Middle East experience with me willingly from the beginning, and given me five incredible daughters at the same time! Thank you for shaping me with your gentle, yet skillful, touch.

When this is over, my only fear is what I have offered can never balance the love that has so freely come my way.

BIBLIOGRAPHY

The research for this book came from a variety of sources, primarily from personal contacts made over the past decade and with whom I maintain regular contact. Some go back further in time. Primary information was gained during my three most recent trips to the Middle East, in December, 2002, and then in January and again in August, 2005. Other sources include articles found in journals and newspapers, many accessible on-line. These are listed in the endnotes.

Below is a collection of worthwhile books on the Middle East, some references noted in this book.

Baer, Robert. 2003. *See No Evil: The True Story of a Ground Soldier in the CIA's War On Terrorism.* New York: Crown Publishing Group.

Bodansky, Yossef. 1993. *Target America—Terrorism in the U.S. Today.* New York: S.P.I. Books.

_____. 2004. *The Secret History of the Iraq War.* New York: HarperCollins.

Boyne, Walter J. 2004. *Operation Iraqi Freedom: What Went Right, What Went Wrong, and Why.* New York: Tor Books.

Bradford, Ernle. 1980. *Thermopylae: The Battle for the West.* Cambridge, Massachusetts: Da Capo Press.

Braude, Joseph. 2003. *The New Iraq: Rebuilding the Country for its People, the Middle East, and the World.* New York: Basic Books.

Brisard, Jean-Charles & Dasquie, Guillaume. 2002. *Forbidden Truth: U.S.-Taliban Secret Oil Diplomacy and the Failed Hunt for*

Bin Laden. New York: Nation's Books.

Chavis, Melody Ermachild. 2003, *Meena, Heroine of Afghanistan*. New York: St. Martins Press.

Claire, Rodger. 2004. *Raid on the Sun: Inside Israel's Campaign that Denied Saddam the Bomb*. New York: Broadway Books.

Cleveland, William L. 2004. *A History of the Modern Middle East*. Boulder, Colorado: Westview Press.

Cohn, Norman. 1957. *The Pursuit of the Millennium*. Bristol, England: J.W. Arrowsmith, Ltd.

Coll, Steve. 2004. *Ghost Wars: The Secret History of the CIA, Afghanistan, and Bin Laden, from the Soviet Invasion to September 10, 2001*. New York: Penguin Press.

Corbin, Jane. 2003. *The Base: Al-Qaeda and the Changing Face of Global Terror*. London: Pocket Books/Simon & Schuster.

Cordesman, Anthony H. 2003. *The Iraq War: Strategy, Tactics, and Military Lessons*. Connecticut: Greenwood Publishing Group.

D'Souza, Dinesh. 2002. *What's So Great About America*. Washington, D.C.: Regnery Publishing.

Feldman, Noah. 2004. *After Jihad: America and the Struggle for Islamic Democracy*. New York: Farrar, Straus, Giroux Publishers.

Gertz, Bill. 2000. *The China Threat: How the People's Republic Targets America*. Washington, D.C.: Regnery Publishing.

_____. 2002. *Breakdown: How America's Intelligence Failures Led to September 11*. Washington, D.C.: Regnery Publishing.

Gold, Dore. 2004. *Hatred's Kingdom: How Saudi Arabia Supports the New Global Terrorism*. Washington, D.C.: Regnery Publishing.

Griffin, Michael. 2003. *Reaping the Whirlwind: Afghanistan, al-Qa'ida and the Holy War*. London: Pluto Press.

Hitchens, Christopher. 2003. *A Long Short War: The Postponed Liberation of Iraq*. New York: Penguin Group.

Hitti, Philip K. 1968. *Makers of Arab History*. New York: Harper Torch Books.

Hoffman, Bruce. 1998. *Inside Terrorism*. New York: Columbia University Press.

Huntington, Samuel P. 1996. *The Clash of Civilizations and the Remaking of World Order*. New York: Simon & Schuster Inc.

James, William. 1958, *The Varieties of Religious Experience*. New York: Mentor Books.

Kessler, Ronald. 2003. *The CIA at War: Inside the Secret Campaign Against Terror*. New York: St. Martin's Press.

Klare, Michael T. 2001. *Resource Wars: The New Landscape of Global Conflict*. New York: Henry Holt Company.

Lewis, Bernard. 1967. *The Assassins: A Radical Sect In Islam*. New York: Basic Books.

_____. 1995. *The Middle East: A Brief History of the Last 2,000 Years*. New York: Touchstone.

_____. 2002. *What Went Wrong? The Clash Between Islam and Modernity in the Middle East*. New York: Perennial Press.

_____. 2003. *The Crisis of Islam: Holy War and Unholy*

Terror. New York: Random House.

Miniter, Richard. 2003. *Losing bin Laden: How Bill Clinton's Failures Unleashed Global Terror.* Washington, D.C.: Regnery Publishing.

_____. 2004. *Shadow War: The Untold Story of How Bush is Winning the War on Terror.* Washington, D.C.: Regnery Publishing.

Moore, Robin. (2003) *The Hunt for bin Laden: Task Force Dagger—On the Ground with the Special Forces in Afghanistan.* New York: Random House.

North, Oliver. 2003. *Operation Iraqi Freedom.* Washington, D.C.: Regnery Publishing.

Parfrey, Adam, (editor). *Extreme Islam: Anti-American Propaganda of Muslim Fundamentalism.* Los Angeles: Feral House, 2001.

Pollack, Kenneth M. 2002. *The Threatening Storm: The Case for Invading Iraq.* New York: Random House.

Prados, John. 2002. *America Confronts Terrorism: Understanding the Danger and How to Think About It; A Documentary Record.* Chicago: Ivan R. Dee Publishing.

Pryce-Jones, David. 1989. *The Closed Circle: An Interpretation of the Arabs.* New York: Harper Perennial.

Qiao Liang, et al. 2002. *Unrestricted Warfare: China's Master Plan to Destroy America.* Panama City, Panama: Pan-American Publishing Company.

Qutb, Sayed. (No date available.) *Milestones.* Damascus: Dar al-Ilm Publishing. (Sayid Qutb was one of the first radical, activist Muslims of the modern era.)

Robinson, Adam. 2001. *Bin Laden: Behind the Mask of the Terrorist*. New York: Arcade Publishing.

Robison, Richard P. 2003. *The Middle East War Process: The Truth Behind America's Middle East Challenge*. Bloomington, Indiana: AuthorHouse Publishers.

Sasson, Jean P. 2004. *Mayada, Daughter of Iraq: One Woman's Survival Under Saddam Hussein*. New York: Penguin Group.

Schweizer, Peter. 1994. *Victory: The Reagan Administration's Secret Strategy that Hastened the Collapse of the Soviet Union*. New York: The Atlantic Monthly Press.

Stark, Rodney. 1996. *The Rise of Christianity*. New Jersey: Princeton University Press.

Tragert, Joseph & Robbins, James S. 2002. *The Complete Idiot's Guide to Understanding Iraq*. New York: Alpha Publishing/Penguin Group.

Verton, Dan. 2003. *Black Ice: The Invisible Threat of Cyber-Terrorism*. Emeryville: McGraw Hill/Osborne.

Weaver, Mary Anne. 1999. *A Portrait of Egypt: A Journey Through the World of Militant Islam*. New York: Farrar, Straus, Giroux Publishers.

Williams, Paul L. 2002. *Al-Qaeda: Brotherhood of Terror*. New York: Alpha Books.

Woodward, Bob. 2002. *Bush at War*. New York: Simon & Schuster.

Ye'or, Bat. 1985. *The Dhimmi: Jews and Christians Under Islam*. New Jersey: Associated University Presses.

_____. 2005. *Eurabia: The Euro-Arab Axis*. New Jersey:

Associated University Presses.

Yergin, Daniel. 1992. *The Prize: The Epic Quest for Oil, Money and Power.* New York: Simon & Schuster

END NOTES

1. See *The Middle East War Process: The Truth Behind America's Middle East Challenge* (2003, AuthorHouse Publishers, by Richard P. Robison).
2. Special to the World Tribune.com: *China Signs a $70 billion Oil Deal with Iran.* November 1, 2004, World Tribune.com. See also: *China's Dangerous Game*, Review and Outlook, the Wall Street Journal, November 11, 2004. Also: *Iran's Power Play*, by Thomas McInerney and Paul Vallely, the Wall Street Journal, September 8, 2004.
3. See: *Attack of the Killer Bras*, by New York Times columnist Nicholas D. Kristof, December 10, 2003 Op-Ed article on the rise of China in the world and the U.S. response.
4. See: *China's Changing Oil Strategy and it Foreign Policy Implications*, Sergei Troush, Visiting Fellow, Center for Northeast Asian Policy Studies, Brookings Institute, Washington, D.C., Fall, 1999, www.brook.edu/fp/cnaps/papers/1999_troush.htm
5. *China's Arms Sales, Motivations and Implications*, by Daniel L. Byman and Roger Cliff, the Rand Corporation special research project paper for the U.S. Air Force, 1999.
6. See: *Fueling the Dragon: China's Race Into the Oil Market*, by Gal Luft, the Institute for the Analysis of Global Security, 2003, www.iags.org/china.htm .
7. See: China's Middle East Strategy, from The Middle East Review of International Affairs Journal, Volume 3, No. 1, March 1999, by Barry Rubin, (www.biu.ac.il/SOC/besa/meria/journal/1999/issue1/jv3n1a4.html) Quote: "American cautions (to China) against the proliferation of weapons of mass destruction do have an effect. Beijing's activities in this area are restrained, but they are not stopped altogether. Sometimes it is more a matter of effective concealment or a slower pace of operations."
8. *China's Choice: Review and Outlook*, The Wall Street Journal, January 21, 2005.
9. President Jimmy Carter, State of the Union Address, before a joint session of Congress, January 23, 1980.

10 *The Associated Press*, March 25, 1992
11 See: *China's Changing Oil Strategy and Its Foreign Policy Implications,* Sergei Troush, Visiting Fellow, Center for Northeast Asian Policy Studies, Brookings Institute, Washington, D.C., Fall, 1999, www.brook.edu/fp/cnaps/papers/1999_troush.htm. Pg 4 reads: "The second important trend is the significantly increasing oil flow from the Middle East to Asian Pacific region, with China, Japan, and Korea the main consumers. According to the chart, almost every second barrel of crude oil produced in the Middle East in 2010 will head to consumers on the other side of the Strait of Malacca (China, Japan, Korea). As a result of these trends, the Middle East's share of China's oil imports, fluctuating roughly about 50%, could conceivably grow to 80% or more in the year 2010. Henceforth, with such a heavy dependence on the Middle East for oil, U.S. strategic domination over the entire (Persian Gulf) region, including the…Strait of Hormuz, will be perceived as the primary vulnerability of China's energy supply…. The key objective of China's oil strategy will be to avoid this strategic vulnerability."
12 According to the Wall Street Journal (Review and Outlook: China's Choice, January 21, 2005) China imports 13.6% of its oil from the Islamic Republic of Iran. That number is growing each year.
13 *The People's Daily,* Beijing, 10/21/02. *China's Oil Security Faces Tests of War: News Analysis. The People's Daily Online* at http://english.peopledaily.com
 See also: *The National Energy Policy report* of May 2001, so-called the "Cheney Report" named by the principal (or best known) author of the study, Richard Cheney, U.S. Vice President. The report states that "by any estimation, Middle East oil producers will remain central to world oil security."
14 *China's Growing Thirst for Oil Remakes the Global Market: Beijing's Buying Keeps Prices High and Could reshape Politics of the Middle East,* by Peter Wonacott, Jeanne Whalen, Bhushan Bahree, The Wall Street Journal, front page, December 3, 2003.
15 *Asia's Reliance on Mideast Grows,* by Michael Richardson, *International Herald Tribune,* London, November 15, 2000, at www.iht.com/articles/1745.html
16 Ibid.

17 *China's Changing Oil Strategy and it Foreign Policy Implications,* Sergei Troush, Visiting Fellow, Center for Northeast Asian Policy Studies, Brookings Institute, Washington, D.C., Fall, 1999, www.brook.edu/fp/cnaps/papers/1999_troush.htm. Pg 12
18 See: *China and the Persian Gulf: Energy and Security,* by John Calabrese, The Middle East Journal, Volume 52, No. 3, Summer, 1998, Pg 361.
19 See: Voice of America report, *China's Arms Sales to the Middle East,* by Erica Benis, Editor: Phil Haynes, December 16, 1996, www.fas.org/news/china/1996/china_3.htm
20 *Central Bankers Shifting Funds from U.S. to Eurozone,* The French Press Agency (AFP), January 24, 2005.
21 *U.S. to Sell $60 Billion in Notes,* by Simon Kennedy, Bloomberg News, as reported in the San Diego Union-Tribune, at www.signonsandiego.com/new/business/20030801-9999_1b1treasury.html
22 Morgan Stanley report on global currencies: *How Far Could, and Should, EUR/USD Go?* January 30, 2003 at www.morganstanley.com/GEFdata/digests/20030130-thu.html
23 *State Sponsors Held Accountable for Terrorism,* AIPAC Issues, September 24, 2001, at www.aipac.org/documents/AIPACmemo0924b.html
24 Elder Mark E. Peterson.
25 Traditional Arab headdress.
26 Edward Said, *Al-Ahram Weekly,* Cairo, Egypt, April 25-May 1, 1996.
27 *Hans Wehr Arabic-English Dictionary,* Spoken Language Services, Inc., Edited by J M. Cowan, Ithaca, New York, 1976, pgs. 198-99.
28 Common Muslim saying, in Arabic, meaning "God is the Most Great" or in this usage, "God has it all in hand."
29 *Makers of Arab History,* by Philip K. Hitti, Harper Torchbooks, New York, 1968.
30 *Madinian Society at the Time of The Prophet,* International Islamic Publishing House and the International Institute of Islamic Thought, 1991.
31 *The Holy Qur'an,* Sura 9: 29.
32 Ibid
33 *The Holy Bible,* Philippians 2:10,11
34 *The Holy Qur'an,* Sura 2: 256.

[35] *World Business Watch*, Zions Bank, Salt Lake City, Utah, *China Is Emerging as an Economic Powerhouse: Is It Part of Your 2003 Plan?* 4th Quarter 2002, pgs 1-2. As a comparison, the growth rate in GNP for the United States over the past decade, a very prosperous period, averaged between 2 to 4 percent per year.

[36] *Iran's New Alliance With China Could Cost U.S. Leverage*, by Robin Wright, The Washington Post, November 17, 2004.

[37] AsiaPulse. Profile: China's Oil Industry, January 2005, www.asiapulse.com

[38] This refers primarily to the original crude oil that is shipped via tanker from the Persian Gulf to Asian refineries. Without oil or gas feedstocks, refineries shut down.

[39] See: *"China's Worldwide Quest for Energy Security,"* by the International Energy Agency, Paris, France, 2000.

[40] See: *China's Growing Thirst for Oil Remakes the Global Market: Beijing's Buying Keeps Prices High and Could reshape Politics of the Middle East*, by Peter Wonacott, Jeanne Whalen, Bhushan Bahree, The Wall Street Journal, front page, December 3, 2003.

[41] Perhaps the world's first monotheistic religion, the religion of the deity *Ahura Mazda* of ancient Iran, established by the holy man Zarathushtra, before Persian lands were ultimately swept by Islam.

[42] Ernle Bradford, *Thermopylae: The Battle for the West* (1980), Da Capo Press, Perseus Books, Cambridge, Massachusetts; page 40.

[43] U.S. Information Agency, Office of Public Liaison, at www.fas.org/news/china/1997/msg00007a.htm

[44] As found in the ending of his "Give me liberty, or give me death" speech, delivered to the Virginia House of Commons, March 23, 1775.

[45] *Iranian Weapons Programs: The Russian Connection*, Hearing before the Committee on Foreign Relations, United States Senate, October 5, 2000, pg. 21, (Italics added), www.fas.org/irp/congress/2000_hr/hr_100500.html

[46] Ibid, pg. 22.(Italics added.)

[47] *The National Interest*, "Pragmatic Theocracy, A Contradiction in Terms?" a report by Ray Takeyh, Spring 2000, Number 59, pg. 100 (Italics added.)

[48] *The Iran Files*, MSNBC, Political Issues, Sources of Instability,

Terrorist Activity: www.msnbc.com/modules/secretempire/iran.asp
49 *Iran Shows Two Faces at Summit*, by John Daniszewski, *The Los Angeles Times*, December 10, 1997.
50 Iran's Ballistic Missile and Weapons of Mass Destruction Programs, Hearing before the International Security, Proliferation, and Federal Services Subcommittee, of the Committee on Governmental Affairs, United States Senate, 106th Congress, Second Session, September 21, 2000, pg. 3, www.fas.org/irp/congress/2000_hr/hr_092100.html
51 *The Christian Science Monitor, Driven by Oil and Spite for U.S., Iran Reaches for Dominance*, by Scott Peterson, April 8, 1997, pg 1, 7.
52 Does the religion of Islam send conflicting signals? Suicide is forbidden by the Islamic faith. The honoring of death in a suicide mission by fundamentalist Islamic sects appears to be a blatant conflict of beliefs. Is not suicide, in which the lives of innocent bystanders are sacrificed, a mockery to God (Allah) and his eternal doctrine? The gift of life to Muslims is a sacred gift, not to be so easily surrendered, nor to be taken from an innocent who happens to be in the wrong place at the wrong time. Yet another example of how corrupt, evil, and non-Islamic these terrorist factions have become.
53 See article "Washington Fears Bombing Reveals Significant Cracks in Saudi Society," The New York Times, June 30, 1996.
54 In the mid-1990s, Iran tested a ship-launched ballistic missile, which changes every equation relative to America's distance from Iran, or any American target worldwide, military or civilian. Iran has several types of mostly Chinese, Russian, and North Korean missile systems, but has been developing an ICBM, the "*Shahab* missile." Shahab 2 has a range of 400-600 kilometers, all the way up to the Shahab 6 (still being developed) with a projected range of 6,000 kilometers (about 4,000 miles).
55 Mullah Ali al-Muttaqi, Kanzu al-Ummah, Beirut, Lebanon, 1985, 1st ed. Vol. 3, pg. 96, Hadith Number 5665.
56 *Al-Taqiyya fi al-Islam* by Dr. Sami N. Makarem, American University of Beirut, Beirut Lebanon.
57 *The Holy Qur'an*, Sura (Chapter) 16 (al-Nahl), Verse 106.
58 Sahih al-Bukhari, *Sahih Muslim Book 30*, #5848, www.bangladesh.com/forums .
59 www.al-islam.org/encyclopedia/chapter6b/3.html

60   ibid.
61   See *Creed of the Shi'a, Explained* at: www.shiabooks.tripod.com/Creed%20of%20the%20Shia/creed_of_the_shia.htm
62   *The Holy Qur'an*, Sura (Chapter) 3 (Ali Imran), Verse 29.
63   Arabic-English Dictionary, Hans Wehr, pp. 95, 1094, 1095 (1976, Edited by J. M. Cowan).
64   See: *The Reliance of the Traveller*, Ahmad ibn Naqib al-Misri; Keller, Amana Publications, 1997.
65   *The Persian Gulf in the Coming Decade, Trends, Threats, and Opportunities*, by D. Byman and J. Wise, The Rand Corporation, Project Air Force, 2002, pg. 66, as quoted in Alterman, *The Gulf States and the American Umbrella*.
66   *The Holy Qur'an*, Sura (Chapter) 2 (al-Baqarah), vs. 256.
67   The mostly pagan days in Arabia prior to the Prophet Muhammad's calling and the spread of Allah's word to the world.
68   *The Holy Qur'an*, Sura (Chapter) 2 (al-Baqarah), vs. 256.
69   Sahih al-Bukhari, *Sahih Muslim Book 30, Volume 7, Book 62, Number 13o*, narrated by "Abdullah."
70   See: http://lexicorient.com/e.o/muta.htm (and) http//i-cias.com/e.o/muta.htm
71   *Lehi in the Desert*, Dr. Hugh Nibley, Bookcraft, 1988, pg. 73.
72   A middle aged Palestinian businessman operating in the Persian Gulf region.
73   A 40 year-old Syrian military officer of upper rank.
74   A 25 year-old U.S. college-educated Jordanian-American.
75   *The Bible*, The Revised Standard Version, Isaiah Chapter 34:14.
76   *The Hadith*, as told to Abu Huraira, Volume 4, Book 55, No. 548.
77   It seemed all Philippine maids were constantly running up these huge "debts," which is odd because they were not usually allowed out of the house alone to shop, and their personal effects were practically non-existent.
78   Jordan Times, *Hijab—A Passport to Liberty*, by Saeda Kilani, 17 December 1990.
79   Ibid.
80   Ibid.
81   Strange that the NOW [National Organization of Women] group, or the ACLU [American Civil Liberties Union] have been absolutely

silent on the many opportunities and freedoms available to women in Afghanistan and in Iraq, and the democratic openings affecting women all over the Arab world in the wake of President Bush's Iraq War. Very strange....

82   *An Interview with Ralph Peters,* by Fredric Smoler, American Heritage Magazine, February-March 2003.
83   *The Middle East War Process,* by Richard Robison, AuthorHouse Publishers, 2003.
84   *Hans Wehr Arabic-English Dictionary,* Spoken Language Services, Inc., Edited by J M. Cowan, Ithaca, New York, 1976, pgs. 667, 672.
85   *The Holy Qur'an,* Sura (Chapter) 4 (al-Nisa'), Verse 34.
86   See: Amnesty International report at www.amnesty.org.au/women/resources-honour-kill.html
87   www.saxakali.com/southasia/honor.htm
88   *Statecraft: Strategies for a Changing World,* Margaret Thatcher, 2003, HarperCollins.
89   As heard on several news and talk programs on which Mr. Friedmann has appeared.
90   In spite of Prime Minister Tony Blair's close relationship with President Bush, even the BBC, it seems, is unwilling to promote or assist American foreign policy objectives in the Mideast.
91   The Atlantic Monthly Online, *All you need is love, How the terrorists stopped terrorism,* by Bruce Hoffman, at: www.theatlantic.com/2001/12/hoffman.htm
92   See "Black Hawala, Financial Crimes and the World Drug Trade," Patrick Jost, U.S. Department of the Treasury, Financial Crimes Enforcement Network (FinCEN), Office of Communications, 2070 Chainbridge Road, Ste. 200, Vienna, VA 22182 USA.
93   *The Christian Science Monitor,* Monday, March 17, 2003, pg. 6.
94   *The London Daily Telegraph,* January 18, 2003, www.telegraph.co.uk/news/main.jhtml?xml=/news/01/18/nids18.xml
95   Sahih al-Bukhari, *Sahih Muslim Book 30,* Volume 3, Book 49, Number 870, as narrated by "Abu Huraira."
96   Not his true name.
97   A raised platform or pulpit in the mosque, usually to the right of the *mihrab,* from which the Imam will offer prayers or speeches to the congregation.

[98] *Colossus: The Price of America's Empire*, Niall Ferguson, The Penguin Group, 2004.

[99] *Security Pact With Russia Bolster's China's Power*, by Bruce A. Elleman and Sarah C.M. Paine, *The International Herald Tribune of London*, August 6, 2001.

[100] China's Worldwide Quest for Energy Security, the International Energy Agency, special report, 1999.

[101] For more detailed numbers and assessment, see: *Growth Exposes China to Oil Supply Shocks, The International Herald Tribune*, London, October 31, 2001, at www.iht.com/articles/37313.html

[102] For example, look how history views Jane Fonda's actions in supporting the North Vietnamese while our nation was at war; her activities over there likely caused American POWs further depredations, torture, and pain at the hands of the North Vietnamese. Ms. Fonda came from a highly respected American Hollywood family. Out of respect for her father, Henry Fonda, Americans bent over backwards to give her the benefit of the doubt. History, however, has not. Today she must live with what she did and no amount of modern "spin" or supposed "apologies" will alter the historical realities. Modern activists should learn from Jane's sad example.

INDEX

A

Abbassids 46
Abd al-Malik 155, 156
Abou Jahjah 144
Abraham 27, 158, 273
Abu Abbas 6
Abu Ghraib 246
Abu Nidal 6
ACLU 207, 298
Adam 29, 175, 176, 177, 178, 188, 286, 287
Admiral Yamamoto 208
Afghanistan xi, 6, 19, 20, 26, 61, 62, 67, 73, 108, 114, 116, 135, 136, 137, 143, 151, 160, 207, 208, 209, 211, 212, 213, 214, 215, 245, 255, 270, 271, 284, 285, 286, 290, 299
Age of Discovery 87
Age of Information 79, 82, 136
Ahmad Chalabi 113
Al-Ahram Weekly 41, 295
al-Ahsa Province 113
al-dahna 115
al-Qaeda 6, 19, 20, 21, 40, 42, 49, 67, 71, 73, 85, 91, 94, 103, 115, 116, 118, 120, 124, 133, 135, 136, 137, 160, 198, 205, 212, 216, 217, 245, 250, 254, 255
Algerian 26
Ali Akbar Rafsanjani 54, 109
Ali Akbar Velayati 102
Ali Khamenei 36, 102, 104, 108, 110
Allah's will 52, 60, 87, 140, 141
alms giving 126
American values 18, 197, 201
Ammar Ibn Yasir 121, 122
Ansar al-Islam 6
Anti-Christ 126, 127
Anwar Sadat 40, 49, 133, 136, 137, 157
Apocalypse Now 245, 246
apostate 22, 68
Aqsa' Brigades 21
Arabia xii, xiii, 4, 6, 8, 19, 21, 26, 38, 39, 43, 51, 52, 53, 57, 58, 65, 67, 68, 71, 74, 86, 104, 111, 113, 136, 139, 152, 155, 160, 198, 213, 214, 244, 247, 253, 254, 256, 278, 284, 291, 292, 298
Arab European League 144
Arab Miracle 24
Arab nationalists 35, 160
Arab powerlessness 41
ARAMCO 113
archaic 48, 176, 232, 236
Ari Fleischer 23
Armenians 73, 157
Armies of Christ 37
arsenal 20
Assad 26, 29, 36, 160
assassin 156, 246
assimilate 56
Assyrian 73
Axis of Evil viii, xii, 101, 105, 291

B

Ba'ath Party 5, 253, 259, 260, 266
Babylon 51
Babylonians 35
Baghdad 30, 41, 44, 48, 61, 111, 114, 199, 208, 209, 265, 266, 278
Baghdad Bob 208, 209
Bali, Indonesia 58
ballistic missiles 105
Bangladesh xiii, 27, 85, 226, 275, 289, 297
Battle of Cannae 271
BBC 224, 299
Bekaa Valley 22
Benelux 43

Bermuda Triangle 40
Biblical 31, 33, 188
biological weapons 72, 98
black gold 4, 198
Black September Organization 248, 249
blockade 65
blood oath 52, 160
boabs 237
bonafides 251
booty 51
Bosnia 5
brainwashing 135
British Empire 31
Britney Spears 57, 188
Brookings Institute 12, 293, 294, 295
Bruce Willis ix, 229, 231
burqa 75
Bush 15, 25, 28, 29, 30, 31, 43, 50, 54, 63, 67, 84, 89, 91, 99, 105, 116, 123, 128, 133, 159, 199, 201, 202, 203, 204, 209, 216, 217, 221, 224, 225, 226, 235, 247, 259, 265, 274, 275, 286, 287, 299
Bush Administration 128, 202, 216, 247, 259
Bush Doctrine 91, 201, 203
Byzantine 48, 128

C

Cairo 30, 44, 125, 133, 148, 149, 153, 171, 181, 225, 236, 237, 249, 251, 295, 303
caliphate 53, 71, 72, 212, 254
capitulation 33, 34
captive 6
Careerism 39, 45
Carter Doctrine 9
Caspian Basin 10, 11, 14, 94, 264
catalyst 51, 55, 56, 57, 74, 144, 198
catbird seat 14
Central Asia 11, 41, 104, 109, 211, 212, 213, 214
Central Intelligence Agency 303

chador 75
Chaldean 73
Charles Martel 54
Cheney (Dick) 10, 247
China Card xii, 8, 95, 289, 291
Christians 5, 52, 53, 55, 60, 68, 72, 73, 74, 75, 76, 77, 86, 87, 126, 127, 138, 141, 156, 157, 168, 182, 226, 287
CIA 8, 109, 128, 129, 247, 248, 283, 284, 285
civilian 26, 98, 253, 297
clandestine 9, 73, 110, 116, 120, 123, 128, 170, 215, 270, 271, 276
cloaked, cloaking 9, 119, 123, 124, 143, 260
Clovis Maksoud 24
club of whiners 32
coalition 17, 42, 92
Cold War 10, 41, 42, 197
Colin Powell 31
colonialism 163
common market 43
communists 35, 136
compromise 27, 39, 135, 155, 156, 157, 199, 214
conspiracy 48, 62, 127, 128, 166
Constantinople 51, 52
Council of Guardians 108, 110
crude 10, 11, 14, 42, 93, 95, 96, 97, 198, 264, 294, 296
Crusader 64, 87, 93
cultural shackles 148, 273
cyberwar 228

D

Damascus 30, 44, 286
Dark Ages 37, 94, 273
Dark Side 29
Dar es-Salaam 57
Dead Sea 43, 44
debt 14, 16, 163, 232
Deceiver 126
deception 82, 119, 120, 122, 123, 124
Declaration of Independence 18

democracy tutorial shop 31
democrat 9, 50
demographic 24, 41, 42, 54, 56
denial 40, 44, 48, 49, 50
Desert Storm 197, 229
dhimmi 53, 73, 74, 75, 76, 77, 287
dhimmitude 77
dhow 37
dirhams 53
Dome of the Rock 156
Dostoyevsky 157
Dr. Ayman al-Zawahiri 21, 63, 67, 250
drought 51, 52, 53
Dubrovka Theater 58
Durfar (Sudan) 73

E

East Jerusalem 27
Edom (Idumea) 176
Edward Said 41, 295
Egyptian Islamic Jihad 49, 63, 133
elite 27, 46, 164, 203, 277
Eminem 232, 233
empire 4, 14, 18, 31, 32, 36, 50, 75, 87, 128, 168, 197, 262, 263, 264, 265, 267, 279, 300
Empire of Japan 4
enemy 6, 20, 21, 22, 34, 39, 44, 61, 65, 83, 85, 91, 93, 102, 104, 112, 118, 119, 120, 121, 123, 177, 207, 208, 209, 220, 221, 222, 223, 226, 228, 243, 244, 245, 246, 248, 249, 256, 265, 270, 271, 272
energy storehouse xi, 4, 8, 198, 290
Enkidu 175
entrepreneurial 28, 37
ethnic cleansing 43, 143
eunuch 85
Euphrates 198, 266
euro 14, 15, 16, 17, 287
European Central Bank 15
European Union 5, 15, 42, 62, 143, 253, 265

Eve 29, 175, 176, 177, 178, 188
expatriates 38
exports 13, 15
extortionists 6

F

fanaticism 25, 101
farsi 224
fascism 131, 134, 138, 227, 276
fasting 126
Fatah 123
Fatamids 46
fatwa(s) 63, 64, 65, 66, 67, 152
FBI 35, 104
feedstocks 97, 296
feel-good diplomacy 34
filipina 182, 183
flashpoint 10, 94
Four Righteous Caliphs 86
frankincense 51
free market 197
Free Trade Zone 28, 30, 43
Fumio Hoshi 17
fundamentalism 40, 119, 133, 286
fundamentalist 18, 26, 48, 101, 103, 120, 123, 127, 134, 136, 138, 158, 206, 212, 213, 297

G

G-8 Summit 106
galley 37
Gamal Nasser 160
Gaza Strip 27, 43
General Musharraf 215, 216
genius 30, 53, 245
genocide 73, 74, 203
Ghauri ballistic missile 215
Ghazali 46, 124
global jihad 18
Great Satan 29, 49, 88, 127, 205, 226
Greece 79, 101, 102
Gulfies 4, 247
Gulf Arabs 4, 97, 153, 254
Gulf of Mexico 8, 11

H

Hadith 44, 119, 121, 150, 153, 170, 175, 178, 297, 298
Hajaj 121
Hamas 21, 42, 73, 109, 118, 124, 244, 253, 254
Hamid Karzai 211
Hamzah Haz 159
Hannibal 271, 272
hard currency 43, 49
harem 101, 170, 185, 230
Hashashiin 246
Hashemite Kingdom (Jordan) 45, 191, 193, 303
Hassan al-Banna 54, 134, 142
hawala banking 250
Heaven 37, 46, 125, 150, 155, 188, 206, 207, 208, 260
hegemony 29, 73, 94, 104, 197, 198, 255
Hejaz 51, 52, 86
Hemmingway (Ernest) 222
Hezbollah 21, 22, 42, 49, 103, 109, 116, 117, 118, 124, 220, 243, 244, 250, 254
Hidden Imam 205, 206, 207
hijab 186, 187, 298
hijacked 124, 143
Hollywood 3, 85, 89, 131, 219, 231, 276, 279, 300
Holy Land 94, 244
honor v, ix, 26, 27, 36, 61, 85, 93, 120, 125, 147, 154, 156, 163, 164, 165, 166, 167, 168, 169, 170, 171, 175, 191, 192, 193, 194, 195, 201, 232, 236, 255, 258, 261, 273, 281, 299
honor killing 154, 191, 192, 193, 195
hope xiii, 19, 25, 27, 43, 47, 77, 80, 106, 116, 126, 143, 145, 152, 164, 175, 189, 203, 206, 216, 241, 270, 271, 272, 276, 280, 282, 289, 292
hopeless appeasers 33

hornet's nest 55
House of Islam xii, 28, 52, 77, 111, 137, 257, 291
House of War 52, 123, 137
hubbly bubbly 172, 173
human rights 29, 189, 194, 203
humiliation 48, 64, 87
Hu Jintao 13
hypocrisy 40, 122, 153, 154, 156, 159, 247, 263

I

"Islam is the Solution" 57, 260
ICBMs 297
IEA (International Energy Agency) 11, 264, 296, 300
illusion 48, 172, 173
imam 46, 49, 112, 124, 131, 152, 205, 206, 207, 299
imperialism 41, 278
imports 11, 12, 17, 92, 95, 97, 230, 264, 294
India 11, 38, 54, 180, 212, 215, 216, 278
information iv, 27, 35, 37, 47, 55, 57, 69, 79, 82, 104, 105, 115, 125, 126, 128, 129, 136, 226, 227, 228, 229, 240, 241, 246, 252, 274, 283, 296
inheritance 14, 24, 27, 29
intelligence 10, 23, 37, 77, 98, 109, 115, 122, 128, 147, 161, 216, 217, 226, 231, 241, 247, 248, 270, 271, 274, 281, 284, 303
International Energy Agency (IEA) 11, 264, 296, 300
internet cafe 230
Iran viii, xii, 6, 8, 9, 11, 12, 16, 17, 19, 21, 22, 23, 26, 28, 29, 34, 36, 48, 49, 54, 55, 56, 88, 95, 97, 98, 99, 101, 102, 103, 104, 105, 106, 107, 108, 109, 110, 111, 112, 113, 114, 115, 116, 117, 118, 120, 124, 132, 137, 151, 153, 157, 160, 198, 204,

207, 213, 214, 220, 243, 244, 248, 256, 264, 278, 289, 291, 293, 294, 296, 297, 303
Iranian Revolutionary Guard 104
Iraq vii, ix, xi, xii, 3, 5, 6, 7, 8, 9, 13, 16, 17, 18, 19, 20, 21, 22, 23, 24, 25, 26, 28, 29, 30, 33, 34, 42, 43, 46, 48, 58, 61, 64, 65, 67, 68, 73, 81, 83, 84, 85, 91, 92, 95, 97, 108, 109, 111, 112, 113, 114, 115, 116, 117, 118, 120, 127, 128, 131, 143, 155, 156, 160, 166, 168, 194, 195, 197, 198, 202, 203, 208, 211, 214, 219, 220, 221, 222, 224, 226, 229, 244, 245, 248, 253, 255, 256, 259, 260, 261, 262, 264, 265, 266, 270, 271, 274, 278, 283, 284, 285, 286, 287, 289, 290, 291, 299, 303
Islamic absolutism 151
Islamic Empire 50, 73, 75, 87
Islamic Jihad 21, 42, 49, 63, 73, 109, 118, 124, 133, 244, 253, 254
Israel 7, 21, 22, 24, 26, 30, 43, 44, 48, 49, 58, 65, 71, 81, 87, 88, 89, 93, 108, 118, 124, 128, 132, 156, 160, 166, 168, 199, 217, 219, 220, 221, 222, 223, 229, 230, 244, 254, 255, 256, 284
Israel's Vietnam 220

J

Jahiliyya 150
Janet Jackson 57
Jane Fonda 199, 300
Japanese Bank for International Cooperation 17
Jazeera (News Agency) 59
jihad 18, 21, 42, 49, 57, 61, 63, 65, 68, 73, 77, 109, 115, 116, 118, 124, 133, 137, 207, 208, 212, 244, 253, 254, 284
Jimmy Carter 9, 224, 293
jinn 26

jizya 53, 74, 75, 76, 87, 88
John Miller 67
John Stuart Mill 23
Jordan First 234, 235
junkies 14

K

Kabul 61, 206
kafirs 137
Karbala 111, 125, 127
Kashmir 26, 212
Kemal Ataturk 42
King Abdullah 45
King Fahd 38
King Hussein 45
King of the Terrorists 159
Kobar Towers 57, 104
Kofi Annan 19
Kosovo 5
Kuala Lumpur 17
Kurd, Kurdish 24, 109, 160, 278
Kurtz 245, 246
Kuwait 4, 5, 26, 43, 111, 179, 182, 183, 207, 247, 303

L

Land of Oz 71, 73
League of Nations 32
legacy 25, 36, 111, 148, 157, 213, 257
Leonidas 101, 102, 104
Lexington, KY 7
liberal 17, 46, 89, 213
liberate 5, 6, 63, 65
Lilith 175, 176
Little Satan 40, 88
Longfellow 243
Louis Freeh 104

M

Madonna 57, 82, 188
madressa 57, 72, 116, 135
Madrid (Spain) 58, 62
Mahathir Mohammad 17
Mahdi 124, 126, 127

make-work programs 39
Malekites 35
Maria (one of Muhammad's wives) 52
Marines 26, 117, 219
Mark E. Peterson 295
Marrakech xiii, 27, 85, 226, 275, 289
martyr 57, 127, 206, 260
Marxist 35
masculinity 83
mastery 30, 37, 66, 107
Maximum Leader 20, 48, 91, 229, 234
Mecca 35, 51, 52, 63, 65, 121, 127, 136, 154, 155, 225
medieval 18, 25, 39, 123, 138, 143, 144, 181, 184, 229, 273
Medina 35, 52, 53, 68, 121
mercantilist 37
Mercenary States 7
Mesopotamia 52
Michael Moore 89, 116
Michael Moore Syndrome 116
Midan Tahrir 148, 171
middlemen 9, 153
Middle East War Process (The) 14, 115, 119, 125, 287, 293, 299, 303
minbar 260
Mindanao 111
misyar 152, 153, 154
mobilize 24
moderates 78, 124, 227
Mohammad Atta 21
Mohammad Khatami 104, 107, 110
Morgan Stanley 15, 295
mosque 63, 65, 76, 116, 132, 155, 225, 226, 232, 233, 260, 262, 275, 299
Mossad 128
Mount Nebo 171
Mount of Olives 171
Mubarak (Hosni) 133, 134, 159
Muhammad Ali 224
Muharama 111, 117, 127

Mujahadin 26, 54, 55, 67, 68, 89, 124, 135, 136, 205, 206, 207, 255, 257
Mukhabarat 5
multi-polar world 13
murderers 6, 7, 124, 167
Muslim Brotherhood 54, 134, 142
Muslim oil 4, 99
mut'a 152, 153, 154, 155
mutawa 139
myopics 244

N

Nairobi 57
NATO 5, 221
Naval War College 263
New Islamic Caliphate 71, 72
New York 33, 59, 61, 67, 133, 135, 203, 251, 257, 283, 284, 285, 286, 287, 288, 293, 295, 297, 299
Niall Ferguson 263, 300
Night Hag 176
Night Ride 156
Nile 27, 128, 131, 132, 236
nonproliferation 106, 107
North Korea 19, 23, 72, 105, 220
North Ossetia 58, 74, 245
North Sea 8, 265, 266
nuclear 9, 10, 12, 19, 72, 88, 98, 105, 106, 109, 115, 200, 215, 216, 228

O

October 6, 1973 40
oil xi, 3, 4, 7, 8, 9, 10, 11, 12, 13, 14, 16, 17, 18, 22, 24, 25, 33, 38, 39, 41, 42, 43, 45, 46, 72, 74, 81, 84, 91, 92, 93, 94, 95, 96, 97, 98, 99, 103, 108, 109, 110, 111, 112, 113, 114, 115, 118, 139, 140, 156, 172, 183, 197, 198, 199, 202, 204, 212, 215, 221, 231, 246, 247, 254, 255,

256, 263, 264, 265, 266, 283, 288, 289, 290, 293, 294, 295, 296, 297, 300
Oil-for-Food Program (UN) 33, 91
OPEC 16, 17, 92, 198
Operation Morning Twilight 219
Organization of the Islamic Conference 110
Ossetia 58, 74, 245
Ottoman Empire (Muslim) 36

P

"People of the Book" 60, 68, 75, 137
pacifist 9, 75, 200
pagan 51, 138, 150, 298
Pahlavi Dynasty 101
Pakistan 58, 159, 198, 206, 211, 212, 213, 214, 215, 216
Palestine 30, 43, 52, 62, 86, 109, 123, 167, 168, 230, 248, 249, 254, 255, 275
paper tigers 67
Paradise 67, 150
parity 13
pasha 87, 172, 173
Patrick Henry xi, 3, 106, 290
Paula Abdul ix, 229, 232, 233
pauper 241
payback 107, 117
Peace Lobby 197, 199
Pearl Harbor 34, 115, 143, 209, 228
penetration xii, 10, 28, 94, 123, 138, 231, 270, 291
Pentagon 200, 209
perception 171, 246
perpetual negotiators 33
Persepolis 101
Persia 51, 101, 102, 105
Persian Gulf xi, xii, 4, 7, 8, 9, 10, 11, 13, 14, 46, 81, 94, 97, 98, 104, 106, 107, 108, 110, 112, 115, 116, 139, 152, 163, 179, 183, 197, 199, 220, 254, 255, 257, 264, 290, 291, 294, 295, 296, 298, 303

petrochemical 39
petrodollars 16, 17, 30
phalanx 105
Philippine 35, 111, 179, 182, 183, 184, 298
Phoenicians 35
Pilgrimage 51, 52, 112, 154
pillage 4, 52
pipeline 43
piracy 203
Pirate Coast 112
PKK 109
Plataea 102
polytheists 76, 138
pop-culture 131
population explosion 57
Porter Goss 128
Portuguese Man of War 37
pragmatic 14, 236, 296
predatory 36, 45, 120, 176
predestination 28, 140, 141
projection 12, 13, 200
prophet 44, 46, 52, 54, 55, 64, 66, 68, 86, 87, 105, 111, 119, 121, 122, 123, 124, 126, 127, 135, 137, 150, 153, 155, 156, 158, 170, 175, 178, 258, 260, 295, 298
prostitutes 114
Putin 106, 107, 263
Pythia 79

Q

qiblah 225
quagmire xiii, 292
Qur'an 68, 74, 76, 88, 111, 121, 126, 139, 142, 154, 158, 191, 193, 194, 295, 297, 298, 299
Qur'anic 53, 66, 88, 122, 188

R

Radio Sawa 224, 275
raiding 51, 52, 53, 112, 244
Ramzi Yusif 35
Rand Corporation 8, 293, 298

Ray Takeyh 107, 296
Reagan (President) 259, 279
reality 4, 5, 11, 27, 30, 48, 50, 61, 85, 97, 109, 118, 132, 133, 134, 141, 145, 154, 157, 161, 166, 169, 171, 177, 178, 179, 199, 209, 220, 227, 230, 246, 247, 255, 257
Red Sea 43, 44, 58, 171
Republican 9, 18, 24, 50, 101, 143, 201, 209
Revolutionary Guard Corps 109
Rice (Condaleeza) 99, 223
Richard the Lion-hearted 93
Righteous Path 136
rising 27, 97, 105, 227, 244, 274
Riyadh 30, 38, 58, 125, 139
roadkill of history 223, 224
Road Map 199
rogue nations 19, 73, 199, 248
Roman Empire 4, 31, 262
Rome 265, 266, 271, 272
Rosie 179, 180, 181, 182
Russia xi, 7, 12, 13, 58, 72, 75, 96, 104, 105, 106, 109, 203, 204, 217, 264, 279, 290, 300
Russian 13, 37, 74, 106, 107, 109, 204, 263, 296, 297

S

S. Makarem (Dr.) 121
sacrifice v, xi, 5, 25, 29, 83, 102, 104, 111, 124, 138, 147, 157, 159, 165, 178, 189, 195, 204, 208, 219, 221, 227, 250, 256, 269, 272, 279, 290
Saddam Hussein vii, viii, 7, 20, 22, 23, 25, 33, 34, 35, 49, 81, 85, 113, 131, 160, 198, 201, 202, 220, 221, 229, 231, 253, 287
safehouse 135, 206
safe haven 6, 7, 20, 91, 109, 207, 212, 214, 263, 270
Sahih Bukhari 121
Saladin 40, 93, 157

sanctions 9, 65, 108, 134, 265
Sayid al-Qutb 286
Sean Penn 199
Seducer 88
self-serving 7, 12, 27, 36, 44, 92, 94, 151, 160, 229, 259, 279
sensory overload 171
September 11th 19, 21, 31, 33, 34, 38, 58, 60, 61, 94, 105, 143, 144, 160, 198, 200, 213, 216, 223, 232, 252
Seventh Generation 27
Seven Heavens 156
sex 170, 171, 175, 177, 183, 184
Shahab missile 297
shame 85, 125, 167, 169, 191, 193, 194, 201, 206, 258, 276
Shanghai Pact 263, 264
Shari'a 137, 150
Shaykh Nasrallah 117
Sheikh Tantawi 152
Sheik Abdul Rahman 133
Shi'a 111, 120, 126, 298
Shi'ite 21, 22, 24, 103, 110, 111, 112, 113, 114, 116, 117, 118, 119, 122, 123, 127, 152, 153, 154, 243, 260, 278
Shi-sha' 172
Shimon Perez 6, 26
Shock and Awe 83, 85, 219
shrewish 175, 176
sigheh 152, 153, 154
Six Days War 48
Sky People 236, 237, 240, 241
slave 101, 138, 177, 179
slavery 179, 183, 203
sleeper cell 135
smoke and mirrors 127, 169, 170, 171, 172, 260
smoking gun 23
soft-targets 215
soldiers xiii, 26, 27, 37, 66, 74, 82, 87, 115, 135, 153, 215, 219, 222, 223, 235, 245, 250, 259, 292

Solution (the) 22, 27, 28, 30, 43, 44, 45, 57, 138, 156, 179, 206, 212, 248, 250, 254, 260, 269
Somalia 67, 160
Southeast Asia 13, 54
Southwest Asia 10, 57, 82, 211, 213, 222
South Lebanon 21, 117, 118, 219, 243
Spain 24, 38, 54, 58, 75, 82, 86, 140, 271, 278
Spice Trail 51, 52
spies 215, 231
spin, spun 45, 81, 124, 134, 300
St. Paul 171
Steven Seagal 230
Straits of Hormuz 204
Straits of Malacca 13
strategic power 4, 8, 17, 18, 93, 198, 289
submission 34, 52, 68, 74, 77, 87, 101, 150
Sudan 6, 26, 48, 65, 73, 74, 98, 151, 160
suicide terrorists 7
Sunni 24, 111, 112, 113, 120, 121, 122, 124, 125, 126, 127, 131, 152, 154, 278
superhighway 43
superpower 4, 13, 88, 95, 98, 143
suuks 254, 262
sweet crude 10, 97, 198
Syria 6, 19, 21, 22, 26, 29, 36, 43, 48, 117, 123, 160, 194, 198, 244, 248, 256, 264, 278

T

"Tehran Spring" 109
Taiwan 10, 263, 264
Taliban 26, 42, 49, 115, 120, 137, 151, 201, 212, 213, 215, 216, 245, 283
tammaya 172, 173
taqiya (taqiyya) viii, xii, 34, 119, 120, 121, 122, 123, 124, 125, 276, 291, 297
Tarik Ramadan 142
Tarim Basin 98
tawhid 123
techno-alliance 30
technology 12, 17, 25, 27, 37, 55, 57, 72, 92, 96, 98, 105, 107, 116, 131, 144, 163, 184, 205, 207, 216, 227, 229, 240, 241, 263, 264, 266, 270, 274
Tehran 4, 8, 30, 99, 103, 104, 109, 110, 125
temporary wife xii, 151, 152, 154, 291
temptress 175
Terror-mongers 27, 31, 33, 58, 71, 85, 199, 255, 257, 279
theocracy viii, 108, 131, 296
Three Iraqi Deficits 24
thugs 26, 30, 105
Tigris 27, 128, 131, 198, 266
Tikriti Clan 29
Timothy McVeigh 216, 217
Tony Blair (British P.M.) 299
Tora Bora 206
totalitarian 4, 12, 151, 185, 213, 214
Trappist Monks 74
trash heap of history 41
treachery 6, 48, 127
treasure 5, 9, 28, 32, 36, 38, 195, 203, 228
tribal cross-dressing 34
tribal logic 155
Tripoli 4, 30
Trojan Horse 28
truth xiii, 3, 14, 24, 25, 37, 50, 68, 69, 74, 107, 114, 119, 124, 126, 128, 144, 184, 221, 247, 257, 263, 273, 277, 283, 287, 289, 292, 293, 303
Turkey 43, 58, 86, 109, 275
TV 25, 57, 83, 88, 118, 131, 149, 158, 159, 160, 161, 172, 226, 239, 260

U

U.N. Security Council 73
U.S. Department of Energy 13
U.S. Fifth Fleet 115, 220
U.S. State Department 105, 224
Uighur Independence Group 217
ulema 65, 66
Umayyad 155
umma 60, 77
Umm Idduniya 3, 289
unemployment 38, 133
United Nations 19, 24, 32, 33, 34, 62, 72, 193, 195, 202, 221, 249
United States iv, vii, viii, xii, xiii, 3, 4, 5, 6, 7, 8, 9, 10, 11, 12, 13, 14, 15, 16, 17, 18, 19, 21, 23, 24, 25, 28, 30, 31, 38, 40, 41, 42, 43, 49, 55, 56, 60, 64, 66, 71, 72, 87, 88, 89, 91, 92, 93, 94, 95, 98, 99, 102, 104, 105, 108, 109, 110, 112, 113, 114, 118, 120, 124, 127, 128, 132, 134, 135, 136, 142, 156, 159, 160, 166, 168, 197, 198, 199, 207, 211, 212, 214, 216, 217, 219, 223, 224, 227, 228, 231, 235, 244, 246, 248, 252, 254, 259, 263, 264, 266, 275, 276, 278, 289, 291, 292, 296, 297
unity 123, 160, 270
UNOCAL 96
uranium 98
USS Cole 57

V

vassals 77
veil 75, 148, 155
vengeance 43, 52, 54, 93, 125, 126, 205, 207, 272
vett 80
victory 28, 36, 40, 42, 48, 54, 58, 83, 84, 91, 102, 203, 209, 221, 222, 225, 231, 241, 270, 271, 272, 279, 287

virgin 79, 152, 206, 236
virility 83
Vision xii, 27, 28, 30, 32, 42, 44, 91, 101, 114, 259, 272, 273, 278, 279, 280, 291

W

Wahhabis 39
Wall Street Journal 11, 293, 294, 296
war vii, ix, xi, xii, xiii, 3, 4, 5, 6, 7, 9, 10, 11, 14, 17, 18, 20, 21, 22, 23, 25, 26, 28, 31, 32, 34, 36, 37, 40, 41, 42, 43, 48, 52, 54, 55, 57, 58, 61, 62, 63, 64, 65, 66, 72, 73, 74, 81, 83, 84, 85, 88, 91, 95, 99, 108, 110, 113, 114, 115, 118, 119, 123, 125, 128, 131, 137, 143, 144, 155, 181, 197, 198, 199, 200, 201, 203, 208, 211, 212, 213, 214, 215, 216, 219, 221, 222, 223, 224, 225, 226, 229, 231, 232, 233, 234, 235, 240, 241, 243, 244, 245, 246, 247, 250, 255, 257, 260, 263, 264, 265, 269, 270, 271, 276, 277, 283, 284, 285, 286, 287, 290, 291, 293, 294, 299, 300, 303
warlords 6, 29, 41, 75, 87, 94, 168, 209, 211, 212, 223
Washington, D.C. 12, 24, 33, 279, 284, 285, 286, 293, 294, 295, 303
wasta 83, 169
weapons of mass destruction 9, 19, 20, 23, 33, 57, 92, 93, 105, 107, 110, 197, 198, 293
West Bank 21, 22, 199, 221, 253, 256, 275
wife of pleasure xii, 151, 152, 291
William Safire 18, 269
WMD 19, 20, 23, 57, 72, 198, 222, 248
Woodrow Wilson 31
World Trade Center 35, 133, 209

X

Xerxes 101, 102

Y

"yes-men" 48
Yahweh 157
Yathrib 52, 121
Yemen 48, 51, 111, 117, 206, 257
yen 15
Yom Kippur 40
youth 27, 56, 59, 67, 82, 83, 84, 85, 142, 211, 212
Yugoslavia 43

Z

Zarqawi 5, 68, 71, 128, 129, 205, 246
Zemin (Jiang) 263
Zion 296
Zionist 64
Zoroastrian 102

ABOUT THE AUTHOR:

Richard Robison is President of The Mideast Source, Inc. (www.mideastsource.com). He has worked in, and written on, the Middle East for over two decades. During the 1980s and early '90s he worked for the U.S. Foreign Service, stationed in Persian Gulf Nations during the Iran-Iraq War (1980-88), also assigned to Washington, D.C. for two years during this period. Later, during Gulf War I (1990-91) he served in the Hashemite Kingdom of Jordan.

In 1991 he assisted the Central Intelligence Agency's Gulf War Task Force. Following the Gulf War (1991), Mr. Robison resigned from the government, returning to the Persian Gulf a private citizen to direct U.S. companies rebuilding Kuwait.

A popular speaker at conventions, on talk shows, at universities, and before professional organizations while promoting his private consulting services and his books, writings, and audio visual products on the Middle East.

Mr. Robison is also the author of *THE MIDDLE EAST WAR PROCESS: The Truth Behind America's Middle East Challenge, a Book of Answers* (AuthorHouse Publishers, www.AuthorHouse.com, March 2003).

In the 1970s, Mr. Robison earned a Bachelor's Degree in Middle East Anthropology, and later a Master's Degree in the Arabic Language and Middle East Area Studies. He attended the American University In Cairo, Egypt on a FLAS Scholarship.

He now assists American companies rebuilding Iraq, and writing and speaking on America's Middle East challenge. The insights he offers are unique, firmly grounded from decades on the inside of Mideast culture, as well as representing corporate America operating abroad. His perspective, more importantly discernment and instinct, was molded working for the U.S. Government in the Middle East and elsewhere. His unique window on the world provides valuable knowledge for all Americans at this critical time.

20